ARCO

GMAT CAT
Answers to the
Real Essay Questions

ARCO

GMAT CAT

Answers to the Real Essay Questions

Mark Alan Stewart, J.D.

Frederick J. O'Toole, Ph.D.

Linda Bomstad, Ph.D.

Macmillan • USA

CONTENTS

About the Authors

Mark Alan Stewart (J.D., B.A. Economics and Business) is an attorney and private test-preparation consultant based in Southern California. He is the author of many ARCO books for GMAT, LSAT, and GRE preparation.

Frederick J. O'Toole (Ph.D. Philosophy, M.A., B.A.) is a Professor of Philosophy at California State Polytechnic University, San Luis Obispo, with over twenty years' experience teaching critical thinking concepts and skills to college students. His areas of specialization include critical thinking, symbolic logic, and history and philosophy of science.

Linda Bomstad (Ph.D. Philosophy, M.A., B.A. English and Philosophy) is an Associate Professor of Philosophy at California State Polytechnic University, San Luis Obispo. Her areas of specialization include business ethics and critical thinking.

Two Other Books by the Authors for Aspiring MBA Students

30 Days to the GMAT CAT 30 one-day lessons for complete GMAT preparation; includes eight mini-tests and one full-length sample GMAT. (*Macmillan USA, 1998*)

Perfect Personal Statements—Law, Business, Medical, and Graduate School Thirty-five great admission essays by *real* applicants to professional and graduate programs; in-depth interviews with admission officials at the top-ranked business, law, and medical schools; strategies, tips, and pitfalls every applicant should know for writing and submitting personal statements. (*Macmillan USA, 1996*)

We Have *All* the Answers!

The *Analytical Writing Assessment* portion of GMAT CAT requires that you compose two essays (each in 30 minutes):

- an *Analysis-of-an-Issue* essay

- an *Analysis-of-an-Argument* essay

The two essay questions that the test presents to you will be selected randomly by the GMAT's computerized testing system from a "bank" of 180 questions.

Here's the good news:

The test-maker (Educational Testing Service) has pre-disclosed its complete "bank" of 180 AWA questions; so you *can* be ready for any of them—if you're willing to make the effort!

Here's even better news:

Sample responses to all 180 AWA questions are right here in this book! (You'll find them in Parts 2 and 3.) Additionally, in Part 1 we're giving you all the tools you need to compose your own high-scoring GMAT essays.

PART 1

Getting Ready for the GMAT Essays

B Y picking up this book, you've taken an important first step toward achieving your highest possible score on the much-feared Analytical Writing Assessment (AWA) portion of the GMAT CAT. If you're like most test-takers, you've been neglecting this portion of the test. Why? Well, probably for one or more of the following reasons:

- *There's no room for guesswork*—in contrast to multiple-choice questions, in which you are occasionally awarded for random and reasoned guesses.

- *It's subjective.* There is no "correct" answer. It's difficult to know what the reader will reward you for and where you stand in relation to other test-takers.

- *It's hard work*, inherently requiring a far more active mind-set than the multiple-choice sections, which you can approach more passively.

- *Preparing for it seems an overwhelming task.* With a total of 180 possible AWA questions, being ready for any of them would seem to require an overwhelmingly arduous effort.

If it's any comfort to you, nearly every other person preparing for the GMAT has the same insecurities about the AWA portion of the exam. So let's face your fears head-on! Before we begin, however, let's make sure you're familiar with the terminology—especially the acronyms—that we'll use here in Part 1:

- **GMAT CAT** *Graduate Management Admission Test, Computer-Adaptive Test.* The GMAT is offered only by computer now (except for some remote locations outside the U.S.), so "GMAT" is now synonymous with "GMAT CAT."

- **GMAC** *Graduate Management Admission Council.* This policy-making organization guides business schools in establishing their admission requirements and guidelines. The GMAC is comprised primarily of administrators from various graduate management schools.

- **ETS** *Educational Testing Service.* This is the organization that produces and administers the GMAT and reports scores to the business schools, all in cooperation with the GMAC.

- **AWA** *Analytical Writing Assessment.* This is the term used by the GMAC and ETS to identify the essay portion of the GMAT, which consists of two distinct sections (identified below).

- **Analysis of an Issue** is the name of one of the two AWA sections; we'll refer to it as the "Issue" section from now on.

- **Analysis of an Argument** is the name of the other AWA section; we'll refer to it as the "Argument" section from now on.

❏ So Many AWA Questions, So Little Time!

Writing essays under timed conditions can be a trying experience and can raise your anxiety to a point where you find it difficult to perform well. Adding to this anxiety is the overwhelming number of possible topics—180 in all. The fact that ETS has pre-disclosed all of the topics actually *increases* test anxiety, since you might feel that you're at a competitive disadvantage unless you're ready for each and every one of the questions. So how can you minimize this anxiety and make sure you're as prepared as possible for the test? Read on!

❏ What You *Shouldn't Do*: Try to Memorize Our Sample Essays

If you actually were to memorize all 180 sample essays in Parts 2 and 3 of this book *and* reproduce any two of them on the actual exam, you would well deserve the highest possible score, just for the effort! Of course, that's our opinion. Unfortunately, that's not the way the folks at ETS and the GMAC view things.

Be forewarned: GMAT readers will have access to this book, and they're likely to recognize plagiarism. There's nothing wrong with borrowing ideas, reasons, and transitional phrases from our sample essays. Rest assured: Many test-takers will use similar ideas, arguments and phrases. Do try, however, to include your own examples, especially in your Issue essay, and be sure that in both essays you express your ideas *in your own words*. Besides, our sample responses are not "the" answers, since there is no "correct" response to any AWA question.

☐ What You *Should* Do: Some Serious Brainstorming

To beat the competition, you need to do some brainstorming for *all* 180 AWA questions so that you are ready for any of them. Here are the steps we suggest:

1. Print out the 90 Issue questions and the 90 Argument questions (see the *Appendix* for how to obtain the questions via the GMAC Web site).

2. Quickly read through all of the questions. Then go back and read each one again. Pause for a minute to ponder the topic. At least three or four ideas will probably pop into your mind; jot them down. At this point, don't try to organize your thoughts or commit to a position on the issues. Just make some quick shorthand notes, then move on to the next topic. Keep your mind as well as your pencil moving!

3. If you have trouble conjuring up ideas for a particular essay, read the corresponding sample response in this book and jot down the points you find clearest, most convincing, or most useful.

4. Save your notes and review them shortly before exam day.

Isn't this strategy awfully time-consuming? Perhaps. But what are your alternatives? Do nothing, and go into the test at a competitive disadvantage? Try to memorize all 180 sample responses in this book so that you can parrot back any one of them on test day? That option's out. We think you'll agree that it's well worth the effort to formulate your ideas ahead of time for each question.

☐ What You Should Also Do: Practice, Practice, Practice!

You could read this book cover to cover ten times and still perform poorly on the actual exam. There's no substitute for putting yourself to the task under simulated exam conditions, especially under the pressure of time. Practice writing as many essays as you reasonably have time for, responding to the official questions. As you do so, keep in mind the following points of advice:

- *Always practice under timed conditions*. This point cannot be overemphasized. Unless you are put under the pressure of time, you really won't be ready for the real exam.

- *Always use a word-processor for your practice tests.* Restrict your use of editing functions to the ones provided on the real exam. (We'll examine the GMAT CAT word-processing features later in Part 1.)

- *Organize your thoughts on paper before you start typing.* Before typing, take a few minutes (five, at most) to outline your response on scratch paper. But don't spend too much time pondering what to write and how to write it. You won't score points unless you start pecking at the keyboard! With the word processor, you can easily edit as you go.

- *Draw on your inventory of "buzz" words.* Try to make use of your favorite transitional and rhetorical words and phrases to help your essay sound convincing and flow naturally from one idea to the next. Remember: The reader will have no idea that you've used the same catch-phrase a hundred times in your practice essays.

- *Save enough time for proofreading.* Save the last two of your 30 minutes to proofread your essay, looking for errors in diction, usage, and grammar. Check the flow of your essay, paying particular attention to transitions. Also check your introductory and concluding paragraphs to make sure they're consistent with each other and with the question.

- *Evaluate your practice essays.* Practicing isn't all that helpful if you keep making the same blunders over and over. After taking each 30-minute essay, use the scorecard on page 8 to evaluate it. Then reflect on your weaknesses, and concentrate on improving in those areas the next time. Don't worry if your essays don't turn out as polished as the samples in Parts 2 and 3 of this book. Concentrate instead on improving *your own* performance.

❏ The GMAT AWA Sections—
Basic Format and Testing Procedures

For each AWA section, your task is to respond in essay form to a specific topic that the exam presents to you. The CAT system stores in its test "bank" 90 distinct Issue questions and 90 distinct Argument questions. For each test-taker, the CAT system randomly select from its bank one question of each type.

The two AWA sections are administered consecutively and always *before* the Quantitative and Verbal sections of the exam. Here's how the AWA sections fit into the overall format of the GMAT CAT:

FORMAT OF THE GMAT CAT

- CAT System Tutorial, Practice, and Demonstration of Competence

- Analytical Writing Assessment (60 minutes)
  Analysis of an Issue (30 minutes, 1 topic)*
  Analysis of an Argument (30 minutes, 1 topic)*

- □ 5-minute break (optional)

- Quantitative Section (75 minutes)**
  Problem Solving (23–24 questions)
  Data Sufficiency (13–14 questions)
  Total number of questions: 37 (28 scored, 9 unscored***)

- □ 5-minute break (optional)

- Verbal Section (75 minutes)**
  Critical Reasoning (14–15 questions)
  Sentence Completion (14–15 questions)
  Reading Comprehension (4 passages, 12–14 questions)
  Total number of questions: 41 (30 scored, 11 unscored***)

Total testing time: *3 hours, 20 minutes*

* The two AWA sections may appear in either order on the exam.

** The Quantitative and Verbal sections may appear in either order, and the different types of questions included within each section are interspersed.

*** Either 9 Quantitative and 11 Verbal questions *or* 10 from each section are unscored—totaling 20 unscored questions on the exam altogether.

You're allowed a maximum of 5 minutes after the second AWA section before moving on to the multiple-choice sections. (No break is provided between the two 30-minute AWA sections.)

The procedural rules for the AWA portion of the GMAT CAT are essentially the same as for the exam's Quantitative and Verbal sections:

- Scratch paper is permitted and provided (the exam supervisor will collect all scratch paper at the conclusion of your exam).

- Pencils are permitted and provided.

- Silent timing devices are permitted (the GMAT CAT interface indicates elapsed time, so you need not bring your own timing device to the test).

■ The CAT system does not allow you to return to either of the two AWA essays once you've moved on. If you've completed either essay before the 30-minute time limit has elapsed, you can proceed immediately to the next section by clicking the appropriate button on the screen (more on the CAT screen a bit later).

❏ Scoring, Evaluation, and Score Reporting

Within one week after the test, your two AWA essays will be read and graded, and your scores will be sent to the schools to which you direct your score reports. The following sections explain how all of this works.

How Your Two Essays Are Scored

Two readers will read and score your Issue essay, and two *different* readers will read and score your Argument essay. All GMAT essay readers are college or university faculty members, drawn from various academic areas, including management education. Each reader evaluates your writing independently of the other readers, and no reader is informed of the others' scores. Each reader will employ a "holistic" grading method in which he or she will assign a single score from 0 to 6 (0, 1, 2, 3, 4, 5 or 6) based on the overall quality of your writing. All four readers employ the same scoring criteria.

Your final AWA score is the average of the four readers' grades (in half-point intervals). Average scores falling midway between half-point intervals are rounded *up*. Here are two examples showing how the AWA scoring system works. Notice in Example 2 that the average of the three grades is 3–3/4, which has been rounded *up* to 4, since 3–3/4 is not a half-point interval.

Example 1

Reader A's evaluation of the Issue essay:	3
Reader B's evaluation of the Issue essay:	2
Reader C's evaluation of the Argument essay:	3
Reader D's evaluation of the Argument essay:	4
AWA score:	3

Example 2

Reader A's evaluation of the Issue essay:	4
Reader B's evaluation of the Issue essay:	3
Reader C's evaluation of the Argument essay:	5
Reader D's evaluation of the Argument essay:	3
AWA score:	4

In addition to your AWA score of 0–6, you will receive a *percentile rank* (0% to 99%) for your AWA performance. A percentile rank of 60%, for example, indicates that you scored higher than 60% of all test-takers and lower than 39% of all test-takers. Percentile ranks are also provided for Quantitative, Verbal, and Total (combined Quantitative and Verbal) scores. According to the GMAC, the percentile rankings corresponding to your Quantitative, Verbal, and Total scores indicate how you performed relative to the entire GMAT test-taking population during the most recent three-year period; however, percentile rank for the AWA score is based only on "more current administrations."

How the Readers Evaluate Your Essays

In evaluating the overall quality of your writing, the readers will consider four general areas of ability:

- **Content:** your ability to present cogent, persuasive, and relevant ideas and arguments through sound reasoning and supporting examples

- **Organization:** your ability to present your ideas in an organized and cohesive fashion

- **Language:** your control of the English language, including diction (word choice and usage) and syntax (sentence structure)

- **Grammar:** your facility with the conventions (grammar and punctuation) of Standard Written English

Which of these areas is most important? Unofficial statements by GMAC representatives suggest that the first two areas are more important than the last two. However, discussions with several former GMAT readers suggest that writing style, grammar, and diction—i.e., your ability to communicate ideas effectively in writing—may influence the reader just as much as the ideas themselves.

So the bottom line is that you should strive to demonstrate competency in all four areas. Of course, if you're weak in one area, you can still achieve a high overall score by demonstrating strength in other areas.

Here are two "scorecards," based on the ETS scoring criteria, to help you gauge your performance as you practice writing AWA essays. Answer "yes," "no," or "maybe" to each of the questions. For each "yes" answer, give yourself a mark of 1. For each "no" answer, give yourself a mark of 0. For each "maybe" answer, give yourself a mark of .5. Total the marks to calculate your score.

Scorecard for Analysis-of-an-Issue Response

- Do you show that you understand and appreciate the complexities of the issue?

- Is your essay well organized, with a clear introduction and conclusion, and logical flow from one point to the next?

- Do you use persuasive examples and/or insightful reasons to support your position?

- Do you present a well-reasoned, articulate analysis of the issue?

- Do you cover the specific tasks called for in the instructions, without digressing from the task or from the issue at hand?

- Do you demonstrate a good command of Standard Written English?

Scorecard for Analysis-of-an-Argument Response

- Do you show that you understand the argument and follow its line of reasoning?

- Do you identify the major problems with the argument, using relevant and reasonable support for your critique?

- Do you develop your ideas logically and connect them smoothly with clear transitions?

- Is your essay well organized, with a clear introduction and conclusion?

- Do you perform all relevant tasks mentioned in the instructions, without digressing from these tasks or from the argument?

- Do you demonstrate a good command of Standard Written English?

Reporting of Scores to Test-Takers and to the Schools

Within one week after you take the GMAT CAT, the AWA readers will grade your essays. An official score report for all sections—including the AWA sections—will be mailed to you about two weeks after testing. Concurrently, ETS will mail a score report to each school to which you direct your score report (reports to as many as five schools are permitted without additional fee). Percentile rankings are not reported to the schools. As this book goes to print, ETS is considering, but has not yet implemented, methods for electronic transmission of scores to the schools. Also, at this time score reports do *not* include test-takers' actual AWA *responses*, although the GMAC is examining possible methods of disclosing AWA responses to the schools.

Note: Unofficial Quantitative, Verbal and Total scores will be available to you at the testing center *immediately* after completing the exam. Of course, no AWA score will be available until the readers have evaluated your essays.

How the Schools Evaluate AWA Scores

Each business school develops and implements its own policies for evaluating AWA and other GMAT scores. Some schools place more relative weight than others on AWA scores, just as various schools place different relative weights on GMAT scores and GPA. By the way, your three most recent GMAT scores are reported by ETS to each business school receiving your scores and transcripts. Most schools *average* reported scores; a minority or schools consider only your *highest* reported score.

☐ The Analysis-of-an-Issue Section— Up Close and Personal

The Issue section is designed to test your ability to communicate your opinion on an issue effectively and persuasively. Your task is to analyze the issue presented, considering various perspectives, and to develop your own position on the issue. *There is no "correct" answer*.

Each Issue question consists of two elements:

- **the topic:** a one- or two-sentence statement about a particular issue
- **the directive:** general guidelines or instructions (one or two sentences) for responding to the statement

Here is a simulated Issue question. This question is similar to the ones on the actual GMAT. Keep in mind, however, that it is *not* one of the official 90 questions, so you won't see this one on the actual exam. (We are not permitted to reprint the actual test questions.)

Simulated Question A   **(Analysis-of-an-Issue)**

(topic)	"In any large business organization, teamwork is the ultimate key to the organization's success."
(directive)	In your view, how accurate is the foregoing statement? Use reasons and/or examples from your experience, observation, and/or reading to explain your viewpoint.

Here is a sample response to this question. As you read the response, keep the following information in mind:

- None of the points asserted in this response are irrefutable, because the issue is far from "black-and-white." It's all a matter of opinion.

- This response is relatively simple in style and language and brief enough (about 325 words) to compose and type in 30 minutes.

- This response received a score of 6 (the highest possible score) by an actual GMAT reader, who evaluated it just for us.

First Response to Question A

Whether a particular business ultimately succeeds or fails depends, of course, on a variety of factors. Nevertheless, because teamwork is an essential ingredient for any large business to succeed, I conclude that in most cases it is probably the pivotal factor.

First, cooperative interaction is an integral part of nearly all company jobs—including jobs performed in relative isolation and those in which technical knowledge or ability, not the ability to work with others, would seem to be most important. For example, scientists, researchers, and even computer programmers must collaborate to establish common goals and coordinate efforts. Even in businesses where individual tenacity and ambition of salespeople would seem to be the key for a firm's success, sales personnel must coordinate efforts with support staff and managers.

Secondly, in my experience the kinds of problems that ultimately undermine an organization are those such as low employee morale, attrition, and diminishing productivity. These problems, in turn, almost invariably result from ill-will among coworkers and their unwillingness to communicate, cooperate, and compromise. Thus, problems in working together as a team pose the greatest threat to an organization's success.

Some might argue that the leadership and vision of a company's key executives is of paramount importance. Yet chief executives of our most successful corporations would no doubt admit that without the cooperative efforts of their subordinates, their personal vision would never become reality. Others might cite the heavy manufacturing and natural-resource industries, where the value of tangible assets—raw materials and capital equipment— are often the most significant determinant of business success. However, such industries are diminishing in significance as we move from an industrial society to an information age.

In sum, although leadership, individual ambition, and even the value of tangible assets play crucial roles in the success of many large business organizations, teamwork is the single ingredient common to all such organizations. It is, therefore, the key one.

Variations on the Directive in Issue Questions

The directives for the 90 Issue questions are all similar, yet they are not all exactly the same. All but a handful of the 90 questions will include essentially one of the following directives (we're paraphrasing):

- Discuss the extent to which you agree or disagree with this statement
- Assess the accuracy of this statement
- Explain the meaning of this quotation (or statement)

The first directive listed above appears most frequently. Directives for the following questions, however, are more idiosyncratic and specific to the opinion stated in the question (question numbers here correspond to the sequence of 90 official questions, as provided by ETS):

- *Question numbers: 1 19 35 48 50 53 78 80 90*

On your exam, be on the lookout particularly for a question among this last group, and be sure that your essay responds to the specific directive.

Remember, however, that regardless of the particular directive, your task is essentially the same for every one of the 90 Issue questions: take a position on an issue and support that position with reasons and/or examples.

Common Themes Among the 90 Issue Topics

Although each of the 90 official Issue topics is distinct, many of them cover similar ground in terms of their theme. We've categorized all 90 topics for you, each according to theme, or issue. Understandably, more topics involve business issues than any other type of issue. To help prioritize your exam preparation, use the following list to concentrate on issues about which you are least knowledgeable.

Note: The categories here are not mutually exclusive; some topics could fall into more than one category. (Question numbers here correspond to the sequence of 90 official questions, as provided by ETS.)

- Business—organizational structure/behavior, management
  Question numbers: 10 14 25 33 35 55 56 76

- Business—productivity, efficiency, and teamwork
  Question numbers: 5 17 21 30 36 51 68 69 72 79

- Business—advertising and marketing
  Question numbers: 44 85 86

- Business—labor and employment issues
  Question numbers: 9 19 27 48 50 60

- Business—ethics
  Question numbers: 18 45 64 70 84

- Business—its overall role and objectives in society
  Question numbers: 42 59 66 82 87 90

- Government's role in regulating business, commerce, speech
  Question numbers: 1 61 71

- Government's role in ensuring the welfare of its citizens
  Question numbers: 13 22 34 41 47 82

- Bureaucracy and "the system"
  Question numbers: 53 63 46

- "Global village" issues
  Question numbers: 2 15 40 65

- Technology and its impact on business and society
  Question numbers: 8 20 26

- Culture and social mores, attitudes, values
  Question numbers: 16 32 38 57 67 78 80 54

- Education
  Question numbers: 12 23 28 37 62

- Learning lessons from history
  Question numbers: 43 88 89

- Keys to individual success
  Question numbers: 6 11 29 39 49 52 81

- Individual power and influence
  Question numbers: 4 24 74

- Personal qualities and values
  Question numbers: 31 73 75 77

The Content of Your Issue Essay

To attain a high score (5 or 6) on the Issue section, be sure to include each of the following substantive elements in your essay:

- Recognition of the issue and its complexity

- A clear statement of your position on the issue and at least two sound reasons to support your position

- At least two relevant examples (from your experience, observation, and/or readings) in support of your position

In formulating your position on an issue, keep in mind the points of advice in this section.

☐ Adopting a Position, or Point-of-View, on the Issue

There is no "correct" answer to any Issue question. Don't waste your time second-guessing what the reader might want to read or trying to guess what the "correct" response (politically or otherwise) to a topic might be. Instead, just be sure to acknowledge various perspectives on the issue and develop a well-supported position on it.

Be sure to adopt a position, or point-of-view, on the issue. The test instructions admonish you to adopt a position on the issue. If you don't happen to have a preconceived stance on the issue, develop one—fast! You can always revert to apathy after finishing your 30-minute writing task. Be sure to agree or disagree, to some extent, with the question's statement. (As for just how quickly you need to commit to a position, see the sidebar at the top of page 14.)

Consider Writing Your Introductory Paragraph *Last*

Don't spend too much time mulling over the topic and debating what position on the issue you should adopt. After jotting down some key reasons in favor of and against the stated opinion, organize those reasons into two or three body paragraphs, and start typing—the *body* of your response. Try to be flexible, allowing your position on the issue to evolve, if necessary, as you type the body of your essay. Through the magic of the word processor, you can wait until the last five minutes or so to determine your stance—or "thesis"—and express it in your introductory and summary paragraphs. (Just be sure it's consistent with the points you made in the body of your response.)

Doesn't this advice fly in the face of all you've been taught about planning essays during a "pre-writing" phase? Well, yes! But so what? The conventional advice pre-dated the word processor and CAT system. Moreover, the GMAT readers won't have any idea whether or how often you changed your mind or cut-and-pasted as you typed your response.

Always acknowledge both sides of the issue. You will not find a single irrefutable statement among the 90 official Issue questions, nor will you find a statement that is utter nonsense, wholly without rational justification or supporting evidence. In this fact lies the crux of your writing task: to persuade the reader that, in spite of the apparent merits of other viewpoints, your position is the best one overall.

Try to "hedge your position" on the issue by qualifying your viewpoint and acknowledging others. In doing so, you won't appear wishy-washy, but rather thoughtful and scholarly! In fact, it's perfectly acceptable to "straddle the fence" and abstain from agreeing or disagreeing—by pointing out, for example, that your agreement (or disagreement) depends on factors or circumstances that the statement fails to consider. By the same token, it's perfectly acceptable to strongly agree or disagree with the stated opinion—as long as your position is well-supported.

It's okay to take a controversial stance on an issue; but avoid coming across as fanatical or extreme. Many of the Issue topics are highly "charged" in the sense that they involve issues about which people tend to have strong opinions one way or the other. Don't worry that the reader may have a personal viewpoint that differs strongly from yours, or that your position may appear somewhat "right-wing" or "left-wing." GMAT readers are trained to be objective! Moreover, business schools are looking for students who are independent thinkers with definite points of view, not mindless automatons.

Avoid inflammatory statements, and don't preach or proselytize. Approach the GMAT Issue essay is an intellectual exercise in which you dispassionately examine various viewpoints. Do *not* use it as a forum for sharing your personal belief system. It is perfectly appropriate to criticize particular behavior, policies, or viewpoints as operating against the best interest of a business or of a society. But refrain from either condemning or extolling based on personal moral grounds. Also avoid demagoguery; do not write anything that might appeal primarily to the reader's emotions or prejudices.

☐ Breadth vs. Depth

Don't try to cover every possible argument, rebuttal, and example. During your first few minutes, jot down on your scratch paper the points and supporting examples you wish to incorporate into your essay. But don't worry if you end up with more points and examples than you have time to discuss in 30 minutes. Nearly all GMAT test-takers find themselves in the same predicament. Choose the broadest, most persuasive, and most relevant ones, and leave the secondary and more tangential points on your scratch paper. Be assured: GMAT readers understand your time constraints and don't expect a comprehensive treatise on the issue—nor do they require one for a high score.

Strive to come across as a generalist, not a specialist. Unless a question explicitly asks you to narrow your discussion, avoid harping on one particular reason that you believe is the most convincing one, or on one example that you think is most illustrative. Try to round out your discussion as fully as possible. To guard against going off on a tangent with a single reason or example, be sure to adhere to an outline or "template," as discussed on pages 17–20.

☐ Using Examples to Support Your Position

It's okay to draw on personal experiences to support your position; but don't overdo it. The directive for each Issue question (with only a few exceptions) explicitly allows you to draw on your own experience to support your position. So it's perfectly acceptable to incorporate into your essay your own experiences at work or elsewhere, and to refer to them in this manner. However, avoid relying too heavily on personal experience. Be sure to show that you are well-read and learned as well. Strive to demonstrate through your essay a breadth of both "real-world" experience and academic knowledge.

Don't try to impress the reader with your technical knowledge of business-related subjects. Resist the temptation to use the Issue essay as a forum to re-capitulate your senior-year thesis. This is not the place to convince the reader of your firm grasp of the finest points of econometrics or macroeconomic theory. That's what your GPA and undergraduate transcripts are for.

Don't try to be a "know-it-all." The Issue essay is not like a game of *Jeopardy!* or *Trivial Pursuit*. You will not score points by recounting statistics or by conjuring up the names of little-known historical figures. By all means, draw on both current and historical events to bolster your position. But try to use examples with which the reader is likely to be somewhat familiar. (Consider this point, however, in light of the one immediately below.)

Avoid hackneyed examples to support your viewpoint. Try to avoid using hackneyed, overused examples to make your point. For instance, among the 90 Issue questions are many opportunities to mention these four names:

- Bill Gates
- Adolph Hitler
- O.J. Simpson
- *Seinfeld*

Examples such as these, however, are the all-too-obvious ones that many other test-takers will resort to. Try to dig a bit deeper, showing the reader a broader, more literate perspective. (We confess, however, that the name "Gates" does appear once among the 90 Issue essays in Part 2).

☐ Brainstorming for Essay Ideas—Recommended Reading

The periodicals listed below feature articles that cover the common Issue themes listed on pages 12 and 13:

- *Inc.:* business ethics, management, leadership, entrepreneurship
- *Forbes:* same themes as those in *Inc.*
- *U.S. News and World Report:* notable current events
- *The Economist:* political and economic ideology
- *Reason:* ideology and culture (loads of "cross-discipline" articles)
- *The New Yorker:* arts, humanities, sociology, popular culture
- *The Futurist:* cultural and technological trends

With this list in hand, head to your local library and rifle through some back issues of these periodicals. You'll come away brimming over with ideas for Issue essays.

Organizing Your Issue Essay

The reader may not understand or appreciate your brilliant and incisive ideas if you present them in an rambling, disorganized fashion. A clear organizational framework, including those all-important "bookends"—an introduction and conclusion—is a necessary ingredient for a high AWA score. This section provides some organizational ideas to keep you on track.

Length. The CAT system imposes neither a minimum nor maximum length for an AWA response (aside from the practical limitation associated with a 30-minute time limit). Do GMAT graders prefer brief or longer essays? Well, it all depends on the essay's quality. An essay that is concise and to-the-point may be more effective than a long-winded, rambling one. In contrast, a somewhat lengthy essay that is nevertheless articulate and that includes many insightful ideas will score higher than a brief essay that lacks substance.

Our experience in writing AWA essays (and we have lots of it!) is that at least 275 words are required to incorporate all of the components of a high-scoring essay. The essays in Parts 2 and 3 range from 275 to 425 words in length, and their average length is about 325 words.

Number of Paragraphs. There is no "correct" or "best" number of paragraphs for an Issue essay. In our view, however, your essay should include separate "introductory" and "summary" paragraphs, as well as at least two "body" paragraphs in which you develop your position. *Note:* You should skip a line between paragraphs, since the TAB key will be disabled. (For details about the CAT word-processing features, see pages 31–42.)

An Organizational Template. The following template spells out our recommended structure in more detail, and most of the sample Issue essays in this book follow this basic pattern.

Keep in mind the following points about this template:

- You do not have to adhere strictly to this format in order to write an effective Issue essay. This is one format that works, but you may find that some other structure works better for you, especially for the middle paragraphs of your essay.

- You might wish to combine the second and third *body* paragraphs of this template into one paragraph, or perhaps omit the second body paragraph (as in the essay on page 21, which includes four paragraphs altogether). The best structure depends on the particular ideas you wish to present and how the ideas "fall into place."

- The numbers of sentences indicated for each paragraph here are merely suggestions or guidelines, not hard-and-fast rules.

- The *transitional phrases* used here are purposely simplistic; do not simply "parrot" them word-for-word in your essay or adopt a mechanistic fill-in-the-blank approach. If you do, your essay might appear stilted, awkward, or contrived.

Introductory Paragraph (2–4 Sentences)

Try to accomplish each of these goals in your introductory paragraph:

- Articulate the issue at hand
- Demonstrate that you understand the complexities of the issue (for example, by recognizing competing interests or various factors)
- State your position on the issue (but do *not* go into your reasoning or give examples in this paragraph; see *Avoid Intro-itis* in the sidebar at the bottom of page 19)

Here's a sample template for the introductory paragraph that accomplishes these goals:

> Whether ——————————————————— depends on ——— ——————————————————————. In my view, ——— ————————————————————.

First Body Paragraph (3–5 Sentences)

Begin to develop your position with your "chief" reason. Always support your rationale with at least one or two examples (from your experience, observations, or readings):

- State your chief reason (one only)
- Provide rationale and evidence to support it

Here's a sample template for the first body paragraph that accomplishes these objectives:

> The main reason for my view is ———————————— ————. For example, ———————————————— ————————————. Also, ————————————————. Finally, ————————————————————.

Second Body Paragraph (3–5 Sentences)

Further develop your position with your "secondary" reason. Support your rationale with at least one example. *Optional:* Acknowledge a counter-argument, then respond to (rebut) it in a way that further supports *your* position:

- State your second reason (one only)

- Provide rationale and/or evidence to support it

- Acknowledge and rebut a counter-argument

Here's a sample template for the second body paragraph that accomplishes these objectives:

Another reason for my view is ——————————————————————.
Specifically, ——————————————————————. Admittedly, ———
——————————————————————. However, ———————————————
——————————————————.

Optional Third (or Alternate Second) Body Paragraph (3–5 Sentences)

Acknowledge a competing viewpoint or counter-argument (and rationale and/or examples that support it), then provide rebuttals to further support *your* position:

- Acknowledge a different viewpoint or a counter-argument

- Provide rationale and/or examples that support it

- Provide a rebuttal

Here's a sample template for the third body paragraph that accomplishes the objectives indicated above:

Some might argue ——————————————————————. Yet ———
——————————————————. Others might cite ———————————
———. However, ——————————————————.

Avoid "Intro-itis."

One common AWA blunder is to devote too much time and too many words to your introductory paragraph. Try to limit your introduction of your Issue essay to 2–3 sentences. Practice writing concise, "punchy" introductions for as many topics as you have time for, so that you can dispense with this task as quickly as possible on exam day. Develop your own template or script so that writing an introduction for any Issue topic becomes almost automatic for you. Read the introductory paragraphs of the 90 essays in Part 2—one right after another. You're sure to pick up some useful technique just by osmosis!

Final (Summary) Paragraph (1–3 Sentences)

Sum up your position, in one to three sentences:

- State the "thrust" or "essence" of your position
- Recapitulate the main points from the body of your essay

Do not include new information or reasons in the summary paragraph. It isn't necessary to come to a conclusion not yet drawn in your essay.

Here's a sample template for the final paragraph that accomplishes the objectives indicated above:

In sum, I agree that —————————————————————————
——————. However, ——————————————; on balance, ————
——————————————————————.

☐ Putting it all Together—an Illustrative Issue Essay

You've already read one response to Simulated Question A on page 10. Here's another response to the same question. As you read it, keep in mind:

- As with the sample response on pages 10–11, this response does not include irrefutable statements. Remember: in the Issue essay, it's all a matter of opinion.

- This response adopts a *contrary* position to the one on pages 10–11 (but a *similar* one to the opinion stated in the question).

- Both responses use similar examples to support their respective positions, but they use these examples to assert different (and opposing) viewpoints.

- Both responses employ a similar organizational structure. We've underlined transitional phrases in this one to emphasize that structure and to help you see how we've applied the template on pages 17–20. (You will not, of course, use underlining in your actual essay.)

- Like the response on pages 10–11, this response is relatively simple in style and language and brief enough (about 325 words) to compose and type in 30 minutes.

- This response received a score of 6 (the highest possible score) from a former GMAT reader, who evaluated it just for us.

Second Response to Question A

Whether a particular business ultimately succeeds or fails depends on a variety of factors. In my view, while teamwork is almost always important, in most instances other factors are more pivotal to a firm's success.

The main reason for my view is simply that it accords with observation and common sense. For example, in many instances it is clearly the policy decisions of key executives that determine whether a firm ultimately succeeds. Notable cases include the turnaround success of Coca-Cola after Roberto Goizueta assumed the position of CEO, and—in contrast—the Apple Computer debacle following the departure of its founding visionary Steve Jobs. Also, consider industries such as financial services, where product differentiation is difficult. It seems to me that a creative marketing ploy or the tenacity of a sales force would the key factor here. Finally, in manufacturing and mining the value of raw materials or capital equipment are surely more significant than the cooperative efforts of employees or, for that matter, any other asset.

Another reason for my view is that technical knowledge and competence would seem to be more fundamental to most jobs. Specifically, without adequate knowledge of the systems, procedures, and vocabulary used in one's department or division, an employee cannot communicate effectively with peers or contribute meaningfully to organizational goals. Admittedly, nearly all jobs in an organization require some cooperative interaction with coworkers, even jobs performed in relative isolation and those calling for a high level of technical knowledge or ability. For instance, researchers, scientists, and computer programmers must agree on specifications and coordinate efforts to meet timelines. However, some substantive knowledge is necessary to perform virtually any job, whereas the ability to work effectively with others is merely helpful.

In sum, I agree that teamwork is an important ingredient for organizational success. However, it is generally not the most important one; on balance, some other factor—perhaps leadership, ambition, tangible assets, or especially technical knowledge—usually plays a more pivotal role.

Now go back to page 10 and read again the first response to Question A. Underline transitional phrases as in the response above. Notice that their overall organization and "flow" is very similar. Also notice that they use the same examples to argue for opposing viewpoints! Remember: In GMAT Issue essays, it's all a matter of opinion, viewpoint, and perspective.

❐ The Analysis-of-an-Argument Section—Up Close and Personal

Argument questions are designed to test your *critical reasoning* and *analytic* (as well as writing) skills. Your task is to critique the stated argument, but *not* to present your own views on the argument's *topic*.

Each Argument question consists of two elements:

- **the argument:** a paragraph-length argument

- **the directive:** specific instructions for analyzing the argument

Here is a simulated Argument question. This question is similar to the ones on the actual GMAT. Keep in mind, however, that it is *not* one of the official 90 questions, so you won't see this one on the actual exam.

Simulated Question B	(Analysis-of-an-Argument)
(argument)	"Eighty percent of the homeless people interviewed in a recent survey said that they prefer to eat and sleep on the streets rather than go to shelters. Surprisingly, this survey proves that contrary to popular opinion, homeless people prefer the discomfort and uncertainty of life on the streets to the comfort and security afforded by shelters."
(directive)	Discuss how logically convincing you find this argument. In your discussion, you should analyze the argument's line of reasoning and use of evidence. It may be appropriate in your critique to call into question certain assumptions underlying the argument and/or to indicate what evidence might weaken or strengthen the argument. It may also be appropriate to discuss how you would alter the argument to make it more convincing and/or discuss what additional evidence, if any, would aid in evaluating the argument.

Here is a sample response to Simulated Question B. As with the sample Issue responses earlier in Part 1:

- This response is relatively simple in style and language and brief enough (about 330 words) to compose and type in 30 minutes.

- This response received a score of 6 (the highest possible score) from a former GMAT reader, who evaluated it just for us!

Response to Question B

Based upon a survey in which 80 percent of the homeless respondents said that they prefer to eat and sleep on the streets rather than go to shelters, the author concludes that all homeless people share this preference. This argument is unconvincing for several reasons.

First of all, the author's conclusion goes beyond the evidence. Only 80 percent of the respondents indicated a preference for eating and sleeping on the streets. Yet the author concludes that all homeless people share this preference. This conclusion is not warranted by the evidence.

Secondly, it is possible that the homeless people interviewed are not representative of the entire population of homeless people. For example, perhaps the survey was conducted in a small rural community rather than a large metropolitan one, or perhaps it was conducted during summer rather than winter. Either fact would raise doubts about the reliability of the survey.

Thirdly, the argument fails to mention how many homeless people were interviewed in the survey or how they were selected. If, for example, only ten people were interviewed, this would be too small a sample to support the conclusion in this case. Lacking information about the sampling method used in the survey, it is impossible to assess the persuasiveness of the argument.

Finally, the author assumes that shelters are more comfortable and secure than the streets. No evidence is offered to support this assumption. It may be the case that the shelters are overcrowded and crime-ridden. If this were so, it would go a long way toward explaining the results of the survey.

In conclusion, the argument is unconvincing as it stands. To make the argument more persuasive, the author would have to modify the conclusion to bring it into line with the evidence and provide information that would ensure that the survey was reliable. Additionally, the author would have to provide evidence to support the assumption that shelters are more secure and comfortable than the streets.

3 Vital Points to Remember About the Argument Section

1. **Your analysis must focus strictly on important logical features of the argument.**

   The official instructions admonish you NOT to present your own views on the topic. Your personal opinions about an issue to which the argument might allude are neither relevant nor useful in the Argument section.

   It is impossible to overstate the importance of this point! Do not confuse your task in the Argument section with your task in the Issue section. Consider, for example, Simulated Question B. An *Issue* question involving homelessness might call for you to present various viewpoints about:

   - how best to solve the problem of homelessness

   - the severity of the problem relative to other social problems

   - who should take responsibility for the problem

   However, such viewpoints are irrelevant to the Argument section, in which you must focus strictly on the *internal* cogency (logical justification) of the stated argument.

2. **The directive is exactly the same for every Argument question.**

   All 90 official Argument questions include *exactly* the same directive. The directive in Simulated Question B (page 22) is essentially the same as the one appearing in the official questions.

3. **Each Argument has been intentionally "loaded" with flaws (fallacies) that you should acknowledge and discuss.**

   In contrast to the instructions for the Issue section, the instructions for the Argument section do *not* state: "There is no correct response." Why not? Well, in creating each argument, the test-makers made sure to incorporate certain logical problems (weaknesses or fallacies) into the argument, in order to give the test-taker something to write about. If you fail to see the more fundamental problems that were "built into" the argument, you will not attain a high score.

   However, beyond acknowledging the key fallacies in an argument, there is no *single* point, reason, explanation, counterexample, etc., that you *must* include in your essay to attain a high score. Also, as in the Issue essay, there is no "correct" or "set" *format* in which to present your response.

The Content Of Your Argument Essay

As suggested by the Argument directive, you should try to accomplish the following tasks in your Argument essay:

- Analyze the argument's line of reasoning and use of evidence
- Evaluate the cogency (logical justification) of the argument
- Support your critique with sound reasons and/or relevant examples
- Discuss what is required to make the argument more persuasive and/or what would help you better evaluate its conclusion

The following checklist should keep you from getting stuck—with nothing worthwhile to write. To set your mental wheels in motion, think about these questions as you read the argument:

- What is the *conclusion* of the argument?
- What *reasons* does the author offer in support of the conclusion?
- What *assumptions* does the author's argument depend upon? (Try to think of at least one.)
- Is the argument logically *convincing*? If "yes," why is it convincing? If "no," why isn't it convincing?
- What additional information/evidence would *strengthen* the argument?
- What additional information/evidence would *weaken* the argument?

Common Reasoning Fallacies in AWA Arguments

It is far beyond the scope of Part 1 to examine *every* type of logical flaw incorporated into the 90 official Arguments. Nevertheless, certain logical fallacies crop up again and again among the Arguments; so in this section we'll identify and examine these "frequent flaws." (By the way, these fallacies also appear on the Verbal section of the GMAT—among the Critical Reasoning questions; so you're doing double-duty in studying them here!)

☐ The Biased-Sample Fallacy

The fallacy of the *biased sample* is committed whenever the data for a statistical inference are drawn from a sample that is *not representative of the population* under consideration. Professional statisticians avoid this error through random sampling and other sampling techniques that are designed to eliminate bias in the data used to support their inferences.

Here is an argument that commits the fallacy of the biased sample:

"In a recent survey conducted on the Internet, eighty percent of the respondents indicated their strong disapproval of government regulation of the content and access of web-based information. This survey clearly shows that legislation designed to restrict the access to or control the content of Internet information will meet with strong opposition from the electorate."

The data for the inference in this argument are drawn from a sample that is not representative of the entire electorate. Since the survey was conducted on the Internet, not all members of the electorate have an equal chance of being included in the sample. Moreover, persons who use the Internet are more likely to have an opinion on the topic than persons who do not. For these reasons the sample is obviously biased.

☐ The Insufficient-Sample Fallacy

The fallacy of the small or insufficient sample is committed whenever too small a sample is used to warrant confidence in the conclusion or whenever greater reliability is attributed to the conclusion than is warranted by the sample size. Professional statisticians avoid this error by choosing samples of sufficient size to reduce the margin of error in the conclusion.

Here's an argument that commits the fallacy of the insufficient sample:

"I met my new boss at work today and she was very unpleasant. Twice when I tried to talk with her she said she was busy and told me not to interrupt her again. Later, when I needed her advice on a customer's problem, she ignored me and walked away. It's obvious that she has a bad attitude and is not going to be easy to work with."

The data for the inference in this argument are insufficient to support the conclusion. Three observations of a person's behavior are not sufficient to support a conclusion about the person's behavior in general. Obviously, the boss could just have been having a bad day or been engrossed in other things.

In many cases involving the insufficient-sample fallacy, the biased-sample fallacy is committed at the same time. Here are some of the official AWA Arguments that suffer from the biased-sample and/or insufficient-sample fallacies (question numbers here correspond to the sequence of 90 official questions):

- *Question Numbers: 7 8 10 26 30 32 43 45 48 51 56 58 64 70 72 83*

☐ The Fallacy of Faulty Analogy

Reasoning by analogy typically proceeds by comparing two things, then reasoning that because they are alike in various ways, and because one of them has a certain characteristic, it is likely that the other has this characteristic as well. The fallacy of *faulty analogy* is committed either:

- when we overlook or ignore relevant dissimilarities between the things being compared, or

- when the similarities between the things compared are not relevant to the characteristic being inferred in the conclusion.

Here's an example of the *first* type of faulty-analogy fallacy:

> "Joyce and Oona have similar tastes in fashion, music, movies and books, and both are vegetarians. Since Joyce is a big fan of the famous French chef Julia Child, it's likely that Oona is too."

In this example, numerous similarities between Joyce and Oona are taken as the basis for the inference, and, *all other things being equal*, the stated conclusion is the correct one to draw. However, if Joyce and Oona, for all their shared characteristics, fail to share similar tastes in food (perhaps Oona likes Thai cuisine, while Joyce prefers French cuisine), this (relevant) dissimilarity between them will weaken the argument considerably.

Here's an example of the *second* type of faulty-analogy fallacy:

> "Professors O'Toole and Stewart are alike in many ways. Both of them are young, handsome and well-liked by their students. O'Toole is an easy grader, so it is likely that Stewart is an easy grader as well."

In this example, the stated similarities between Professors O'Toole and Stewart are irrelevant to the characteristic stated in the conclusion. Obviously, age and appearance have no relevance to one's grading practices, and a professor may be well-liked for many other reasons besides being an easy grader.

Here are some of the AWA Arguments that suffer from the fallacy of faulty analogy (question numbers here correspond to the sequence of 90 official questions, as provided by ETS):

- *Question Numbers: 1 13 24 37 50 55 63 66 71 85 86 88*

☐ The "After This, Therefore Because of This" Fallacy

This fallacy is by far the most common form of *causal reasoning* error, and it is the most common such error found among the AWA Arguments. This is the fallacy of concluding on insufficient grounds that because some event X comes *after* some other event Y, X must have *caused* Y. Many common bad-luck superstitions are examples of this fallacy (e.g., the black cat crossing one's path, walking under ladders, etc.).

The error in arguments that commit this fallacy is that their conclusions are causal claims that are not sufficiently substantiated by the evidence. In most instances of this fallacy, the only evidence that is offered to support the causal claim is a temporal relationship between two conditions or events; the one that occurs first is identified as the cause, the one that follows is identified as the effect. Typically, the causal connection between the two events is implausible given our general understanding of the world.

Here are two examples of the "after this, therefore because of this" fallacy:

"Ten minutes after walking into the auditorium, I began to feel sick to my stomach. There must have been something in the air in that building that caused my nausea."

"The stock market declined shortly after the election of the president, thus indicating the lack of confidence the business community has in the new administration."

In the first example, a causal connection is posited between two events simply on the basis of one occurring before the other. Without further evidence to support it, the causal claim based on the correlation is premature.

The second example is typical of modern news reporting. The only evidence offered in this argument to support the implicit causal claim that the decline in the stock market was caused by the election of the president is the fact that election preceded the decline. While this may have been a causal factor in the decline of the stock market, to argue that it is the cause without additional information and auxiliary hypotheses that make the causal connection plausible is to commit the "after this, therefore because of this fallacy."

Here are some of the AWA Arguments that suffer from the "after this, therefore because of this" fallacy (question numbers here correspond to the sequence of 90 official questions, as provided by ETS):

- *Question Numbers: 2 11 14 22 44 52 83*

☐ The False Dichotomy Fallacy

The *false dichotomy* fallacy, also known as the *false dilemma* fallacy, is committed when one assumes without warrant that there are only two alternatives and reasons that since one of the alternatives is false or unacceptable the other must be true or accepted. Of course, in cases where there are in fact only two alternatives, and this fact is obvious or can be justified, this pattern of reasoning is highly effective and acceptable. Typically, in arguments in which this fallacy occurs no evidence is offered to support the claim that there are only two alternatives available and a little reflection reveals that this claim is not self evident. This fallacy is commonly referred to as the "black-and-white" fallacy.

Here is an example of the false-dichotomy fallacy:

"Either we put convicted child molesters in jail for life or we risk having our children become their next victims. We certainly can't risk this, so we had better lock them up for the rest of their lives."

The argument above assumes that there are only two possible alternatives open to us. No evidence is offered to support this claim and a little reflection reveals that it is not obviously the case. While child molestation is a difficult problem to deal with, it is unlikely that the only solution to the problem is the one mentioned in the argument. It is also unlikely that this is the only way that we can protect our children from becoming the victims of convicted offenders.

Here are some of the AWA Arguments that suffer from the false-dichotomy fallacy (question numbers here correspond to the sequence of 90 official questions, as provided by ETS):

- *Question Numbers: 28 29 73 87 89*

☐ The "All Things are Equal" Fallacy

The *all things are equal* fallacy is committed when it is assumed without justification that background conditions have remained the same at different times or at different locations. In most instances this is an unwarranted assumption for the simple reason that things rarely remain the same over extended periods of time, and things rarely remain the same from place to place.

At the top of page 30 is an example of the "all things are equal" fallacy:

"Two years ago when it when it rained for three days in a row the river jumped its banks and flooded the town. The latest weather

> forecast predicts that it will rain for at least three days, so it looks as though the town will be flooded again this year too."

The assumption operative in this argument is that nothing has changed in the two year interim since the last flood. No evidence or justification is offered for this assumption. Moreover, it is just as likely an assumption that things *have* changed and that measures were put in place to avoid a reoccurrence of the flooding.

Here are some of the AWA Arguments that suffer from the "all things are equal" fallacy (question numbers here correspond to the sequence of 90 official questions, as provided by ETS):

- *Question Numbers: 2 59 87*

☐ The Fallacy of Equivocation

The *fallacy of equivocation* occurs when a key word or phrase that has more than one meaning is employed in different meanings throughout the argument. Since the truth of the premises and the conclusion is in part a function of the meanings of the words in the sentences that express them, a shift in meaning of key terms in the argument will enable one to draw conclusions from premises that do not in fact support them.

Here's an example of an argument that commits the fallacy of equivocation.

> "Logic is the study of arguments, and since arguments are disagreements, it follows that logic is the study of disagreements."

In this example, the word "argument" is employed in two different meanings. In the first premise "argument" is used to mean "a discourse in which reasons are offered in support of a claim"; in the second premise "argument" is defined as meaning "a disagreement." If we adopt the second meaning, the first premise is false. If we adopt the first meaning, the second premise is false. Either way, the premises simply fail to provide support for the conclusion.

Here are some of the AWA Arguments that suffer from the fallacy of equivocation (question numbers here correspond to the sequence of 90 official questions, as provided by ETS):

- *Question Numbers: 21 36 57 85*

Organizing Your Argument Essay

As with the Issue essay, there is no single "correct" way to organize an Argument essay. In our view, however, your essay should include separate "introduction" and "conclusion" paragraphs, as well as at least two "body" paragraphs in which you develop your critique of the stated argument. The following template spells out this structure in more detail, and each of the sample Argument essays in this book follow this basic pattern.

As with the Issue essay, you do not have to adhere strictly to this format in order to write an effective Argument essay. You may find that some other form works better for you, especially for the body of your essay. Also, the numbers of sentences indicated for each paragraph here are merely suggestions or guidelines, not hard-and-fast rules.

(*Note:* The *transitional phrases* used here are purposely simplistic; do not simply "parrot" them word-for-word in your essay or adopt a mechanistic fill-in-the-blank approach. If you do, your essay might appear stilted or contrived.)

Introductory Paragraph (2–4 Sentences)

Try to accomplish three goals in your introductory paragraph:

- Briefly restate the argument

- Briefly trace the argument's line of reasoning

- Indicate the extent to which the argument is logically convincing

Here's a sample template for the first paragraph that accomplishes these goals:

> The author concludes that ———————————— because ————
> ————————————————————. The author's line of
> reasoning is that ————————————————————
> ————. This argument is unconvincing for several reasons.

First Body Paragraph (3–5 Sentences)

In the first body paragraph your goal is to critique *one* of the following:

- The reasoning of the argument

- One of the premises of the argument

- One of the assumptions of the argument

Here's a sample template for this paragraph that accomplishes this goal:

> First of all, —————————— is based upon the questionable assumption
> that ————————————————————. However, ——————————
> ————————————Moreover, ———————————————————.

Second Body Paragraph (3–5 Sentences)

In this paragraph your goal is to critique *one* of the following:

- The reasoning of the argument
- One of the premises of the argument
- One of the assumptions of the argument

Here's a sample template for this paragraph that accomplishes this goal:

> Secondly, the author assumes that ————————————————————
> ——————————. However, ————————————————————. It seems
> equally reasonable to assume that ————————————————————.

Third (and Fourth) Body Paragraph (Optional; 3–5 Sentences)

In this paragraph your goal is to critique *one* of the following:

- The reasoning of the argument
- One of the premises of the argument
- One of the assumptions of the argument

Here's a sample template for this paragraph that accomplishes this goal:

> Finally *[Thirdly]*, ——————— the author fails to consider————————
> ——————————————— For example, ————————————————
> ———————————. Because the author's argument lacks ———————————.

Final Paragraph (2–4 Sentences)

In the final paragraph your goals are to:

- Summarize your critique of the argument
- Discuss how the argument could be improved or strengthened

Here's a sample template for the final paragraph that accomplishes these goals:

In conclusion, to convince me that ————————————, the author
would have to provide evidence that ——————————————
————. Without this additional evidence, I am not convinced that ————
——————————————————.

□ Putting It All Together—an Illustrative Argument Essay

You've already seen one Argument question and response (pages 22–23). Now here's another. In reading the response, focus on how well it follows the advice just given for writing a good Argument essay. Also keep in mind:

- The response strictly follows the organizational template presented above. We've underlined transitional phrases in the response to "underscore" this feature. (You won't use underlining on the actual exam, of course.)

- The response is simple in style and language and brief enough (about 325 words) to compose and type in 30 minutes.

- The response received a score of 6 (the highest possible score) from a former GMAT reader, who evaluated it just for us.

Simulated Question C	(Analysis-of-an-Argument)

"Most environmentalists believe that the 'information superhighway' does not pose a serious threat to the environment. But what they fail to see is that the information superhighway will enable millions of people to work at home, far from the office. In other words, it will enable them to flee the cities and the suburbs and take up residence in areas that have hitherto been unpopulated and unspoiled. This dispersal of the populace portends an environmental disaster of the first magnitude."

Discuss how logically convincing you find this argument. In your discussion, you should analyze the argument's line of reasoning and use of evidence. It may be appropriate in your critique to call into question certain assumptions underlying the argument and/or to indicate what evidence might weaken or strengthen the argument. It may also be appropriate to discuss how you would alter the argument to make it more convincing and/or discuss what additional evidence, if any, would aid in evaluating the argument.

The author concludes that the information superhighway poses a serious threat to the environment because it will emancipate millions of people from traditional work places. The author's line of reasoning is that once emancipated, these workers will migrate into previously unpopulated and unspoiled areas, resulting in an environmental disaster of the first magnitude. This argument is unconvincing for several reasons.

First of all, the author's prediction of environmental disaster is based upon the questionable assumption that most people would prefer to live in unpopulated and remote areas. However, the author offers no evidence to support this crucial assumption. Moreover, given that most people are gregarious by nature, the truth of this claim is highly unlikely.

Secondly, the author assumes that most people live in cities and suburbs only because of the proximity to work and that, given the opportunity, they would move. Again, however, the author provides no evidence to support this questionable assumption. It seems equally reasonable to assume that people live in cities and suburbs for other reasons as well, such as the proximity to entertainment and cultural events.

Finally, the author fails to consider the environmental benefits this technology might bring. For example, transmitting information uses much less energy than transporting commuters, so it will save precious natural resources and be less polluting. It may turn out that the environmental advantages of this technology far outweigh the disadvantages. Because the author's argument lacks a complete analysis of the situation, the author's forecast of environmental disaster cannot be taken seriously.

In conclusion, to convince me that the information superhighway poses a threat to the environment, the author would have to provide evidence that, given the opportunity, most people would in fact move to remote and unspoiled areas. Additionally, the author would have to show that the adverse effects of this migration would outweigh the benefits of this technology. Without this additional evidence, I am not convinced that the information superhighway poses a serious threat to the environment.

Now go back to page 23 and read again the response to Simulated Question B. Underline transitional phrases as in the response above. You'll notice that although different transitional words and phrases are used in the two essays, their overall organizational structure is *very* similar!

❑ Finding an Appropriate and Persuasive Style

According to GMAC officials, GMAT readers are instructed to place *less weight* on writing style and mechanics than on content and organization. This doesn't mean, however, that your writing style won't influence the reader or affect your AWA score. Indeed, it will! If your writing style is poor, the reader will be predisposed to award a lower score, regardless of the ideas you present and how you organize them. To attain a high AWA score (5 or 6), your writing must be:

- Concise (direct and to-the-point, not wordy or verbose)

- Correct in grammar, mechanics, and usage (conforming to the requirements of Standard Written English)

- Persuasive in style (using rhetorical devices effectively)

- Varied in sentence length and structure (to add interest and variety as well as to demonstrate maturity and sophistication in writing style)

All of this is easier said than done, of course. Don't worry if you're not a "natural" when it comes to writing effective prose. Few GMAT test-takers are. A person's writing style develops over many years, of course. Nevertheless, you *can* improve your style in a few weeks to prepare for the GMAT. Here are some specific style-related guidelines for writing AWA essays.

To help your ideas flow from one to the next, develop an arsenal of rhetorical and transitional "buzz" words (and phrases). Many of the same rhetorical and transitional devices appear over and over among the essays in Parts 2 and 3. By reading these sample essays, the devices they employ can become part of your writing style as well. As you read the essays, highlight your favorite "buzz" phrases, then review them later and add them to your own rhetorical inventory.

Maintain a somewhat formal tone, avoiding slang and colloquialisms. Don't try to be hip or informal in your essays. Try to convey a somewhat formal tone through your choice of words. If your essay sounds conversational in tone, it's probably a bit too informal for the GMAT. Avoid colloquialisms and jargon, whether in quotes or not. Otherwise, instead of hitting a "home run" with your essay, you'll be "out of luck" with the GMAT readers, and you'll have to "snake" your way in to a "bottom-barrel" MBA program. Get the idea?

Don't try to make your point with humor or sarcasm. Avoid puns, double-meanings, and humor. Not that the GMAT readers don't have a sense of humor. It's just that they leave it at the door when they enter ETS regional offices to do their work. (That sentence exhibits just the sort of "humor" you should avoid in your GMAT essays.) Sarcasm is entirely inappropriate for your GMAT essays. Also, avoid coming across as flippant (disrespectful).

Use rhetorical questions for stylistic effect. Rhetorical questions are posed to help make a point, not to elicit a response. They can be quite effective, especially in Issue essays. Yet how many test-takers think to incorporate them into their essays? Not many. (By the way, we just posed a rhetorical question.) If you do pose a rhetorical question, just be sure to provide an answer to it!

Use Latin and other non-English terms sparingly. One of the primary skills being tested in the AWA sections is your capacity with Standard Written *English*. So try to avoid non-English words. However, the occasional use of Latin terms and acronyms—for example, *per se, de facto, ad hoc, i.e.,* and *e.g.*—is perfectly acceptable. Non-English words used commonly in academic writing—such as *vis-à-vis, caveat* and *laissez faire*—are acceptable as well. Just don't overdo it.

Note: The rules of Standard Written English require that Latin and other foreign terms be italicized (or underlined). However, the CAT word processor does not allow you to incorporate these attributes or special accent marks (as in *vis-à-vis,* for example). So leave such words as is, but be sure they are terms that most educated people are familiar with.

Don't try too hard to impress the reader with your vocabulary. There's nothing wrong with demonstrating a well-educated vocabulary. But don't put the reader off by using obscure words that he is she is unlikely to be familiar with. Avoid technical terminology understood only by specialists and scholars in a specific field. In particular, don't assume that the GMAT readers know the language of economists; in all likelihood, they don't.

It's okay to refer to yourself, at your option. Self-references—singular as well as plural—are perfectly acceptable, though optional. Just be consistent:

- "*I* disagree with…"

- "In *my* view,…"

- "Without additional evidence, *we* cannot assume that…"

Be sure your references to the source of the statement or argument are appropriate. The first time you refer to the source, be specific *and* correct—e.g., "this editorial," "the ad," "the vice president," or "ACME Shoes." If no specific source is provided, try using "speaker," "statement" or "claim" in your Issue essay, and "author" or "argument" in your Argument essay. Also, it's okay to save keystrokes by using an occasional pronoun. Be sure, however, that your pronouns are appropriate and consistent:

- "The *speaker* argues….*Her* line of reasoning is…; but *she* overlooks…"

- "To strengthen *its* conclusion, the *board* must…. *It* must also…"

☐ Coping with the CAT System and Computer "Interface"

During the GMAT CAT, you must record your essay responses electronically, with the word processor built into the CAT system. (Unless the GMAC decides otherwise in the future, handwritten responses will not be permitted.) Before we look at the CAT word-processing features and limitations, let's examine the features built into the CAT interface that are common to all sections of the exam. (These features are illustrated in the "screen shot" on page 38.)

The CAT Titlebar

A dark "titlebar" will appear across the top of the computer screen *at all times* (you cannot hide the titlebar) during *all* test sections. The title bar displays three items:

- *left corner:* time elapsed for the current section
- *middle:* the name and number of the test section [for the AWA sections, you'll probably see "Section 1 (or 2): Analytical Writing 1 (or 2)"]
- *right corner:* the current question number and total number of questions on the current section (nothing is displayed here, however, for the AWA sections)

The CAT Toolbar

A series of six buttons appear in a "toolbar" across the bottom of the computer screen *at all times* (you cannot hide the toolbar) during *all* test sections.

Quit Test. Click on this button to STOP the test and CANCEL your scores for the entire test. If you click here, a dialog box will appear on the screen, asking you to confirm this operation.

Exit Section. Click on this button if you finish the section before the allotted time expires and wish to proceed immediately to the next section. A dialog box will appear on the screen, asking you to confirm this operation.

Time. Click on this button to display/hide the *time remaining* in the section. Since the time *elapsed* is displayed in any event (in the upper left corner), you probably won't need this additional feature, unless you forget what the time limit is for the current section.

Time elapsed

CAT Title bar

Name and Number
of Text Section

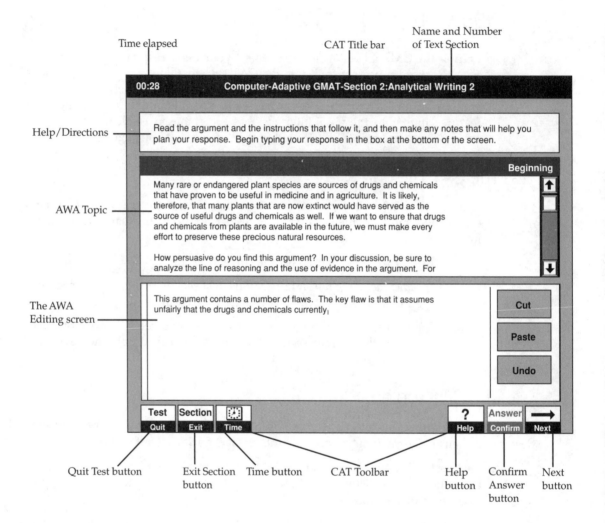

Help/Directions

00:28   **Computer-Adaptive GMAT-Section 2:Analytical Writing 2**

Read the argument and the instructions that follow it, and then make any notes that will help you plan your response. Begin typing your response in the box at the bottom of the screen.

Beginning

AWA Topic

Many rare or endangered plant species are sources of drugs and chemicals that have proven to be useful in medicine and in agriculture. It is likely, therefore, that many plants that are now extinct would have served as the source of useful drugs and chemicals as well. If we want to ensure that drugs and chemicals from plants are available in the future, we must make every effort to preserve these precious natural resources.

How persuasive do you find this argument? In your discussion, be sure to analyze the line of reasoning and the use of evidence in the argument. For

The AWA
Editing screen

This argument contains a number of flaws. The key flaw is that it assumes unfairly that the drugs and chemicals currently

Cut

Paste

Undo

Test	Section	▦		?	Answer	→
Quit	Exit	Time		Help	Confirm	Next

Quit Test button

Exit Section
button

Time button

CAT Toolbar

Help
button

Confirm
Answer
button

Next
button

Help. Click on this button to display/hide the directions at the top of the screen. By default, the directions are displayed (as in the screen shot on page 38). Assuming you will already be familiar with the directions, you should hide them at all times to allow for more test material on your screen without scrolling up and down using the vertical scroll bar.

Confirm Answer. When you click on the "Next" button to proceed to the next question, a dialogue box will appear on your screen asking you to confirm your response. Once you confirm your response, the next question is presented, and you cannot go back and change your response to the prior question. If you do not wish to confirm your response, disable the "confirm" function by clicking on the "Confirm Answer" icon. Click on the icon again to enable the function. If the icon is dark, the function is enabled; if the icon appears light, the function is disabled. [*Note:* The "confirm answer" function is automatically disabled during the AWA section.]

Next. Click on this button to proceed to the next question. As noted above, a "confirm answer" dialogue box will then appear.

The AWA Word-Processing Features

For each of the two 30-minute AWA questions, you will be provided with a blank editing screen on which to enter your response (as in the screen shot on page 38), using the editing functions provided by the CAT word-processor. These functions are examined in this section.

◻ Navigation and Editing—Available Keyboard Commands

Here are the navigational and editing keyboard keys available in the CAT word processor:

Backspace	removes the character to the left of the cursor
Delete	removes the character to the right of the cursor
Home	moves the cursor to the beginning of the line
End	moves the cursor to the end of the line
Arrow Keys	move the cursor up, down, left, or right
Enter	inserts a paragraph break (starts a new line)
Page Up	moves the cursor up one page (screen)
Page Down	moves the cursor down one page (screen)

□ Common Keyboard Commands Not Available

Certain often-used features of standard word-processing programs are not available in the CAT word processor. For example, no keyboard commands are available for:

TAB— disabled (does not function)

Beginning/end of line

Beginning/end of paragraph

Beginning/end of document

□ Mouse-Driven Editing Functions

In addition to editing keys, the CAT word processor includes mouse-driven "cut," "paste," and "undo." Drag-and-drop cut-and-paste is not available.

Selecting text you wish to cut or copy. You select text the same way as with standard word-processing programs: either (1) hold down your mouse button while sweeping the I-beam on the screen over the desired text, or (2) hold down the SHIFT key and use the navigation keys to select text.

The "Cut" Button. If you wish to delete text but want to save it to a temporary "clipboard" for pasting elsewhere, select that text (see above) then click on the "Cut" button. (The CAT word processor stores only one "cut" text selection at a time in its memory.) Cutting text is not the same as deleting it. When you delete text (using the "delete" key), you cannot paste it elsewhere in your document (but see *The "Undo" Button* below).

The "Paste" button. If you wish to move text from one position to another, select and cut the text, then reposition your cursor where you want the text to go, and click on the "Paste" button. (The CAT word processor stores only one "cut" text selection at a time in its memory.)

The "Undo" button. Click on this button to undo the most recent "delete," "cut," or "paste" that you performed. (The CAT word processor stores only your most recent "delete," "cut," or "paste." Multiple "undo" is not available.)

The vertical scrollbar. Drag the square button on the vertical scrollbar (located just to the right of the editing screen) up and down to scroll up and down your essay. To minimize the amount of scrolling you must do, be sure to hide the directions (click on the "Help" icon) that otherwise appear just below the Titlebar at the top of the screen. Notice that a vertical scroll bar also appears to the right of the AWA *question.* Be sure to scroll all the way down to make sure that you have read the entire question.

The CAT System: Tutorial, Practice, and Demonstration of Competence

To ensure that you are comfortable with the Computer-Adaptive Test (CAT) System, before the test begins the CAT System will lead you through a tutorial (at your option), as well as giving you the opportunity to practice using the system by responding to sample questions (also at your option). During the tutorial, you will learn how to:

- Use the mouse
- Scroll the screen display up and down
- Select and change a response
- Confirm a response and move to the next question
- Access the on-line help
- Access the directions for the current test section
- Access the on-screen timing clock
- Use the AWA word-processing features

To further ensure that you are sufficiently capable of handling the computerized aspect of the GMAT CAT, before beginning the actual timed exam you must demonstrate adequate competence in performing the tasks listed above. While the tutorial and practice questions are optional, demonstration of competence with the CAT System is *required* before testing begins.

Fonts, attributes, and hyphenation. The type of "font" appearing on the screen as you type your response cannot be altered. The text size can be altered, but only with a special "Zoomtext" option, available only upon request *in advance*. Attributes—such as bold, italics, and underlining—are not available. For titles of books and movies, and for other proper nouns that would otherwise be italicized or underlined, we suggest using either quotation marks or nothing at all. If you use Latin terms, such as *per se*, or other foreign words which should otherwise be italicized, don't worry that you cannot italicize them in your CAT response. Just leave them as is. The readers understand the limitations of the CAT word processor. Neither an automatic nor manual hyphenation feature is provided by the CAT word processor (and the essays in Parts 2 and 3 do not include hyphenation).

Do fast typists and computer-literate test-takers have an advantage on the AWA section? In developing the CAT word-processor, ETS has taken every measure to eliminate any advantage test-takers with extensive word-processing experience might have on the test. The word processor used for the AWA is *very* basic, incorporating only the few simple editing features described above, which can be quickly and easily mastered. The tutorial, practice, and required demonstration of competence prior to the test further ensure a level playing field for all test-takers (see the sidebar above). Notwithstanding the efforts of

ETS to eliminate any advantage that certain test-takers might have, a test-taker who is experienced with "cut-and-paste" mouse operations or who is a fast and accurate typist may in fact be at a *slight* advantage.

Can slow typists obtain permission to produce *handwritten* essays? No, except for test-takers who suffer from a physical handicap that adversely affects their ability to use both hands for typing. However, the GMAC and ETS may modify the rules in the future. Check with the GMAC for its current policy.

By the way: Test-takers use only the mouse (not the keyboard) during the Quantitative and Verbal sections, so no keyboard commands are involved during those sections.

PART 2

Sample Responses to the *Real*
Analysis-of-an-Issue
Questions

PART 2 includes sample responses to all 90 Analysis-of-an-Issue questions. The responses are numbered sequentially from 1 to 90, corresponding to the sequence of questions in the ETS question "bank." (See the *Appendix* for details about downloading the questions via the GMAC Web site.) As you study these responses, keep these facts in mind:

- These essays are *not* actual responses by GMAT test-takers; they are responses that *we* wrote. And they are not, of course, "the" answers; there is no one "correct" response to any AWA question.

- These essays were written under timed conditions. However, we did go back and fine-tune them to make them better models for you to study. So don't be concerned if your essays aren't as polished as these. Be realistic about what *you* can produce in 30 minutes.

- These essays are intended to provide you with substantive, organizational, and stylistic ideas for composing your Issue essay; but they are *not* for copying word-for-word. Be forewarned: GMAT graders will be on the lookout for plagiarism.

- The AWA question to which each essay responds is referenced by number *and* by a brief identifying phrase (in the shaded box above the response). We've included these phrases to help you match each response to its corresponding question. These phrases are *not* substitutes for or summaries of the official questions. Be sure to obtain and read the actual questions as well!

Issue No. 1   Censorship of television and radio programs

The extent to which the broadcast media should be censored for offensive language and behavior involves a conflict between our right as individuals to freely express ourselves and the duty of government to protect its citizenry from potential harm. In my view, our societal interest in preventing the harm that exposure to obscenity produces takes precedence over the rights of individuals to broadcast this type of content.

First of all, I believe that exposure to obscene and offensive language and behavior does indeed cause similar behavior on the part of those who are exposed to it. Although we may not have conclusive scientific evidence of a cause-effect relationship, ample anecdotal evidence establishes a significant correlation. Moreover, both common sense and our experiences with children inform us that people tend to mimic the language and behavior they are exposed to.

Secondly, I believe that obscene and offensive behavior is indeed harmful to a society. The harm it produces is, in my view, both palpable and profound. For the individual, it has a debasing impact on vital human relationships; for the society, it promotes a tendency toward immoral and antisocial behavior. Both outcomes, in turn, tear apart the social fabric that holds a society together.

Those who advocate unbridled individual expression might point out that the right of free speech is intrinsic to a democracy and necessary to its survival. Even so, this right is not absolute, nor is it the most critical element. In my assessment, the interests served by restricting obscenity in broadcast media are, on balance, more crucial to the survival of a society. Advocates of free expression might also point out difficulties in defining "obscene" or "offensive" language or behavior. But in my view, however difficult it may be to agree on standards, the effort is worthwhile.

In sum, it is in our best interest as a society for the government to censor broadcast media for obscene and offensive language and behavior. Exposure to such media content tends to harm society and its citizenry in ways that are worth preventing, even in light of the resulting infringement of our right of free expression.

Issue No. 2	Energy sources and international cooperation

The speaker asserts that an international effort is needed to preserve the world's energy resources for future generations. While individual nations, like people, are at times willing to make voluntary sacrifices for the benefit of others, my view is that international coordination is nevertheless necessary in light of the strong propensity of nations to act selfishly, and because the problem is international in scope.

The main reason why an international effort is necessary is that, left to their own devices, individual nations, like people, will act according to their short-term motives and self-interest. The mere existence of military weapons indicates that self-interest and national survival are every nation's prime drivers. And overconsumption by industrialized nations of natural resources they know to be finite, when alternatives are at hand, demonstrates that self-interest and short-sightedness extend to the use of energy resources as well. Furthermore, nations, like people, tend to rationalize their own self-serving policies and actions. Emerging nations might argue, for example, that they should be exempt from energy conservation because it is the industrialized nations who can better afford to make sacrifices and who use more resources in the first place.

Another reason why an international effort is required is that other problems of an international nature have also required global cooperation. For example, has each nation independently recognized the folly of nuclear weapons proliferation and voluntarily disarmed? No; only by way of an international effort, based largely on coercion of strong leaders against detractors, along with an appeal to self-interest, have we made some progress. By the same token, efforts of individual nations to thwart international drug trafficking have proven largely futile, because efforts have not been internationally based. Similarly, the problem of energy conservation transcends national borders in that either all nations must cooperate, or all will ultimately suffer.

In conclusion, nations are made up of individuals who, when left unconstrained, tend to act in their own self-interest and with short-term motives. In light of how we have dealt, or not dealt, with other global problems, it appears that an international effort is needed to ensure the preservation of natural resources for future generations.

Issue No. 3   **Hierarchical vs. flat organizational structure**

Which is a better way to classify and reward employees of a business: a "flat" organizational structure or a hierarchical structure? The speaker prefers a "flat" structure in which distinctions between employees based on education or experience are not used as a basis for monetary rewards. I strongly disagree with the speaker's view, for two reasons.

In the first place, the speaker's preference for a "flat" structure is based upon the claim that cooperation and collegiality among employees is more likely under this system than under a hierarchical one. However, this claim ignores our everyday experience in human interaction. Disagreements among coworkers are inevitable. Without a clear authoritative figure to resolve them and to make final decisions, disputes are more likely to go unresolved and even worsen, thereby undermining cooperation, congeniality and, ultimately, productivity and profit.

In the second place, whether or not collegiality and cooperation are best fostered by a flat organizational structure is beside the point. My main reason for rejecting an organizational structure that does not distinguish workers in terms of their abilities or experience is that under such a system workers have little incentive to improve their skills, accomplish their work-related goals, or assume responsibility for the completion of their assigned tasks. In my experience, human motivation is such that without enticements such as money, status or recognition, few people would accomplish anything of value or assume responsibility for any task. A flat system actually might provide a distinct disincentive for productivity and efficiency insofar as workers are not held accountable for the quality or quantity of their work. By ignoring human nature, then, a company may be harming itself by encouraging laziness and complacency.

In sum, the speaker's opinion that a "flat" organizational structure is the best way to promote collegiality and cooperation among employees runs contrary to common sense about how people act in a work environment, and in any case provides a feeble rationale for the preference of one organizational structure over another.

Issue No. 4	Manifestations of power

This quote means essentially that people admire powerful individuals who do not use their power to the utmost to achieve their goals but rather use only the minimum amount required to attain them. While this view is admirable in the abstract, the statement is inaccurate in that it fails to reflect how people actually behave.

The popularity of "revenge" movies aptly illustrates that many people are not impressed with individuals who use restraint when exercising their power. In these movies the protagonist is typically portrayed as having certain physical abilities that would enable him to easily defeat the various adversaries he encounters. In the initial confrontations with these individuals he typically refrains from using his abilities to defeat them. The audience, however, soon grows tired of this, and when the hero finally loses control and completely demolishes his opponent, they burst into applause. This homey example strongly suggests that many people are more impressed with the use of power than with the restraint of its use.

The Gulf War provides another example of a situation where restraint in the use of power was not widely acclaimed. When the allied forces under the command of General Schwartzkoff showed restraint by not annihilating the retreating Iraqi army, the general was widely criticized by the public for not using the force available to him to eliminate this potential enemy once and for all. This example shows once again that people are often not impressed by individuals who exhibit restraint in using their power.

In conclusion, the examples cited above clearly indicate that, contrary to the view expressed in the quote, many—if not most—people are more impressed with individuals who utilize their power to the utmost than with those who exercise restraint in the use of their power.

Issue No. 5   **Sharing decision-making**

Which is a more productive method of performing a group task: allowing all group members to share in the decision making, duties and responsibilities, or appointing one member to make decisions, delegate duties and take responsibility? The speaker's opinion is that the first method is always the best one. In my view, however, each of these alternatives is viable in certain circumstances, as illustrated by two very different examples.

A jury in a criminal trial is good example of a group in which shared decision-making, duties, and responsibility is the most appropriate and effective way to get the job done. Each member of the jury is on equal footing with the others. While one person is appointed to head the jury, his or her function is to act as facilitator, not as leader. To place ultimate authority and responsibility on the facilitator would essentially be to appoint a judge, and to thereby defeat the very purpose of the jury system.

By way of contrast, a trauma unit in a hospital is a case in which one individual should assume responsibility, delegate duties and make decisions. In trauma units, split-second decisions are inherently part of the daily routine, and it is generally easier for one person to make a quick decision than for a team to agree on how to proceed. One could argue that since decisions in trauma units are typically life-and-death ones, leaving these decisions to one person is too risky. However, this argument ignores the crucial point that only the most experienced individuals should be trusted with such a burden and with such power; leaving decisions to inexperienced group members can jeopardize a patient's very life.

In conclusion, I agree that in some situations the best way to accomplish a task is through teamwork—sharing responsibility, duties and decision making. However, in other situations, especially those where quick decisions are necessary or where individual experience is critical, the most effective means is for one individual to serve as leader and assume ultimate responsibility for completing the job.

Issue No. 6   The definition of success

The speaker here defines success simply as the ability to choose how to spend one's life. Under this definition, people who have the freedom to do whatever they want at any time they choose would presumably be the most successful ones, while those who have no such freedom would be the biggest failures. Viewing the definition in this light reveals three serious problems with it.

The chief problem with this definition of success is that by the definition nearly all people would be regarded as failures. The reason for this is simple. Most people have extremely limited choices in what they can do and when they can do it. In other words, unrestricted freedom of choice is a luxury only a few people—perhaps a handful of tyrannical dictators and ultra-wealthy individuals—can afford.

Secondly, people who have a high degree of freedom in choosing their lifestyle often acquire it through means that would not earn them the accolade of being successful. For example, lottery winners or people who inherit a great deal of money may be able to spend their life in any way they choose, but few people would regard them as successful merely due to their financial fortune.

A third reason this definition of success is unacceptable is that it repudiates some of our basic intuitions about success. For most people, success is related to achievement. The more you achieve, the more successful you are; conversely, the less you achieve the less successful you are. Defining success in terms of freedom of choice ignores this intuition.

In sum, the proposed definition of success is far too limiting, and it belies our intuition about the concept. I think most people would agree with me that success is better defined in terms of the attainment of goals.

Issue No. 7   **Giving advice to other people**

Is the best way to advise people to simply find out what they want and help them attain it? In my view, this method is generally not the best way to proceed in advising others; it ignores the plain truth that many people do not know what they want and do not know what is best for themselves.

My main reason for rejecting this technique is that people very rarely have any clear idea of what they want. This applies not only to consumer items such as clothing, cars and luxury items but also to what they want out of life in general. In fact, numerous studies have shown that most people cannot list the ten things they want most out of life, even if given considerable time to think about it.

My second reason for rejecting this method is that more often than not what people want is not what is best for them. Parents continually face this problem when advising their children. For example, suppose a child wants to quit school and get a job. Surely, the parents would be derelict in helping their child attain this want instead of convincing the child that continuing education would be in his or her best interest.

Admittedly, following the proposed advising method would result in a high rate of compliance, since the person being advised would act consistently with his or her own will by following the advice. However, as noted above, acting according to what one wants is not necessarily desirable. Proponents of this method might also point to college counselors as models of this technique. However, college counselors should not necessarily be held up as models for advising people generally, let alone as models for advising students.

In conclusion, I do not agree that the best way to advise people is to find out what they desire and help them achieve it. In my estimation the pitfalls of such a technique outweigh any of its potential advantages.

Issue No. 8   Monetary systems

The prospect of converting the world's monetary system of metal coins and printed paper into a computerized system of credits and debits is intriguing. Opponents of the idea regard a digital economy as a dangerous step toward a totalitarian society in which an elite class dominates an information-starved lower class. My view, however, is that conversion to a digital economy has far-reaching economic and social virtues that outweigh the potential risk of misuse by a political elite.

Supporters of the idea of "digital cash" view the move to a digital economy as the next logical step toward a global system of free trade and competition. Herein lies the main virtue of a digital economy. In facilitating trade among nations, consumers worldwide would enjoying a broader range of goods at more competitive prices.

In addition, a digital economy would afford customers added convenience, while at the same time saving money for businesses. Making purchases with electronic currency would be simple, fast, and secure. There would be no need to carry cash, and no need for cashiers to collect it. A good example of the convenience and savings afforded by such a system is the "pay and go" gasoline pump used at many service stations today. Using these pumps saves time for the customer and saves money for the business.

A third benefit of such a system is its potential to eliminate illegal monetary transactions. Traffickers of illegal arms and drugs, dealers in black-market contraband, and counterfeiters all rely on tangible currency to conduct their activities. By eliminating hard currency, illegal transactions such as these would be much easier to track and record. As a result, illegal monetary transactions could be virtually eliminated. A related benefit would be the ability to thwart tax evasion by collecting tax revenues on transactions that otherwise would not be recorded.

To sum up, I think it would be a good idea to convert current monetary systems into a system of electronic accounts. The economic benefits, convenience and savings afforded by such a system, along with the potential to reduce crime, far outweigh the remote possibility of a significant social or political shift toward totalitarianism.

Issue No. 9   Employees' personal lives

Should employees leave their personal lives entirely behind them when they enter the workplace, as the speaker suggests here? While I agree that employees should not allow their personal lives to interfere with their jobs, the speaker fails to consider that integrating personal life with work can foster a workplace ambiance that helps everyone do a better job, thereby promoting success for the organization.

Engaging coworkers in occasional conversation about personal interests and activities can help build collegiality among coworkers that adds to their sense of common purpose on the job. Managers would be well advised to participate in and perhaps even plan the sharing of personal information—as a leadership tool as well as a morale booster. An employee feels valued when the boss takes time to ask about the employee's family or recent vacation. The employee, in turn, is likely to be more loyal to and cooperative with the boss. Company-sponsored social events—picnics, parties, excursions, and so forth—also help to produce greater cohesiveness in an organization, by providing opportunities for employees to bond with one another in ways that translate into better working relationships.

Admittedly, employees should guard against allowing their personal life to impinge upon their job performance or intrude on coworkers. Excessive chatting about non-business topics, frequent personal telephone calls, and the like, are always distracting. And romances between coworkers are best kept confidential, at least to the extent they disrupt work or demoralize or offend other employees. By the same token, however, employees who are too aloof—sharing nothing personal with others—may be resented by coworkers who perceive them as arrogant, unfriendly or uncooperative. The ill-will and lack of communication that is likely to result may ultimately harm the organization.

In the final analysis, employees should strike a careful balance when they mix their personal lives with their jobs. Although there are some circumstances in which bringing one's personal life to the job may be counterproductive, for many reasons it is a good idea to inject small doses of personal life into the workplace.

Issue No. 10	Process vs. product

The question at hand is whether the process of making or doing something is ultimately more important than the final product. Process may not always be more important than product, but it often is. A process may provide an opportunity for new and important discoveries with ramifications far beyond the current product; moreover, a process can often be an important end in and of itself for those engaged in it.

New discoveries are often unexpectedly made during routine processes. Such was the case with Alexander Fleming in 1928, who while conducting an unremarkable study of bacteria, discovered inadvertently that mold growing on one of his cultures was killing the bacteria. His ordinary process led to an unexpected and remarkable end: the development of penicillin.

Process also offers opportunities for refining old methods and inventing new ones. For example, as the defense industry slowed down after the cold war, many methods and technologies for weapons production proved useful in other areas—from commercial aviation to medical technology. The same has been true of technologies developed for the space program, which now find broad application in many other fields.

Finally, in my observation and experience, people become caught up in processes primarily for the challenge and enjoyment of the activity, not merely to produce some product. Once the process has culminated in a final product, the participants immediately search for a new process to involve themselves with. From a psychological standpoint, then, people have a need to busy themselves with meaningful activities—i.e., processes. So most processes can fittingly be characterized as ends in themselves insofar as they fulfill this psychological need.

In sum, the process of making or doing something frequently has implications far beyond the immediate product. For this reason, and because process fills a basic human need, I strongly agree with the speaker's assertion the process is ultimately more important than product.

Issue No. 11   **Personal failings of great achievers**

Perhaps in some instances the personal failings of great achievers are unimportant relative to the achievements. In many cases, however, the relative significance of personal failings can be very great, depending on two factors: (1) the extent to which the failing is part of the achievement process itself, and (2) the societal impact of the achiever's failing apart from his or her own success.

Personal failings and achievement are often symbiotically related. The former test the would-be achiever's mettle; they pose challenges—necessary resistance that drives one to achieve despite the shortcoming. Personal failings may also compel one to focus on one's strengths, thereby spawning achievement. For example, poor academic or job performance may propel a gifted entrepreneur to start his or her own business. In the arts, a personal failing may be a necessary ingredient or integral part of the process of achieving. Artists and musicians often produce their most creative works during periods of depression, addiction, or other distress. In business, insensitivity to the "human" costs of success has bred grand achievements, as with the questionable labor practices of the great philanthropist Andrew Carnegie.

A second type of personal failing is one that is unrelated to the achievement. Modern politics is replete with examples: the marital indiscretions of the great leader John F. Kennedy and the paranoia of the great statesman Richard Nixon, to name just two. Were the personal failings of these two presidents less "important" than their achievements? In the former example, probably so. In the latter example, probably not since it resulted in the Watergate scandal—a watershed event in American politics. In cases such as these, therefore, the societal impact of shortcoming and achievement must be weighed on a case-by-case basis.

In sum, history informs us that personal failings are often part-and-parcel of great achievements; even where they are not, personal shortcomings of great achievers often make an important societal impact of their own.

Issue No. 12	Education as the key to success

Which factor offers more opportunities for success in our society: education or money and property? In my view, education has replaced money and property as the main provider of such opportunities today. I base my view on two reasons. First, education—particularly higher education—used to be available only to the wealthy but now is accessible to almost anyone. Second, because of the civil-rights movement and resulting laws, businesses are now required to hire on the basis of merit rather than the kinds of personal connections traditionally common among the wealthy.

Education probably always played a key role in determining one's opportunities for success. But in the past, good post-secondary education was available mainly to the privileged classes. Because money and property largely determined one's access to higher education, money and property really were the critical factors in opening doors to success. However, higher education is more egalitarian today. Given our vast numbers of state universities and financial-aid programs, virtually anyone who meets entrance requirements for college can obtain an excellent college education and open up windows of opportunity in life.

Another reason those opportunities will be open to educated young people from middle-class and poorer backgrounds is that hiring is more meritocratic today than ever before. In principle, at least, we have always been a society where all people are equal; yet in the past, children of the wealthy and well-connected could expect to obtain higher-status jobs and to receive better pay. But the laws and programs resulting from our civil-rights struggles have produced a modern business climate in which jobs are available on an equal-opportunity basis, and in which candidates have a legal right to be judged on the merit of their educational background and experience.

In conclusion, education is probably the main factor in opening doors to success for young people in our society. The fact that education has supplanted money and property in this role is owing to a more egalitarian system of higher education, as well as to more merit-based hiring practices that generally value individual education over family fortune or connections.

Issue No. 13   Responsibility for preserving the natural environment

While nearly everyone would agree in principle that certain efforts to preserve the natural environment are in humankind's best interest, environmental issues always involve a tug of war among conflicting political and economic interests. For this reason, and because serious environmental problems are generally large in scale, government participation is needed to ensure environmental preservation.

Experience tells us that individuals (and private corporations owned by individuals) tend to act on behalf of their own short-term economic and political interest, not on behalf of the environment or the public at large. For example, current technology makes possible the complete elimination of polluting emissions from automobiles. Nevertheless, neither automobile manufacturers nor consumers are willing or able to voluntarily make the short-term sacrifices necessary to accomplish this goal. Only the government holds the regulatory and enforcement power to impose the necessary standards and to ensure that we achieve such goals.

Aside from the problems of self-interest and enforcement, environmental issues inherently involve public health and are far too pandemic in nature for individuals to solve on their own. Many of the most egregious environmental violations traverse state and sometimes national borders. Environmental hazards are akin to those involving food and drug safety and to protecting borders against enemies; individuals have neither the power nor the resources to address these widespread hazards.

In the final analysis, only the authority and scope of power that a government possesses can ensure the attainment of agreed-upon environmental goals. Because individuals are incapable of assuming this responsibility, government must do so.

Issue No. 14   Importance to an organization of a clear hierarchy

The speaker claims that all organizations should include a clear hierarchy of accountability because any other structure would work against human nature and therefore prove fruitless in the end. This claim gives rise to complex issues about human nature and the social structures best suited to it. In my view, the claim assumes a distortedly narrow view of human nature, ignoring certain aspects of it that are undermined by hierarchical structure in ways that ultimately hurt the organization.

First, the organizational structure the speaker recommends undermines the nexus between worker and product that facilitates efficiency and productivity. When employees are responsible for just their small component of work, they can easily lose sight of larger organizational goals and the importance of their role in realizing these goals. In turn, workers will feel alienated, unimportant, and unmotivated to do work they are proud of. These effects cannot help but damage the organization in the end.

Second, compartmentalizing tasks in a hierarchical structure stifles creativity. An acquaintance of mine worked for a company which had established a rigid organizational barrier between designers and engineers. The designers often provided the engineers with concepts that were unworkable from an engineering standpoint. Conversely, whenever an engineer offered a design idea that allowed for easier engineering, the designers would simply warn the engineer not to interfere. This is a typical case where organizational barriers operate against creativity, harming the organization in the end.

Third, strict hierarchy undermines the collegiality and cooperation among coworkers needed for a sense of common purpose and pride in accomplishment. The message from the designers to the engineers at my friend's company produced just the opposite—resentment between the two departments, low morale among the engineers whose creative suggestions were ignored, and ultimate resignation to do inferior work with an attitude that developing ideas is a waste of time.

In sum, the speaker seems to assume that humans are essentially irresponsible and unmotivated, and that they therefore need external motivation by way of a layered bureaucratic structure. The speaker misunderstands human nature, which instead requires creative exercise and sense of purpose and pride in accomplishment. By stifling these needs with organizational barriers, the organization is ultimately worse off.

Issue No. 15   Children and the Internet

The issue here is whether an international effort to regulate children's access to adult material on the Internet is worthwhile. In my view, nations should attempt to regulate such access by cooperative regulatory effort. I base this view on the universality and importance of the interest in protecting children from harm, and on the inherently pandemic nature of the problem.

Adults everywhere have a serious interest in limiting access by children to pornographic material. Pornographic material tends to confuse children—distorting their notion of sex, of themselves as sexual beings, and of how people ought to treat one another. Particularly in the case of domination and child pornography, the messages children receive from pornographic material cannot contribute in a healthy way to their emerging sexuality. Given this important interest that knows no cultural bounds, we should regulate children's access to sexually explicit material on the Internet.

However, information on the Internet is not easily contained within national borders. Limiting access to such information is akin to preventing certain kinds of global environmental destruction. Consider the problem of ozone depletion thought to be a result of chloroflourocarbon (CFC) emissions. When the government regulated CFC production in the U.S., corporations responsible for releasing CFC's into the atmosphere simply moved abroad, and the global threat continued. Similarly, the Internet is a global phenomenon; regulations in one country will not stop "contamination" overall. Thus, successful regulation of Internet pornography requires international cooperation, just as successful CFC regulation finally required the joint efforts of many nations.

Admittedly, any global regulatory effort faces formidable political hurdles, since cooperation and compliance on the part of all nations—even warring ones—is inherently required. Nevertheless, as in the case of nuclear disarmament or global warming, the possible consequences of failing to cooperate demand that the effort be made. And dissenters can always be coerced into compliance politically or economically by an alliance of influential nations.

In sum, people everywhere have a serious interest in the healthy sexual development of children and, therefore, in limiting children's access to Internet pornography. Because Internet material is not easily confined within national borders, we can successfully regulate children's access to adult materials on the Internet only by way of international cooperation.

Issue No. 16   **Public architecture as a reflection of society**

The extent to which new public buildings reflect societal values and attitudes depends on whether one considers a building's intended function or its design. In the former sense, new public buildings do mirror society, while in the latter sense they do not.

The intended uses of new public buildings says something about our priorities and values as a society. For example, proliferation of public cultural centers and schools reflects a societal concern for the arts and education, respectively, while new prison construction indicates a heightened concern for safety and security.

The design of new public buildings, however, fails to mirror society, for two reasons. First, modern democratic states do not have the luxury of making cultural "statements" at any expense. Functionality and fiscal accountability dictate the face of public architecture today. Second, public participation in the process is limited. New buildings typically reflect the architect's eccentric vision or the preference of a few public officials, not the populace's values and attitudes. In England, for example, Prince Charles oversees and approves the design of new public buildings. The resulting conventional designs suggest his unwillingness to break from tradition. Yet it would seem unfair to assign his lack of vision to English society. In Denver, the controversial design of a new airport met with public outcry for its appearance, expense, and lack of functionality. Does the airport reflect the values of Denver's denizens? Probably not.

In conclusion, while modern public buildings seem to reflect the values and attitudes of a society in their function, they do not necessarily do so in their design.

Issue No. 17   Time management and flexibility

The speaker claims that a detailed time-management plan fails to afford adequate flexibility to deal with the unexpected at the workplace. He seems to offer an either/or choice between planning one's time rigidly, by detailing important daily as well as long-term plans, and not planning at all; and he prefers the second choice. The speaker's claim is overly simplistic, since it is possible for a detailed time-management plan to also provide flexibility.

Working at any job without a detailed road map for the immediate and longer-term can trivialize the efforts of both employees and organizational units so that all their efforts become aimless. The only sensible way proceed is to consider first one's most important long-term objectives; then an organizational unit and its employees can order daily and weekly tasks according to how much each adds to the achievement of those objectives. With a broader perspective, workers can eliminate from the list those daily activities that may seem urgent or may be most enjoyable but don't really contribute to long-term job goals or to organizational objectives.

A detailed time-management system need not be inflexible. Knowing which items to eliminate from a "to-do" list gives a time-management plan its flexibility. When the unexpected arises, it can be judged according to its role in fulfilling long-term goals. If what at first seemed urgent turns out not to be important, it can be deferred to another time or ignored altogether. But if something unexpected needs handling in order to fulfill an important business or life plan, it will take priority over lesser activities in the daily or weekly schedule. For instance, I might have a meeting planned for one o'clock with coworkers to decide the location of an awards banquet, and find out at noon that an important client is thinking of switching to our competitor but wants to talk with me first. I can easily discern that the banquet meeting is less important than a critical meeting with a valuable client.

In conclusion, effective time management must involve a detailed scheduling of tasks. But it also requires determining which tasks are more central than others to the satisfaction of long-term objectives. This way, the daily or weekly schedule becomes not just a list of tasks to check off, but a flexible plan that can accommodate important urgencies while allowing us to bypass less significant scheduled tasks and ignore unimportant interruptions.

Issue No. 18	Corporations—making money vs. serving society

We take for granted that a primary objective and obligation of a corporation is to maximize profits. But does this mean a corporation cannot also fulfill its obligations to society? The speaker claims that the two duties necessarily conflict. In my view, however, a corporation's duties to maximize shareholder wealth and to serve society will at times coincide and at times conflict; and when they do conflict, neither takes automatic precedence over the other.

Beyond the obvious duty to maximize shareholder wealth, corporations indeed owe a duty to serve society, especially the immediate community, which permits corporations to operate in exchange for an implicit promise that the corporations will do no harm and will bring some benefit to the community. These duties can often be fulfilled together. For example, a successful corporation brings jobs and related economic benefit to the community. And, by contributing to community activities and charities in other ways, the corporation gains a reputation for social responsibility that often helps it become even more successful.

However, at times these duties do conflict. Consider, for instance, a company that unknowingly leaks into the ground a toxic substance that threatens to contaminate local groundwater. While the company may favor an inexpensive containment program, community leaders may want the company to go further by cleaning up and restoring their environment—even if the expense will force the company to leave and take jobs from the community. Whatever the company decides, it should not assume that protecting profits automatically outweighs social obligation. In many instances it does not, as highly-visible tobacco, automobile safety, and asbestos liability cases aptly illustrate. Such examples reveal a limit as to how far a corporation can ethically go in trading off the well-being of the community for the sake of its own profits.

In sum, corporations have duties both to do well and to do good. Although conflict between these duties is not inevitable, it does occur. Determining which duty takes precedence in time of conflict requires careful consideration of all the ethical ramifications of each alternative.

Issue No. 19   Hiring criteria for entry-level jobs

In recruiting for entry-level jobs, should employers stress a broad liberal arts education, a technical business background, or should employers favor neither one over the other? In my view, while the ideal job candidate has significant academic experience in both realms, whether employers should favor one type of background over the other depends on the nature of the particular job and the anticipated length of employment.

First, a strong business background is more critical for some entry-level jobs than for others. Fledgling accountants, financial analysts, and loan officers cannot perform optimally without a solid academic background in accounting, finance, and banking. Even in sales of financial products and services, new employees need extensive technical knowledge to educate the customer and to be effective salespeople. However, in other entry-level positions—such as personnel, advertising and marketing—technical business knowledge may not be as critical as a broad experience with various types of people and an enlightened view of different cultures.

Second, the employer's hiring decision should also depend on the anticipated length of employment. In recruiting short-term workers, especially for positions that are labor intensive and where judgment and experience are not of paramount importance, the applicant who is strongly business-oriented may be the better choice. On the job, this applicant will probably be more pragmatic, and spend less time pondering the job and more time doing it. However, an employer looking for a long-term employee may be better served by hiring an applicant with a strong liberal arts background. By way of their more general education, these applicants have acquired a variety of general, transferable skills. They may be more adept than their colleagues with business-only backgrounds at recognizing and solving management problems, dealing with business associates from different cultures, and viewing issues from a variety of perspectives. All of these skills contribute to a person's lifelong ability to adapt to and even anticipate changes that affect the company, and to move easily into new positions as such changes demand.

In sum, recruiters for entry-level jobs should avoid preferring one type of applicant over another in all cases. Instead, recruiters should consider the immediate technical demands of the job as well as the prospect of advancement and long-term employment within the company.

Issue No. 20   The role of automation in our lives

In some respects humans serve machines, while in other respects machines serve us by enhancing our lives. While mechanical automation may have diminished our quality of life on balance, digital automation is doing more to improve our lives than to undermine our autonomy.

Consider first mechanical automation, particularly assembly-line manufacturing. With automation came a loss of pride in and alienation from one's work. In this sense, automation both diminished our quality of life and rendered us slaves to machines in our inability to reverse "progress." Admittedly, mechanical automation spawned entire industries, creating jobs, stimulating economic growth, and supplying a plethora of innovative conveniences. Nevertheless, the sociological and environmental price of progress may have outweighed its benefits.

Digital automation has brought its own brand of alienation. Computer automation, and especially the Internet, breeds information overload and steals our time and attention away from family, community, and coworkers. In these respects, digital automation tends to diminish our quality of life and create its own legion of human slaves. On the other hand, by relegating repetitive tasks to computers, digital technology has spawned great advances in medicine and physics, helping us to better understand the world, to enhance our health, and to prolong our lives. Digital automation has also emancipated architects, artists, designers, and musicians, by opening up creative possibilities and by saving time. Perhaps most important, however, information technology makes possible universal access to information, thereby providing a democratizing influence on our culture.

In sum, while mechanical automation may have created a society of slaves to modern conveniences and unfulfilling work, digital automation holds more promise for improving our lives without enslaving us to the technology.

Issue No. 21   Rewarding employees—job performance vs. tenure

According to the statement, in order to ensure high productivity, companies should base their employees' salaries and job security solely on job performance, and not on length of service to the company. I agree that salary increases and job security are powerful incentives to high achievement and should generally go to those who do the best work. However, to ensure employee productivity, companies must also reward tenured employees with cost-of-living raises—though not with job security.

On the one hand, rewarding average job performance with large pay increases or promises of job security is a waste of resources—for two reasons. First, complacent employees will see no reason to become more productive. Secondly, those normally inclined to high achievement may decide the effort isn't worthwhile when mediocre efforts are amply compensated. Companies should, therefore, adjust their pay schedules so that the largest salaries go to the most productive employees.

On the other hand, employees who perform their jobs satisfactorily should be given regular, though small, service-based pay increases—also for two reasons. First, the cost of living is steadily rising, so on the principle of fair compensation alone, it is unjust to condemn loyal employees to de facto salary reductions by refusing them cost-of-living raises. Secondly, failure to adjust salaries to reflect the cost of living may be counterproductive for the firm, which will have difficulty attracting and retaining good employees without such a policy.

In the final analysis, the statement correctly identifies job performance as the single best criterion for salary and job security. However, the statement goes too far; it ignores the fact that a cost-of-living salary increase for tenured employees not only enhances loyalty and, in the end, productivity, but also is required by fairness.

Issue No. 22	Government's responsibility regarding the arts

The speaker here argues that government must support the arts but at the same time impose no control over what art is produced. The implicit rationale for government intervention in the arts is that, without it, cultural decline and erosion of our social fabric will result. However, I find no empirical evidence to support this argument, which in any event is unconvincing in light of more persuasive arguments that government should play no part in either supporting or restricting the arts.

First, subsidizing the arts is neither a proper nor necessary job for government. Although public health is generally viewed as critical to a society's very survival and therefore an appropriate concern of government, this concern should not extend tenuously to our cultural "health" or well-being. A lack of private funding might justify an exception; in my observation, however, philanthropy is alive and well today, especially among the new technology and media moguls.

Second, government cannot possibly play an evenhanded role as arts patron. Inadequate resources call for restrictions, priorities, and choices. It is unconscionable to relegate normative decisions as to which art has "value" to a few legislators and jurists, who may be unenlightened in their notions about art. Also, legislators are all too likely to make choices in favor of the cultural agendas of those lobbyists with the most money and influence.

Third, restricting artistic expression may in some cases encroach upon the constitutional right of free expression. In any case, governmental restriction may chill creativity, thereby defeating the very purpose of subsidizing the arts.

In the final analysis, government cannot philosophically or economically justify its involvement in the arts, either by subsidy or sanction. Responsibility lies with individuals to determine what art has value and to support that art.

Issue No. 23   Should our schools teach values?

The speaker asserts that schools should teach only academic skills, and not ethical or social values. I agree with the speaker insofar as instruction on certain moral issues is best left to parents and churches. However, in my view it is in the best interests of a democratic society for schools to teach at least the values necessary to preserve freedom and a democratic way of life, and perhaps even additional values that enrich and nurture a society and its members.

We all have in interest in preserving our freedom and democratic way of life. At the very least, then, schools should provide instruction in the ethical and social values required for our democracy to survive—particularly the values of respect and tolerance. Respect for individual persons is a basic ethical value that requires us to acknowledge the fundamental equality of all people, a tenet of a democratic society. Tolerance of differences among individuals and their viewpoints is required to actualize many of our basic constitutional rights—including life, liberty, pursuit of happiness, and freedom of speech and religion.

While respect and tolerance are the minimal values that schools should teach, the list should ideally go further—to include caring, compassion, and willingness to help one another. A democracy might survive without these values, but it would not thrive. Respect and tolerance without compassion, it seems to me, breed a cool aloofness that undermines our humanity, and leaves those in the worst position to suffer more and suffer alone—an unhealthy state for any society.

Admittedly, schools should avoid advocating particular viewpoints on controversial moral issues such as abortion or capital punishment. Instruction on issues with clear spiritual or religious implications is best left to parents and churches. Even so, schools should teach students how to approach these kinds of issues—by helping students to recognize their complexity and to clarify competing points of view. In doing so, schools can help breed citizens who approach controversy in the rational and responsible ways characteristic of a healthy democracy.

In sum, schools should by all means refrain from indoctrinating our young people with particular viewpoint on controversial questions of morality. However, it is in a democratic society's interest for schools to inculcate the democratic values of respect and tolerance, and perhaps even additional values that humanize and enrich a society.

Issue No. 24	Power and influence—business vs. government

Historical examples of both influential public officials and influential business leaders abound. However, the power of the modern-era business leader is quite different from that of the government official. On balance, the CEO seems to be better positioned to influence the course of community and of nations.

Admittedly, the opportunities for the legislator to regulate commerce or of the jurist to dictate rules of equity are official and immediate. No private individual can hold that brand of influence. Yet official power is tempered by our check-and-balance system of government and, in the case of legislators, by the voting power of the electorate. Our business leaders are not so constrained, so their opportunities far exceed those of any public official. Moreover, powerful business leaders all too often seem to hold de facto legislative and judicial power by way of their direct influence over public officials, as the Clinton Administration's fund-raising scandal of 1997 illuminated all too well.

The industrial and technological eras have bred such moguls of capitalism as Pullman, Rockefeller, Carnegie, and Gates, who by the nature of their industries and their business savvy, not by force of law, have transformed our economy, the nature of work, and our very day-to-day existence. Of course, many modern-day public servants have made the most of their opportunities—for example, the crime-busting mayor Rudolph Giuliani and the new-dealing President Franklin Roosevelt. Yet their impact seems to pale next to those of our modern captains of industry.

In sum, modern business leaders, by virtue of the far-reaching impact of their industries and of their freedom from external constraints, have supplanted lawmakers as the great opportunists of the world and prime movers of society.

Issue No. 25   **Hiring capable people as a key business strategy**

Is the most effective management approach to hire the best people, then to give them as much autonomy as possible to serve the firm's goals? This strategy would certainly enhance an employee's sense of involvement, purpose and personal worth. It would also benefit the firm by encouraging employees to work creatively and productively. But the strategy requires two constraints to operative effectively.

First, the strategy must be constrained by strong leadership that provides clear vision and direction. Simply putting the most capable people together and letting them loose on projects will provide neither. Thinking so involves the mistaken assumption that just because the parts of a whole are good, the collection of the parts into a whole will be equally good. Business organizations are more than just the sums of their excellent parts; to be similarly excellent, the organization must also be unified and cohesive. And it is strong and visionary leadership that provides these two ingredients.

Second, the strategy must be constrained by an organizational structure that brings all individual efforts together as a coherent whole. Of course, structure can be crippling; heavily layered, overly bureaucratic organizations probably stifle more creative productivity than they inspire. Still, individuals will be capable at some things and not others, so some organization of efforts is always called for. The moderate—and perhaps optimal—approach would be to create a structure that gives individuals some authority across areas relating to their field of expertise, while reserving final authority for higher-level managers. For example, no individual in a finance department should have much authority over a design department. However, within the design department, individual researchers, artists, drafters, and engineers can all contribute meaningfully to one another's projects, and a flexible organizational structure would allow them to do so.

In sum, the advice to hire the best people and give them wide authority requires modification. Hiring capable people and granting them some concurrent authority across areas related to their expertise is better advice. Moreover, solid leadership and a cohesive organizational structure are prerequisites—both are needed to coordinate individual efforts toward the accomplishment of common goals.

Issue No. 26   **Location: still the key to business success**

In retail, or "storefront," business, location is still a key ingredient of business success. The extent to which this will continue to be true, given the inexorable growth of Internet commerce, will vary among industries.

In more traditional retail sectors, such as clothing, cosmetics, and home improvement, an in-person visit to a retail store is often necessary—to try on clothes for fit, compare fragrances, or browse among a full selection of textures, colors, and styles. Also, activities such as shopping and dining out are for many consumers enjoyable experiences in themselves, as well as excuses to get out of the house and mingle with others in their community. Finally, shipping costs for large items such as appliances and home-improvement items render home shopping impracticable. Thus, burgeoning technologies pose no serious threat to Main Street, and location will continue to play a pivotal role in the fate of many retail businesses.

Nevertheless, technology-related industries are sure to move away from physical storefronts to virtual ones. Products that can be reduced to digital "bits and bites," such as books and magazines, recordings, and software applications, are more efficiently distributed electronically. Computer hardware will not disappear from Main Street quite so quickly, though, since its physical look and feel enters into the buying decision. Computer superstores should continue to thrive alongside companies such as Dell, which does not distribute through retail stores.

In conclusion, consumer demand for convenient location will continue with respect to certain tangible products, while for other products alternative distribution systems will gradually replace the storefront, rendering location an obsolete issue.

Issue No. 27   **Job satisfaction and security**

I agree that job satisfaction is an important factor in determining whether a company will be successful in the long term. However, other factors typically play just as vital a role in the ultimate success or failure of a business. At the same time, job security is becoming decidedly unimportant for many employees and, in any event, often leads to substandard job performance.

I agree that business success is more likely when employees feel satisfied with their jobs. Employees who dislike the workplace or their jobs are not likely to reach their potential performance levels; they may tend to arrive late for work, perform their tasks in an unimaginative and sluggish manner, or take excessive sick leave. Nevertheless, a firm's long-term success may equally result from other factors— such as finding a market niche for products, securing a reputation for quality products and services, or forming a synergistic alliance with a competitor. This list hardly exhausts all the factors that can contribute to a firm's ultimate success, and no one of them—including job satisfaction—is pivotal in every case.

While job satisfaction clearly boosts employee morale and contributes to the overall success of a company, the same cannot be said for job security. Admittedly, an employee worried about how secure his or her job is might be less creative or productive as a result. By the same token, however, too much confidence in the security of one's job can foster complacency which, in turn, may diminish employees' creativity and productivity. Moreover, many employees actually place job security relatively low on the list of what they want in a job. In fact, more and more workers today are positively uninterested in long-term job security; instead, they are joining firms for the sole purpose of accomplishing near-term professional goals, then leaving to face the next challenge.

To sum up, the claim at issue overrates the importance of job satisfaction and security by identifying them as the key factors in a company's long-term success. Job satisfaction among employees is very important, but it is not clearly more important than many other factors. At the same time, job security is clearly less important, and even unimportant in some cases.

Issue No. 28   **Should schools teach consumerism?**

This argument is untenable for two reasons. First, the claim that high-quality ads are used to promote low-quality products is unsupported empirically and by common sense. Second, undue attention by schools to consumerism is unnecessary and inappropriate, especially for younger students.

Regarding the first reason, empirical evidence does not suggest that high-quality advertising is used to promote low-quality products. To the contrary, companies that produce low-quality products seem to resort to low-budget, poor-quality ads, especially in broadcast media. Firms that take pride in the quality of their products are far more likely also to produce ads they can be proud of. Furthermore, high-quality products are more likely to succeed in the marketplace and thereby generate the revenues needed to ensure high production value in advertising.

As for the second reason, it is not the job of our schools to breed legions of smart shoppers. Teachers should devote class time to examining the marketplace of ideas, not that of consumer goods and services, which students spend sufficient time examining outside the classroom. Admittedly, consumerism and advertising may be appropriate topics for college-level marketing and psychology courses. However, undue focus on media and materialism may give younger students a distortedly narrow view of the world as little more than a flea market. Additionally, revealing the deceptive side of the advertising business may breed unhealthy cynicism among youngsters, who need positive messages, not negative ones, during their formative years.

In sum, the premise that high-quality ads tout low-quality products is specious at best; in any event, for schools to provide extensive training in consumerism would be to assign them an inappropriate role and to foster in impressionable minds a distortedly narrow and unhealthy view of the world.

Issue No. 29   Focusing on the task rather than the result

This advice means fundamentally that if we focus our attention on the details of a project rather than on the end product, the result will be better than if we proceed the other way around. Admittedly, this advice has some merit; by focusing on the details at hand one is less likely to become discouraged by the daunting or overwhelming tasks ahead in an ambitious project. Otherwise, however, I think this advice is poor.

The central problem with this advice is that focusing attention completely on the task at hand without reference to how that task is related to the end product would be virtually impossible to do. The reason for this is simple. Without some reference to a goal or a result we would have no idea of what task to perform in the first place. As a result, the various tasks we engage in would be somewhat random and, in turn, no matter how diligent and careful we were in performing them the likelihood of producing worthwhile or successful end products would be minimal.

To ensure good results, one should instead take a balanced approach to the task at hand. By a balanced approach I mean paying attention to both the desired result and the specific tasks that are required to achieve it. House building provides a good example of this approach. The house plan not only contains a rendering of the finished product but also contains detailed drawings and descriptions of each of the specific components required to ensure a successful result. Moreover, the order of the tasks is determined with reference to this result. In my estimation, virtually all successful projects proceed in the fashion illustrated in this example.

In sum, I don't think that the advice offered in the statement is worth following. In my view, following this advice is more likely to produce unsuccessful results than successful ones.

Issue No. 30   Should employees take work home with them?

According to this statement, companies would be well advised to discourage employees from working overtime or from taking projects home, since employees are more productive when they return to the job after a break from their work. While I agree with this policy in general, on some occasions the company stands to benefit more from asking employees to forego leisure time than from insisting they be rested and refreshed when they come to work.

In the normal course of business operations, companies benefit when they discourage employees from putting in long hours or from taking work home. Breaks from work provide opportunities to enjoy outside interests and activities, and to spend important time with friends and family. Employees who make time for relationships and leisure activities will find that they return to the job refreshed and with new perspectives on the challenges they face at work. Both of these factors contribute to clearer focus on the task at hand and greater efficiency.

At the same time, every organization is familiar with the press of crucial deadlines and other crisis situations. At such times a company should call upon employees to work overtime, and even to take projects home, especially when doing so might make the difference between the business' success or failure. Moreover, it is in the company's best interest to reward the devoted worker accordingly—not in order to encourage workaholic habits but rather to foster good-will and loyalty.

In sum, I agree that encouraging employees to make a habit of working after hours or taking work home is generally counterproductive for an enterprise. Nevertheless, in exceptional situations, especially where the company is at great risk, calling on employees to forego their ordinary schedules and to work overtime is well justified.

Issue No. 31   Financial gain as a factor in choosing a career

Financial gain is certainly one factor to consider when selecting a career. But many people do not, and should not, focus on this factor as the main one. The role that money plays in career choice should depend on the priorities, goals and values of the particular person making the choice.

The main problem with selecting a career primarily on the basis of money is that for many people to do so would be to ignore one's personal values, needs, and larger life goals. Indeed, many people appreciate this notion when they choose their career. For example, some people join one of the helping professions, such as nursing, teaching or social work, well aware that their career will not be financially lucrative. Their choice properly stems from an overriding altruistic desire, not from an interest in financial gain. Others choose to pursue intellectual or creative fulfillment—as writers, artists, or musicians—knowing that they are trading off dollars for non-tangible rewards. Still others forego economic gain to work as full-time parents; for these people, family and children are of paramount importance in life. Finally, many people subordinate economic prospects to their desire to live in a particular location; these people may place a high value on recreation, their physical health, or being near a circle of friends.

Another problem with focusing primarily on money when selecting a career is that it ignores the notion that making money is not an end in and of itself, but rather a means of obtaining material goods and services and of attaining important goals— such as providing security for oneself and one's family, lifelong learning, or freedom to travel or to pursue hobbies. Acknowledging the distinction, one may nevertheless select a career on the basis of money—since more money can buy more goods and services as well as the security, freedom, and time to enjoy them. Even so, one must strike a balance, for if these things that money is supposed to provide are sacrificed in the pursuit of money itself, the point of having money—and of one's career selection—has been lost.

In conclusion, economic gain should not be the overriding factor in selecting a career. While for a few people the single-minded pursuit of wealth may be fulfillment enough, most people should, and indeed do, temper the pursuit of wealth against other values, goals, and priorities. Moreover, they recognize that money is merely a means to more important objectives, and that the pursuit itself may undermine the achievement of these objectives.

Issue No. 32   Advertisements as reflections of a nation's ideas

In order to determine whether advertisements reflect a nation's ideas, it is necessary to determine whether advertisements present real ideas at all, and, if so, whose ideas they actually reflect. On both counts, it appears that advertisements fail to accurately mirror a nation's ideas.

Indisputably, advertisements inform us as to a nation's values, attitudes, and priorities—what activities are worthwhile, what the future holds, and what is fashionable and attractive. For instance, a proliferation of ads for sport-utility vehicles reflects a societal concern more for safety and machismo than for energy conservation and frugality, while a plethora of ads for inexpensive on-line brokerage services reflects an optimistic and perhaps irrationally exuberant economic outlook. However, a mere picture of a social more, outlook, or fashion is not an "idea"—it does not answer questions such as "why" and "how"?

Admittedly, public-interest advertisements do present ideas held by particular segments of society—for example, those of environmental and other public-health interest groups. However, these ads constitute a negligible percentage of all advertisements, and they do not necessarily reflect the majority's view. Consequently, to assert that advertisements reflect a nation's ideas distorts reality. In truth, they mirror only the business and product ideas of companies whose goods and services are advertised and the creative ideas of advertising firms. Moreover, advertisements look very much the same in all countries, Western and Eastern alike. Does this suggest that all nations have essentially identical ideas? Certainly not.

In sum, the few true ideas we might see in advertisements are those of only a few business concerns and interest groups; they tell us little about the ideas of a nation as a whole.

Issue No. 33   **Earning respect as a leader**

People are more likely to accept the leadership of those who have shown they can perform the same tasks they require of others. My reasons for this view involve the notions of respect and trust.

It is difficult for people to fully respect a leader who cannot, or will not, do what he or she asks of others. President Clinton's difficulty in his role as Commander-in-Chief serves as a fitting and very public example. When Clinton assumed this leadership position, it was well-known that he had evaded military service during the Vietnam conflict. Military leaders and lower-level personnel alike made it clear that they did not respect his leadership as a result. Contrast the Clinton case with that of a business leader such as John Chambers, CEO of Cisco Systems, who by way of his training and experience as a computer engineer earned the respect of his employees.

It is likewise difficult to trust leaders who do not have experience in the areas under their leadership. The Clinton example illustrates this point as well. Because President Clinton lacked military experience, people in the armed forces found it difficult to trust that his policies would reflect any understanding of their interests or needs. And when put to the test, he undermined their trust to an even greater extent with his naive and largely bungled attempt to solve the problem of gays in the military. In stark contrast, President Dwight Eisenhower inspired nearly devotional trust as well as respect because of his role as a military hero in World War II.

In conclusion, it will always be difficult for people to accept leaders who lack demonstrated ability in the areas under their leadership. Initially, such leaders will be regarded as outsiders, and treated accordingly. Moreover, some may never achieve the insider status that inspires respect and trust from those they hope to lead.

| Issue No. 34 | Potential benefits of mandatory public service |

The potential benefits of mandatory public service must be weighed against administrative problems and concerns about individual liberty. On balance, the costs to a nation and to the participants would probably exceed the benefits.

Admittedly, a colorable argument can be made for mandatory public service. It would help alleviate "free-rider" problems, where those who do not contribute benefit from the efforts of those who do. It would mitigate pressing social problems—with education, public health and safety, and the environment. It might instill in participants a sense of civic duty, community, and individual responsibility. Finally, it has worked on a smaller scale, particularly in urban areas, where renewal projects succeed in making communities safer, healthier, and more prosperous.

Far more compelling, however, are the arguments against mandatory public service. First, who would make assignments and decide what projects are worthwhile, and how would compliance be assured? Resolving enforcement issues would require government control, in turn requiring increased taxes and/or cuts in other social programs, thereby nullifying the benefits of mandatory public service. Second, a mandatory system would open the floodgates to incompetence and inexperience. Finally, the whole notion seems tantamount to Communism insofar as each citizen must contribute, according to his or her ability, to a strong state. Modern history informs us that such systems do not work. One could argue that mandatory public service is simply a tax in the form of labor rather than dollars. However, compulsory labor smacks of involuntary servitude, whereas financial taxes do not.

In conclusion, logistical and philosophical barriers to mandating public service outweigh its potential benefits for the nation as well as for participants.

Issue No. 35	Short-term thinking as a business disease

I agree with the speaker that decisions and actions of businesses are too often "infected" by short-sighted motives. Admittedly, attention to immediate results and short-term goals may be critical, and healthy, for survival of a fledgling company. However, for most established businesses, especially large corporations, failure to adequately envision the long-term implications of their actions for themselves and for others is all-too common and appropriately characterized as a "disease."

The business world is replete with evidence that companies often fail to envision the long-term implications of their actions for themselves. Businesses assume excessive debt to keep up with booming business, ignoring the possibility of a future slowdown and resulting forfeiture or bankruptcy. Software companies hastily develop new products to cash in on this year's fad, ignoring bugs and glitches in their programs that ultimately drive customers away. And manufacturers of inherently dangerous products cut safety corners to enhance short-term profits, failing to see the future implications: class-action liability suits, criminal sanctions, and shareholder revolts.

Similarly, businesses fail to see implications of their actions for others. Motivated only by the immediate bottom line, movie studios ignore the deleterious effects that movie violence and obscenity may have on their patrons and on the society at large. Captains of the energy industry pay lip service to environmental ramifications of unbridled energy use for future generations, while their real concern is with ensuring near-term dependence on the industry's products or services. And manufacturers of dangerous products do a long-term disservice to others, of course, by cutting corners in safety and health.

In sum, I think the criticism that businesses are too concerned with immediate results and not concerned enough with the long-term effects of their actions and decisions is for the most part a fair assessment of modern-day business.

Issue No. 36   **Teamwork vs. individual energy and commitment**

The relationship between teamwork and individual strength, energy, and commitment is complex; whether they operate in a complementary or antagonistic manner depends on: (1) the goals toward which the traits are directed, (2) the degree of emphasis on teamwork, and (3) the job of the individual within an organization.

A person's ability to work effectively in a team is not inconsistent per se with personal strength, energy, and commitment. If exercised in a self-serving manner— for example, through pilfering or back stabbing—these traits can operate against the organization. Conversely, if directed toward the firm's goals, these traits can motivate other team members, thereby advancing common goals. World War II generals Patton and Rommel understood this point and knew how to bring out the best individual qualities in their troops, while at the same time instilling a strong sense of team and common purpose.

Nevertheless, overemphasizing teamwork can be counterproductive for an organization. A successful team requires both natural leaders and natural followers; otherwise, a team will accomplish little. Undue emphasis on teamwork may quell initiative among natural leaders, thereby thwarting team goals. Also, teamwork can be overemphasized with a commissioned sales force of highly competitive and autonomic individuals. Overemphasis on teamwork here might stifle healthy competition, thereby defeating a firm's objectives. In other organizational areas, however, teamwork is critical. For example, a product-development team must progress in lock-step fashion toward common goals, such as meeting a rollout deadline.

In sum, individual strength, commitment, and energy can complement a strong team approach; as long as individual autonomy is not undermined, all can operate in a synergistic manner to achieve an organization's goals.

Issue No. 37   Education—science vs. arts and humanities

Because scientific knowledge is increasingly important in our technological world and in the practical world of jobs and careers, schools should devote sufficient time to teaching mathematics and science. This is not to say, however, that schools should devote less time to the arts or humanities. To the contrary, in a technological age the study of arts and humanities is probably more important than ever—for three reasons.

First of all, studying the arts and humanities can help students become better mathematicians and scientists. For example, recent studies of cognitive development show that studying music at an early age can strengthen a child's later grasp of mathematics. And understanding philosophical concepts has helped scientists recognize their own presuppositions, and frame their central questions more accurately.

Secondly, studying the creative and intellectual achievement of others helps inspire our own creativity and intellectual questioning. This is particularly important in an era dominated by technology, where we run a serious risk of becoming automatons who fit neatly into the efficient functioning of some system.

Finally, technology is valuable as an efficient means to our important goals. But neither technology, nor the science on which it is founded, decides which goals are best, or judges the moral value of the means we choose for their attainment. We need the liberal arts to help us select worthwhile ends and ethical means.

In conclusion, schools should not devote less time to the arts and humanities. These areas of study augment and enhance learning in mathematics and science, as well as helping to preserve the richness of our entire human legacy while inspiring us to further it. Moreover, disciplines within the humanities provide methods and contexts for evaluating the morality of our technology and for determining its proper direction.

Issue No. 38   Everyday courtesy as an endangered art

The speaker claims that simple courtesy and good manners are disappearing from modern life, and that the quality of our lives is therefore deteriorating. While I do encounter frequent instances of discourtesy and bad manners, I also encounter many instances of the opposite behavior. For this reason, and because negative experiences tend to be more memorable and newsworthy, I find the speaker's claim to be dubious.

Most people encounter multiple instances of ordinary courtesy and good manners every day—simple acts such as smokers asking whether anyone minds if they light up, people letting others with fewer items ahead in grocery-store lines, and freeway drivers switching lanes to accommodate faster drivers or those entering via on-ramps. Admittedly, most people also encounter discourtesy or poor manners on a daily basis—people using obscene language in public places where young children are present, and business associates intentionally ignoring phone calls, to name a few. However, such acts do not prove that good manners and courtesy are disappearing; they simply show that both courtesy and discourtesy abound in everyday life. Thus, the claim that courtesy and good manners are disappearing grossly distorts reality.

Another reason that the claim is suspect is that we tend to remember negative encounters with people more so than positive ones, probably because bad experiences tend to be more traumatic and sensational, if not more interesting to talk about. The news stories that the media chooses to focus on certainly support this rationale. However, the fact that we remember, hear about, and read about discourtesy more than about courtesy shows neither that discourtesy is increasing nor that courtesy is decreasing. It simply shows that negative experiences leave stronger impressions and tend to be more sensational. In fact, I suspect that if one were to tally up one's daily encounters with both types of behavior, one would conclude that good manners and courtesy are far more prevalent than the opposite behavior.

In conclusion, the speaker's claim that common courtesy and good manners are disappearing is not born out by everyday experience. I suspect the speaker has failed to consider that negative experiences leave stronger impressions on our memory and are more interesting to relate to others than positive ones.

Issue No. 39   **Professional success and personal sacrifices**

Are professional success and a fulfilling personal life mutually exclusive? Probably not, although it is more difficult today to achieve both.

Undeniably, today's professionals must work long hours to keep their heads above water, let alone to get ahead in life financially. This is especially true in Japan, where cost of living, coupled with corporate culture, compel professional males to all but abandon their families and literally to work themselves to death. While the situation here in the states may not be as critical, the two-income family is now the norm, not by choice but by necessity.

However, our society's professionals are taking steps to remedy the problem. First, they are inventing ways—such as job sharing and telecommuting—to ensure that personal life does not take a back seat to career. Second, they are setting priorities and living those hours outside the workplace to their fullest. In fact, professional success usually requires the same time-management skills that are useful to find time for family, hobbies, and recreation. One need only look at the recent American presidents—Clinton, Bush, Reagan and Carter—to see that it is possible to lead a balanced life which includes time for family, hobbies, and recreation, while immersed in a busy and successful career. Third, more professionals are changing careers to ones which allow for some degree of personal fulfillment and self-actualization. Besides, many professionals truly love their work and would do it without compensation, as a hobby. For them, professional and personal fulfillment are one and the same.

In conclusion, given the growing demands of career on today's professionals, a fulfilling personal life remains possible—by working smarter, by setting priorities, and by making suitable career choices.

Issue No. 40   Our role as citizens of the world

With the growth of the global economy and the need for international cooperation, every human being has assumed a role as citizen of the world. Does this mean that our roles as citizens of our respective nations are thereby superseded by our role as world citizens, as the speaker suggests? Not at all. Good citizenship at one level is often compatible with good citizenship at another. In fact, being a good citizen in one social domain can help one be a better citizen in another.

Good global citizenship is not incompatible with good citizenship at other levels. Consider, for example, one's efforts as a citizen to preserve the natural environment. One particular person might, for example: (1) lobby legislators to enact laws preserving an endangered redwood forest, (2) campaign for nationally-elected officials who support clean air laws, and (3) contribute to international rainforest preservation organizations. This one person would be acting consistently as a citizen of community, state, nation and world.

Admittedly, conflicting obligations sometimes arise as a result of our new "dual" citizenship. For example, a U.S. military official with an advisory role in a United Nations peace-keeping force might face conflicting courses of action—one that would secure U.S. military interests, and another that would better serve international interests. However, the fact that such a conflict exists does not mean that either action is automatically more obligatory—that is, that one's role as either U.S. citizen or world citizen must invariably supersede the other. Instead, this situation should be resolved by carefully considering and weighing the consequences of each course of action.

Moreover, being a good citizen in one social context can often help one be a better citizen in another. For example, volunteering to help underprivileged children in one's community might inspire one to work for an international child-welfare organization. And inculcating civic values—such as charity and civic pride—may give rise to personal traits of character that transfer to all social domains and contexts.

In sum, although our "dual" citizenship may at times lead to conflicts, one role need not automatically take precedence over the other. Moreover, the relationship between the two roles is, more often than not, a complementary one—and can even be synergistic.

Issue No. 41   Penalties for damaging the natural environment

Imposing heavy penalties on those who pollute or destroy the environment is one way to preserve our environment. But it is not the only way; nor is it the best way. Penalties may elicit grudging compliance, but other approaches—those that instill a sense of genuine commitment—are likely to be more effective in the long term.

Admittedly, motivating compliance with environmental regulations by way of penalties will serve environmental goals up to a point. The deterrent effect of these remedies cannot be denied. Yet it should not be overstated. Some businesses may attempt to avoid punishment by concealing their activities, bribing (lobbying) legislators to modify regulations, or moving operations to jurisdictions that allow their environmentally harmful activities. Others might calculate the trade-off between accepting punishment and polluting, budget in advance for anticipated penalties, then openly violate the law. My intuition is that this practice is a standard operating mode among some of our largest manufacturers.

A better way to ensure environmental protection is to inculcate a sense of genuine commitment into our corporate culture—through education and through shareholder involvement. When key corporate executives become committed to values, the regulations associated with those values become a codification of conscience rather than obstacles to circumvent. The machinations and maneuverings described earlier will thereby be supplanted by thoughtful concern about all the implications of one's actions. Moreover, commitment-driven actions are likely to benefit the environment over and above what the law requires. For example, while a particular regulation might permit a certain amount of toxic effluents, businesses committed to environmental protection may avoid harmful emissions altogether.

Instilling a genuine sense of commitment through education and shareholder action is not just a better approach in theory, it is also less costly overall than a compliance-driven approach. Regulatory systems inherently call for legislative committees, investigations and enforcement agencies, all of which adds to the tax burden of the citizens whom these regulations are designed to protect. Also, delays typically associated with bureaucratic regulation may thwart the purpose of the regulations, since environmental problems can quickly become very grave.

In sum, penalties for violating environmental-protection laws are essentially expensive band-aids. A commitment-based approach, involving education and shareholder activism, can instill in corporate culture a sense an environmental conscience, resulting in far more effective environmental protection.

Issue No. 42   Reacting to changing environmental standards

The speaker argues that because scientists continually shift viewpoints about how our actions affect the natural environment, companies should not change their products and processes according to scientific recommendations until the government requires them to do so. This argument raises complex issues about the duties of business and about regulatory fairness and effectiveness. Although a wait-and-see policy may help companies avoid costly and unnecessary changes, three countervailing considerations compel me to disagree overall with the argument.

First, a regulatory system of environmental protection might not operate equitably. At first glance, a wait-and-see response might seem fair in that all companies would be subject to the same standards and same enforcement measures. However, enforcement requires detection, and while some violators may be caught, others might not. Moreover, a broad regulatory system imposes general standards that may not apply equitably to every company. Suppose, for example, that pollution from a company in a valley does more damage to the environment than similar pollution from a company on the coast. It would seem unfair to require the coastal company to invest as heavily in abatement or, in the extreme, to shut down the operation if the company cannot afford abatement measures.

Secondly, the argument assumes that the government regulations will properly reflect scientific recommendations. However, this claim is somewhat dubious. Companies with the most money and political influence, not the scientists, might in some cases dictate regulatory standards. In other words, legislators may be more influenced by political expediency and campaign pork than by societal concerns.

Thirdly, waiting until government regulations are in place can have disastrous effects on the environment. A great deal of environmental damage can occur before regulations are implemented. This problem is compounded whenever government reaction to scientific evidence is slow. Moreover, the EPA might be overburdened with its detection and enforcement duties, thereby allowing continued environmental damage by companies who have not yet been caught or who appeal penalties.

In conclusion, despite uncertainty within the scientific community about what environmental standards are best, companies should not wait for government regulation before reacting to warnings about environmental problems. The speaker's recommended approach would in many cases operate inequitably among companies; moreover, it ignores the political-corruption factor as well as the potential environmental damage resulting from bureaucratic delay.

Issue No. 43   The importance of studying history

Examining history makes us better people insofar as it helps us to understand our world. It would seem, therefore, that history would also provide useful clues for dealing with the same social ills that have plagued societies throughout history. On balance, however, the evidence suggests otherwise.

Admittedly, history has helped us learn the appropriateness of addressing certain issues, particularly moral ones, on a societal level. Attempts to legislate morality invariably fail, as illustrated by Prohibition in the 1930s and, more recently, failed federal legislation to regulate access to adult material via the Internet. We are slowly learning this lesson, as the recent trend toward legalization of marijuana for medicinal purposes and the recognition of equal rights for same-sex partners both demonstrate.

However, the overriding lesson from history about social ills is that they are here to stay. Crime and violence, for example, have troubled almost every society. All manner of reform, prevention, and punishment have been tried. Today, the trend appears to be away from reform toward a "tough-on-crime" approach. Is this because history makes clear that punishment is the most effective means of eliminating crime? No; rather, the trend merely reflects current mores, attitudes, and political climate. Also undermining the assertion that history helps us to solve social problems is the fact that, despite the civil-rights efforts of Martin Luther King and his progenies, the cultural gap today between African-Americans and white Americans seems to be widening. It seems that racial prejudice is here to stay. A third example involves how we deal with the mentally-ill segment of the population. History reveals that neither quarantine, treatment, nor accommodation solves the problem, only that each approach comes with its own trade-offs.

To sum up, while history can teach us lessons about our social problems, more often than not the lesson is that there are no solutions to many social problems— only alternate ways of coping with them.

Issue No. 44   **When to invest in high-quality advertising**

The speaker claims that high-quality ads can sell almost anything, and that companies should accordingly invest heavily in such advertising. I agree that the quality of an ad can in some instances play a pivotal role in a product's success or failure in the marketplace. However, the speaker overgeneralizes, for advertising is far more critical in some businesses and for some products than for others.

Certain types of businesses benefit greatly from investing in high-quality advertising. Fledgling companies, for example, may require an extensive top-notch advertising campaign to achieve the name recognition that older competitors already enjoy. Even established companies may need an expensive ad campaign when introducing new products or venturing into new markets. Companies selling products that hold no utilitarian value perhaps stand to gain the most from an extensive high-quality advertising effort. Consider, for example, the kinds of products that are marketed by means of the most extensive and expensive advertising: beer, cigarettes, soft drinks, and cosmetics. None of these products has any utility. Their success depends on consumers' fickle tastes, their emotions, and their subjective perceptions. Accordingly, influencing consumer attitudes through popular and appealing ads is about the only way to increase sales of such products.

In some industries, however, substantial investment in high-quality advertising simply does not make sense from a cost-effectiveness viewpoint. Pharmaceutical companies, for example, might be better off limiting their advertising to specialized publications, and focus instead on other kinds of promotional programs, such as the distribution of free samples. And widespread, flashy advertising would probably have a limited effect on overall sales for companies such as Deere and Caterpillar, whose name recognition and long-standing reputations for quality products are well established and whose customers are unlikely to be swayed by sensational ads.

In sum, the speaker overgeneralizes. Not all companies have an equal need to invest heavily in high-quality advertising. Companies with new products and products that have little utility stand to benefit most from expensive, high-quality advertising. But other companies, especially those whose customers are businesses rather than consumers, would be better off focusing on product quality and reputation, not on sensational advertising.

Issue No. 45   Ethical business conduct and maximizing profits

The speaker claims that following high ethical standards is the best way to maximize profits in the long run. However, this claim seems to be more of a normative statement than an empirical observation. The issue is more complex than the speaker suggests. In my observation, the two objectives at times coincide but at other times conflict.

In many ways behaving ethically can benefit a business. Ethical conduct will gain a company the kind of good reputation that earns repeat business. Treating suppliers, customers and others fairly is likely to result in their reciprocating. Finally, a company that treats its employees fairly and with respect will gain their loyalty which, in turn, usually translates into higher productivity.

On the other hand, taking the most ethical course of action may in many cases reduce profits, in the short run and beyond. Consider the details of a merger in which both firms hope to profit from a synergy gained thereby. If the details of the merger hinge on the ethical conviction that as few employees as possible should lose their jobs, the key executives may lose sight of the fact that a leaner, less labor-intensive organization might be necessary for long-term survival. Thus, undue concern with ethics in this case would results in lower profits and perhaps ultimate business failure.

This merger scenario points out a larger argument that the speaker misses entirely—that profit maximization is per se the highest ethical objective in private business. Why? By maximizing profits, businesses bestow a variety of important benefits on their community and on society: they employ more people, stimulate the economy, and enhance healthy competition. In short, the profit motive is the key to ensuring that the members of a free market society survive and thrive. While this argument might ignore implications for the natural environment and for socio-economic justice, it is a compelling argument nonetheless.

Thus the choice to follow high ethical standards should not be made by thinking that ethical conduct is profitable. While in some cases a commitment to high ethical standards might benefit a company financially, in many cases it will not. In the final analysis, businesses might best be advised to view their attempts to maximize profits as highly ethical behavior in itself.

Issue No. 46   Bureaucracy's impact in business and government

Contrary to the statement's premise, my view is that businesses are less likely than government to establish large bureaucracies, because businesses know that they are more vulnerable than government to damage resulting from bureaucratic inefficiencies. My position is well supported by common sense and by observation.

First, public administrators lack the financial incentives to avoid bureaucratic waste. In contrast, inefficiencies in a private corporation will reduce profits, inflicting damage in the form of job cuts, diminishing common-stock value, and reducing employee compensation. These are ample incentives for the private firm to minimize bureaucratic waste.

Second, there is almost no accountability among government bureaucrats. The electorate's voting power is too indirect to motivate mid-level administrators, whose salaries and jobs rarely depend on political elections. In contrast, private corporations must pay strict attention to efficiency, since their shareholders hold an immediate power to sell their stock, thereby driving down the company's market value.

Third, government is inherently monopolistic, large, and unwieldy; these features breed bureaucracy. Admittedly, some corporations rival state governments in size. Yet even among the largest companies, the profit motive breeds a natural concern for trimming waste, cutting costs, and streamlining operations. Even virtual monopolies strive to remain lean and nimble in order to maintain a distance from upstart competitors. When government pays lip service to efficiency, shrewd listeners recognize this as political rhetoric designed only to pander to the electorate.

In the final analysis, financial incentives, accountability, and competition all distinguish private business from government, both in terms of their likelihood of establishing large bureaucracies and in terms of the damage that these bureaucracies can inflict on the organization.

Issue No. 47   Responsibility for preventing environmental damage

The responsibility for preventing environmental damage should be shared by government, private industry and individuals alike. The primary obligation, however, belongs to individuals. Moreover, within organizations like the government or a corporation, responsibility should be increasingly distributed to individuals according to level of authority.

The primary obligation to preserve the environment belongs to individuals for the reason that assigning responsibility to a government or corporation is problematic. This is because abstract entities like these do not fulfill the usual criteria for being responsible. An entity can shoulder responsibility only if it can be held accountable for its actions. Furthermore, being held accountable for an action requires that the entity act willingly and on the basis of conscious intentions. But governments and businesses are abstractions, having neither will nor consciousness beyond that of the individuals within them.

Still, we can make some sense of treating corporations and governments as if they were individuals. They are individuals under the law, and therefore subject to laws, penalties, and lawsuits. They can even be identified as beneficiaries in wills. Nevertheless, when responsibility is vaguely allocated to abstract entities like governments or corporations, it becomes easy for those within such organizations to cover individual actions that result in devastation to the environment. Consider the famous case of the Exxon Valdez accident and oil spill off the Alaskan coast. While it was easy to single out Captain Hazelwood and determine his blameworthiness the night of the mishap, it was not so easy to identify those responsible at higher levels. Someone was responsible for hiring Hazelwood; others should have known about his drinking or other job-related problems. Thus when we do assign responsibility to governments or business organizations, it must be clearly distributed to individuals in relevant lines of authority within the organization.

In conclusion, individuals are mainly responsible for protecting the environment. And while it makes some sense in a vague way to talk about the similar responsibilities of government and industry, in the end such obligations will belong to individuals within them. Therefore, some individuals will assume greater shares of responsibility for the environment, since they act in positions of authority on behalf of government or industry.

Issue No. 48   Assessing personality traits in hiring employees

In the hiring process, it is more difficult to assess personality and work habits than to determine work experience and educational background. Even so, it is important to try and judge the less quantifiable characteristics of a prospective colleague or employee—such as honesty, reliability, creativity, self-motivation, and the capacity to get along and work well with others. If it doesn't seem obvious that these are important qualities in a coworker, then consider the alternatives.

First of all, dishonest or unreliable workers harm an organization in many ways. Dishonest employees impose costs on a company whether they steal on the grand or small scale; just taking a few days of unwarranted sick leave here and there can add up to significant lost productivity. And lying about progress on a project can result in missed deadlines and even lost contracts. Unreliability works the same way; if an employee cannot meet deadlines or fails to appear at important meetings, the organization will suffer accordingly.

In addition, coworkers who lack motivation or creativity take some of the life out of an organization. To the extent that employees simply plug along, the company will be less productive. In contrast, employees who have imagination and the motivation to implement ideas are productive and can spark those around them to greater achievement.

Finally, employees who cannot get along with or work well with others can as well be detrimental to the organization. The mere presence of a troublemaker is disruptive; moreover, the time such people spend on petty disagreements is time away from getting the job done successfully. In addition, those who cannot smoothly coordinate their efforts with others will end up making things more difficult for everyone else.

In conclusion, it may not be easy to judge the personality traits and work habits of prospective employees, but it certainly is worth the effort to try. Having coworkers who are honest, reliable, creative, self-motivated, compatible with one another and good team players will greatly enhance everyone's work life, and benefit a organization in the most significant way—with greater productivity.

Issue No. 49   **Hard work as the key to success**

There is no doubt that hard work contributes to success. Yet a person can work awfully hard and still achieve very little. In order to bring about success, hard work has to be directed by clear goals and the knowledge of how to reach them. Moreover, imagination, intelligence and persistence can be equally important to success.

Individual success is gauged by the extent to which one reaches important personal goals. And it takes careful planning to set goals and discover the best means of realizing them. Before hard work even begins, therefore, considerable time and effort should be spent on planning.

Intelligence and imagination play important roles in planning. Imagination helps one to envision new solutions to problems, and new means by which to achieve goals. Intelligence helps one research and critically evaluate the possibilities that imagination has provided. Together, imagination and intelligence can even help one avoid certain kinds of hard work, by producing more efficient ways to accomplish goals.

Finally, persistence is crucial to success. Sometimes rewards do not come quickly—even when one has carefully set goals, creatively and intelligently planned ways to achieve them, and worked hard according to plan. Tradition has it, for example, that Thomas Edison made thousands of attempts to create a lightbulb before he was finally successful. In the face of countless failures, he refused to quit. In fact, he considered each failure a successful discovery of what not to do!

In conclusion, it is true that there is no substitute for hard work. But hard work is an ingredient of success, and not the key. Hard work can produce real accomplishment only if it is directed by a plan involving some idea of one's goals and the means to them. And a good plan, as well as its successful implementation, require imagination, intelligence and persistence.

Issue No. 50   Responding to employee performance

Unsatisfactory employee performance demands appropriate response from a manager or supervisor. The question is, what is appropriate? Some managers might claim that verbal abuse and intimidation are useful in getting employees to improve. While this may be true in exceptional cases, my view is that the best managerial responses generally fulfill two criteria: (1) they are respectful; and (2) they are likely to be the most effective in the long run.

Treating employees with respect is important in all contexts. Respect, in the most basic sense, involves treating a person as equal in importance to oneself. For a manager or supervisor, this means recognizing that occupying a subordinate position does not make a worker a lesser person. And it means treating subordinates as one would want to be treated—honestly and fairly. Using threats or verbal abuse to elicit better employee performance amounts to treating a worker like the office copy machine—as an object from which to get what one wants.

Moreover, while verbal abuse might produce the desired reaction at a particular time, it is likely to backfire later. Nobody likes to be abused or intimidated. If such methods were the general practice in an office or division, overall morale would probably be low. And it is unlikely that employees would give 100 percent to managers who so obviously disregarded them.

More beneficial in the long run would be careful but clear feedback to the worker about specific deficiencies, along with ideas and encouragement about improvement. In addition, supervisors should allow employees to explain the problem from their point of view and to suggest solutions. Of course, a supervisor should never mislead a subordinate into thinking that major problems with work performance are insignificant or tolerable. Still, an honest message can be sent without threats or assaults on self-esteem.

In conclusion, supervisors should avoid using verbal abuse and threats. These methods degrade subordinates, and they are unlikely to produce the best results in the long run. It is more respectful, and probably more effective overall, to handle cases of substandard work performance with clear, honest and supportive feedback.

We ordinarily think, as the speaker does here, that the presence of competition is always healthy for business because it sparks efficiency and innovation. While competition is generally good for business in these respects, the speaker here ignores the many problems that can accrue from attempting to keep up with or beat a competitor, and that may be decidedly detrimental to a business.

Admittedly, competition among businesses can occasion all sorts of improved practices. The need for competitive product pricing can motivate effective micro-management of production and marketing costs. Competition for market share can spark invention and innovation in product design that lead to the cutting edge of technology. External competition is known to inspire team spirit within an organization, thereby yielding greater productivity. And competition can challenge a company to streamline operations, thereby improving efficiency.

But taken too far, attempting to keep up with or beat competitors brings about detrimental results for a company. In some cases, companies compromise product quality by switching to inferior, less expensive materials in order to keep prices competitive. Other times, plant managers ignore important employee-safety measures just to save money. And companies are even known to trade off consumer safety in the interest of competition. Perhaps the paradigmatic case involved the Ford Pinto, where Ford management rejected an inexpensive retrofit that would have saved hundreds of lives in rear-end collisions, solely in order to shave a few dollars off the car's sticker price, thereby enhancing the car's competitiveness.

Competition can even bring about large-scale social change that some consider undesirable. For instance, the emergence of large, efficient factory farms has resulted in the virtual disappearance of family farming in the U.S. And it isn't clear that the factory farms always improve farming practices. In the case of the tomato, the old homegrown kind are far superior in taste and texture to the tough, underripe version that has been genetically engineered for machine picking in huge quantity.

In conclusion, competition frequently motivates changes that are beneficial in many ways. But competition is a double-edged sword that can also result in inferior or unsafe products and dangerous working conditions for employees. Moreover, large competitors can swallow up smaller concerns without yielding noticeably better products or practices.

Issue No. 52	Achieving success by setting goals

I agree generally that setting new goals in small increments above past accomplishments is a reliable path to achieving those goals. I think anyone would be hard-pressed to find fault with this advice. Nevertheless, in some exceptional instances, a more dramatic "leap-frog" approach may be more appropriate, or even necessary, to achieve a significant goal.

The virtues of setting goals in small, easily-attainable increments are undeniable. Overwhelming challenges are reduced to readily attainable tasks. A psychological boost is afforded by each intermediate success, helping to ensure that the achiever won't become discouraged and give up. Each step in this process can raise one's level of aspiration, and in manageable proportions that make success more likely. Moreover, this approach can be used by anyone—a sedentary office worker who decides to complete the New York Marathon; a paralegal who wishes to become a surgeon; or a small business owner who aspires to become CEO of a Fortune 500 Company.

In some instances, however, the step-by-step approach is not adequate. For example, many great creative achievements—in art, music, and literature—are made not by the achiever's disciplined setting of incremental goals, but rather by a spontaneous flash of brilliance and intense creativity. Another exception to this approach is the case of the ultra-successful actor, model, or even socialite who might suddenly leap-frog to his or her goal through serendipity. Third, for those who have already achieved great things, taking baby steps toward the next goal would only frustrate them and slow them down. Suppose, for example, a recent gold medalist in the Olympic Games' 100-meter sprint wishes to become a member the football franchise that won last year's Super Bowl. What small, incremental accomplishments are needed to achieve his goal? None, aside from a phone call by his agent to the front office of the team. Admittedly, these are exceptional cases; yet they do exist.

In conclusion, setting modest but increasingly higher goals is generally good advice. Yet this approach may be inappropriate or inadequate under certain exceptional circumstances.

Issue No. 53   User-unfriendly systems in today's society

If one focuses on systems such as financial services and telecommunications, where emerging technologies have the greatest impact, one sees increasing user-friendliness. However, in other systems—public and private alike—inefficiencies, roadblocks, and other "unfriendly" features still abound. One such example is the U.S. health-care delivery system.

To a large extent, the user-unfriendly nature of health-care delivery stems from its close tie to the insurance industry. Service providers and suppliers inflate prices, knowing that insurance companies can well afford to pay by passing on inflated costs to the insured. Hospital patients are often discharged prematurely merely because insurance fails to cover in-patient care beyond a certain amount or duration. In the extreme, patients are sometimes falsely informed that they are well or cured, just so that the facility can make room for insured patients. Insurance providers reject claims and coverage intentionally and in bad faith when the insured has suffered or is statistically likely to suffer from a terminal or other long-term—and costly—illness. Insurance companies also impose extreme coverage exceptions for pre-existing conditions. Both tactics are designed, of course, to maximize insurance company profits at the expense of the system's user. Finally, new medical technologies that provide more effective diagnosis and treatment are often accessible only to the select few who can afford the most comprehensive insurance coverage.

The consequences of these user-unfriendly features can be grave indeed for the individual, since this system relates directly to a person's physical well-being and very life. For example, when a claim or coverage is wrongfully denied, lacking financial resources to enforce their rights, an individual customer has little practical recourse. The end result is to render health care inaccessible to the very individuals who need it most. These user-unfriendly features can be deleterious on a societal scale as well. An unhealthy populace is an unproductive one. Also, increased health-care costs place an undue burden on bread-winning adults who feel the squeeze of caring for aging parents and for children. Finally, these features foster a pervasive distrust of government, big business, and bureaucracy.

In sum, today's "point-and-click" paradigm inaccurately portrays the actual functionality of many systems, including our health-care delivery system, which is well-entrenched in self-interest and insensitivity to the needs of its users.

Issue No. 54   Commercial success of films and television programs

Clearly, most popular films and television shows are superficial and/or include a certain amount of violence or obscenity. Just as clearly, popularity leads to commercial success. But can we conclude that these productions are overly influenced by commercial interests? Perhaps not, since some popular films and television shows are neither superficial, obscene, nor violent. Closer scrutiny, however, reveals that most such productions actually support, not disprove, the thesis that commercial interests dictate movie and television content.

One would-be threat to the thesis can be found in lower-budget independent films, which tend to focus more on character development and topical social issues than on sensationalism. Recently, a few such films have supplanted Hollywood's major studio productions as top box-office hits. Does this mean that profit potential no longer dictates the content of films. No; it simply suggests that the tastes and preferences of the movie-going public are shifting.

A second ostensible challenge to the thesis can be found in companies such as Disney, whose productions continue to achieve great popularity and commercial success, without resort to an appeal to baser interests. Yet it is because these productions are commercially successful that they proliferate.

The only cogent challenge to the thesis is found in perennial television favorites such as "Nova," a public television show that is neither commercially supported nor influenced. However, such shows are more in the nature of education than entertainment, and for every one program like "Nova" there are several equally popular—and highly superficial—programs.

With few exceptions, then, commercial success of certain films and television shows is no accidental byproduct of popularity; it is the intentional result of producers' efforts to maximize profits.

Issue No. 55   Should bosses tell workers how to do their job?

I agree that supervisors should under most circumstances merely tell subordinates what to do, but not necessarily how to do it. Of course, employees need adequate training in order to do a job. But beyond that, trusting employees to discover and develop their own methods for meeting a supervisor's expectations can produce surprising rewards that outweigh any pitfalls of such an approach.

First of all, restraint in directing the how-to aspect of a project signals the supervisor's confidence in an employee's intelligence and abilities. Sensing this confidence, the subordinate will often respond with his or her best work. This phenomenon lends truth to the adage that people rise to the level of what others expect from them.

Secondly, by allowing a subordinate to decide how best to attain an objective, a supervisor imparts a larger share of responsibility for the project to the subordinate. This alleviates some of the burden from the supervisor, who may have more time for other tasks as a result. At the same time, when the subordinate shares in the responsibility, he or she will probably feel more accountable for how the job turns out. The result is likely to be better job performance.

Thirdly, directing every step of a project often blocks a worker's own creativity, as well as creating animosity. Except in the training of a new worker with little or no experience, it would be naive and arrogant for any supervisor to assume there is one and only one best way—the supervisor's own way—to get a job done. A bright, competent subordinate is likely to resent being led by the hand like a child. Allowing employees to choose their own means and methods will spark their ingenuity in ways that enhance productivity now and in the future, and will foster goodwill and mutual respect in the workplace.

In sum, telling a subordinate how to do a job is rarely the best management approach. Instead, supervisors should assign tasks without directing each step. When employees are left to choose methods for completing work, they will be bolstered by the supervisor's trust, motivated to greater creativity and inclined to feel accountable for outcomes.

Issue No. 56   The secret of business: keeping an important secret

This statement is ambiguous. It could mean, literally, that business success depends on knowing more than anyone else about one's operations, products and markets. Or it could be a subtle recommendation to acquire privileged information, by whatever means, to use for one's own advantage. I agree with the statement in the first sense. However, I strongly disagree with many implications of the second possible meaning.

It goes without saying that competitive edge in business is a function of knowledge. It is crucial to fully understand the technology and uses of one's products; and it is prudent to micromanage operations, knowing as much as possible about the small details that can add up to a significant economic difference. It is also prudent, and legitimate, to take every measure to protect that knowledge as trade secrets, since they often play a pivotal role in a firm's competitiveness.

But the advice to know something that nobody else does could easily become distorted. If taken another way, the advice could recommend that one dig up dirt in order to damage or discredit a rival. It could also be taken to recommend stealing trade secrets or other inside information from a competitor in order to gain an unfair business advantage. All of these tactics are unfair; and some also violate civil and criminal laws. Moreover, the recommendation to find and use any information, even unfairly or illegally, can backfire. People who follow such advice risk civil liability, criminal prosecution, and the loss of an important business asset—their good reputations.

In sum, I agree with the statement up to the point that it validates detailed and even proprietary knowledge as a key to competitiveness. Insofar as the statement sanctions unfair practices, however, following it would be unethical, bad for business, and damaging to the character and reputation of the perpetrator.

Issue No. 57   **Respecting one another's differences**

In determining whether we are becoming more respectful of one another's differences, one must examine both overt actions and underlying motives, as well as examining whether our differences are increasing or decreasing. The issue, therefore, is quite complex, and the answer is unclear.

Disrespect for one another's differences manifests itself in various forms of prejudice and discrimination. Since the civil rights and feminist movements of the 60s and 70s, it would seem that we have made significant progress toward eliminating racial and sexual discrimination. Antidiscriminatory laws in the areas of employment, housing, and education, now protect all significant minority groups—racial minorities and women, the physically challenged and, more recently, homosexuals. Movies and television shows, which for better or worse have become the cynosure of our cultural attention, now tout the rights of minorities, encouraging acceptance of and respect for others.

However, much of this progress is forced upon us legislatively. Without Title 10 and its progenies, would we voluntarily refrain from the discriminatory behavior that the laws prevent? Perhaps not. Moreover, signs of disrespect are all around us today. Extreme factions still rally around bigoted demagogues; the number of "hate crimes" is increasing alarmingly; and school-age children seem to flaunt a disrespect toward adults as never before. Finally, what appears to be respect for one another's differences may in fact be an increasing global homogeneity—that is, we are becoming more and more alike.

In sum, on a societal level it is difficult to distinguish between genuine respect for one another's differences on the one hand and legislated morality and increasing homogeneity on the other. Accordingly, the claim that we are becoming more respectful of one another's differences is somewhat dubious.

Issue No. 58   **The final objective of business**

This quotation suggests that the ultimate purpose of business is to streamline and mechanize work, thereby minimizing it, so that people can make a living but still have time for other things in life. The assumptions behind this view of business are that the value of work is entirely instrumental, and that our work lives are distinct from the rest of our lives. I disagree with both assumptions.

Admittedly, work is to a large extent instrumental in that we engage in it to provide for our basic needs while leaving time and resources for other activities—raising families, participating in civic life, traveling, pursuing hobbies, and so forth. And these activities normally take place away from the workplace and are distinct from our work. However, for most people, work is far more than a means to these ends. It can also be engaging, enjoyable and fulfilling in itself. And it can provide a context for expressing an important part of one's self. However, work will be less of all these to the extent that it is streamlined and mechanized for quick disposal, as the quotation recommends. Instead, our jobs will become monotonous and tedious, the work of drones. And we might become drone-like in the process.

In addition, work can to some extent be integrated with the rest of our lives. More and more companies are installing on-site daycare facilities and workout rooms. They are giving greater attention to the ambiance of the breakroom, and they are sponsoring family events, excursions and athletic activities for employees as never before. The notion behind this trend is that when a company provides employees with ways to fulfill outside needs and desires, employees will do better work. I think this idea has merit.

In conclusion, I admit that there is more to life than work, and that work is to some extent a means to provide a livelihood. But to suggest that this is the sole purpose of business is an oversimplification that ignores the self-actualizing significance of work, as well as the ways it can be integrated with other aspects of our lives.

Juvenile delinquency is clearly a serious social problem. Whether businesses must become more involved in helping to prevent the problem depends, however, on the specific business—whether it is culpable in creating the problem and whether its owners' collective conscience calls for such involvement.

Although parents and schools have the most direct influence on children, businesses nonetheless exert a strong, and often negative, influence on juveniles by way of their advertisements and of the goods they choose to produce. For example, cigarette advertisements aimed at young people, music and clothing that legitimize "gang" sub-culture, and toys depicting violence, all sanction juvenile delinquency. In such cases perhaps the business should be obligated to mitigate its own harmful actions—for example, by sponsoring community youth organizations or by producing public-interest ads.

In other cases, however, imposing on a business a duty to help solve juvenile delinquency or any other social problem seems impractical and unfair. Some would argue that because business success depends on community support, businesses have an ethical duty to give back to the community—by donating money, facilities, or services to social programs. Many successful businesses—such as Mrs. Field's, Ben & Jerry's, and Timberland—have embraced this philosophy. But how far should such a duty extend, and is it fair to impose a special duty on businesses to help prevent one specific problem, such as juvenile delinquency? Moreover, businesses already serve their communities by enhancing the local tax base and by providing jobs, goods and services.

In the final analysis, while businesses are clearly in a position to influence young people, whether they should help solve juvenile delinquency is perhaps a decision best left to the collective conscience of each business.

Issue No. 60   Access to personal information about employees

Determining whether employers should have access to personal information about employees requires that the interests of businesses in ensuring productivity and stability be weighed against concerns about equity and privacy interests. On balance, my view is that employers should not have the right to obtain personal information about current employees without their consent.

A business' interest in maintaining a stable, productive workforce clearly justifies right of access to certain personal information about prospective employees. Job applicants can easily conceal personal information that might adversely affect job performance, thereby damaging the employer in terms of low productivity and high turnover. During employment, however, the employee's interests are far more compelling than those of the employer, for three reasons.

First, the employer has every opportunity to monitor ongoing job performance and to replace workers who fail to meet standards, regardless of the reason for that failure. Second, allowing free access to personal information about employees might open the floodgates to discriminatory promotions and salary adjustments. Current federal laws—which protect employees from unfair treatment based on gender, race, and marital status, may not adequately guard against an employer's searching for an excuse to treat certain employees unfairly. Third, access to personal information without consent raises serious privacy concerns, especially where multiple individuals have access to the information. Heightening this concern is the ease of access to information which our burgeoning electronic intranets make possible.

In sum, ready access to certain personal information about prospective employees is necessary to protect businesses; however, once hired, an employee's interest in equitable treatment and privacy far outweighs the employer's interest in ensuring a productive and stable workforce.

Issue No. 61   Government as a necessary burden on business

I agree with the statement insofar as government systems of taxation and regulation are, in general, a great burden to business, and I agree that government constraints are needed to prevent serious harms that would result if business were left free in the singular pursuit of profit. However, I think the speaker states the obvious and begs the more relevant question.

Is government "at best" a "tremendous burden" on business, as the speaker claims? I think one would be hard-pressed to find any small business owner or corporate CEO who would disagree. Businesses today are mired in the burdens that government has imposed on them: consumer and environmental protection laws, the double-tiered tax structure for C-corporations, federal and state securities regulations, affirmative action requirements, anti-trust laws, and so on. In focusing solely on these burdens, one might well adopt a strict laissez faire view that if business is left free to pursue profit the so-called invisible hand of competition will guide it to produce the greatest social benefit, and therefore that the proper nexus between business and government is no nexus at all.

Is government, nevertheless, a "necessary" burden on business, as the speaker also claims? Yes. Laissez faire is an extreme view that fails to consider the serious harms that business would do—to other businesses and to the society—if left to its own devices. And the harms may very well exceed the benefits. In fact, history has shown that, left entirely to themselves, corporations can be expected not only to harm the society by making unsafe products and by polluting the environment, but also to cheat one another, exploit workers, and fix prices—all for profit's sake. Thus, I agree that government constraints on business are necessary burdens.

Ideally, the government should regulate against harmful practices but not interfere with the beneficial ones. But achieving this balance is not a simple matter. For instance, I know of a business that was forced by government regulation of toxic effluents to spend over $120,000 to clean up an area outside of its plant where employees had regularly washed their hands. The 'toxin' in this case was nothing more than biodegradable soap. This example suggests that perhaps the real issue here is not whether government is a necessary burden on business—for it clearly is—but rather how best to ensure that its burdens don't outweigh its benefits.

In sum, the speaker's two assertions are palpable ones that are amply supported by the evidence. The more intriguing question is how to strike the best balance between government regulation and laissez faire business activity.

Issue No. 62   Education—teaching about the human community

This view of education seems to recommend that schools stress the unity of all people instead of their diversity. While I agree that education should include teaching students about characteristics that we all share, doing so need not necessarily entail shifting focus away from our differences. Education can and should include both.

On the one hand, we are in the midst of an evolving global community where it is increasingly important for people to recognize our common humanity, as well as specific hopes and goals we all share. People universally prefer health to disease, being nourished to starving, safe communities to crime-riddled ones, and peace to war. Focusing on our unity will help us realize these hopes and goals. Moreover, in our pluralistic democracy it is crucial to find ways to unify citizens from diverse backgrounds. Otherwise, we risk being reduced to ethnic, religious or political factions at war with one another, as witnessed recently in the former Yugoslavia. Our own diverse society can forestall such horrors only if citizens are educated about the democratic ideals, heritage, rights and obligations we all have in common.

On the other hand, our schools should not attempt to erase, ignore, or even play down religious, ethnic or cultural diversity. First of all, schools have the obligation to teach the democratic ideal of tolerance, and the best way to teach tolerance is to educate people about different religions, cultures and so on. Moreover, educating people about diversity might even produce a unifying effect—by promoting understanding and appreciation among people from all backgrounds.

In conclusion, while it may appear paradoxical to recommend that education stress both unity and diversity, it is not. Understanding our common humanity will help us achieve a better, more peaceful world. Toward the same end, we need to understand our differences in order to better tolerate them, and perhaps even appreciate them. Our schools can and should promote both kinds of understanding by way of a balanced approach.

Issue No. 63   Government bureaucracy

At first glance, it would seem that increased bureaucracy creates obstacles between the citizens and those who govern, thereby separating the two groups. Closer examination reveals, however, that in many ways government bureaucracy actually bridges this gap, and that new technologies now allow for ways around the gap.

First of all, many government bureaucracies are established as a response to the needs of the citizenry. In a sense, they manifest a nexus between citizens and government, providing a means of communication and redress for grievances that would not otherwise be available. For example, does the FDA, by virtue of its ensuring the safety of our food and drugs, separate us from the government? Or does the FHA, by helping to make home ownership more viable to ordinary citizens, thereby increase the gap between citizens and the government? No; these agencies serve our interests and enhance the accessibility of government resources to citizens.

Admittedly, agencies such as these are necessary proxies for direct participation in government, since our societal problems are too large and complex for individuals to solve. However, technology is coming forward to bridge some of the larger gaps. For example, we can now communicate directly with our legislators by e-mail, visit our lawmakers on the Web, and engage in electronic town hall meetings. In addition, the fact that government bureaucracies are the largest employers of citizens should not be overlooked. In this sense, bureaucracies bridge the gap by enabling more citizens to become part of the government.

In the final analysis, one can view bureaucracies as surrogates for individual participation in government; however, they are more accurately viewed as a manifestation of the symbiotic relationship between citizens and the government.

Issue No. 64   Goal of business: profit vs. public welfare

I agree that business has some obligation to the community and society in which it operates. As it stands, however, the statement permits one to conclude that this obligation should take precedence over the profit objective. By allowing for this interpretation, the speaker fails to appreciate the problems associated with shouldering business with an affirmative duty to ensure the public's well-being.

The primary reason why I agree business should have a duty to the public is that society would be worse off by exonerating business from social responsibility. Left entirely to their own self-interest, businesses pollute the environment, withhold important product information from consumers, pay employees substandard wages, and misrepresent their financial condition to current and potential shareholders. Admittedly, in its pursuit of profit business can benefit the society as well—by way of more and better-paying jobs, economic growth, and better yet lower-priced products. However, this point ignores the harsh consequences—such as those listed earlier—of imposing no affirmative social duty on business.

Another reason why I agree business should have a duty to the public is that business owes such a duty. A business enters into an implied contract with the community in which it operates, under which the community agrees to permit a corporation to do business while the business implicitly promises to benefit, and not harm, the community. This understanding gives rise to a number of social obligations on the part of the business—to promote consumer safety, to not harm the environmental, to treat employees and competitors fairly, and so on.

Although I agree that business should have a duty to serve the pubic, I disagree that this should be the primarily objective of business. Imposing affirmative social duties on business opens a Pandora's box of problems—for example, how to determine, (1) what the public interest is in the first place, (2) which public interests are most important, (3) what actions are in the public interest, and (4) how business' duty to the public might be monitored and enforced. Government regulation is the only practical way to deal with these issues, yet government is notoriously inefficient and corrupt; the only way to limit these problems is to limit the duty of business to serve the public interest.

In sum, I agree that the duty of business should extend beyond the simple profit motive. However, its affirmative obligations to society should be tempered against the pubic benefits of the profit motive and against the practical problems associated with imposition of affirmative social duties.

Issue No. 65   Multinational corporations and global homogeneity

Although global homogeneity in a broader sense may not be as inexorable as the speaker here suggests, I agree that multinational corporations are indeed creating global sameness in consumer preferences. This homogeneity is manifested in two concurrent megatrends: (1) the embracing of American popular culture throughout the world, and (2) a synthesis of cultures, as reflected in consumer preferences.

The first trend is toward Americanization of popular culture throughout the world. In food and fashion, once a nation's denizens "fall into the Gap" or get a taste of a Coke or Big Mac, their preferences are forever Westernized. The ubiquitous Nike "swoosh," which nearly every soccer player in the world will soon don, epitomizes this phenomenon. In media, the cultural agendas of giants such as Time-Warner now drive the world's entertainment preferences. The Rolling Stones and the stars of America's prime-time television shows are revered among young people worldwide, while Mozart's music, Shakespeare's prose, and Ghandi's ideology are largely ignored.

A second megatrend is toward a synthesis of cultures into a homogenous stew. The popularity of "world music" and of the "New Age" health care and leisure-time activities aptly illustrate this blending of Eastern, Western and third-world cultures. Perhaps nowhere is the cultural-stew paradigm more striking, and more bland, than at the international "food courts" now featured in malls throughout the developed world.

These trends appear inexorable. Counter-attacks, such as Ebonics, rap music, and bilingual education, promote the distinct culture of minority groups, but not of nations. Further homogenization of consumer preferences is all but ensured by falling trade barriers, coupled with the global billboard that satellite communications and the Internet provide.

In sum, American multinationals have indeed instigated a homogeneous global, yet American-style, consumerism—one which in all likelihood will grow in extent along with free-market capitalism and global connectivity.

Issue No. 66 Products liability

In determining whether manufacturers should be accountable for all injuries resulting from the use of their products, one must weigh the interests of consumers against those of manufacturers. On balance, holding manufacturers strictly liable for such injuries is unjustifiable.

Admittedly, protecting consumers from defective and dangerous products is an important and worthwhile goal. No doubt nearly all of us would agree that health and safety should rank highly as an objective of public policy. Also, compelling a high level of safety forces manufacturers to become more innovative in design, use of materials, and so forth. Consumers and manufacturers alike benefit, of course, from innovation.

However, the arguments against a strict-liability standard are more compelling. First, the standard is costly. It forces manufacturers to incur undue expenses for overbuilding, excessive safety testing, and defending liability law suits. Consumers are then damaged by ultimately bearing these costs in the form of higher prices. Second, the standard can be unfair. It can assign fault to the wrong party; where a product is distributed through a wholesaler and/or retailer, one of these parties may have actually caused, or at least contributed to, the injury. The standard can also misplace fault where the injured party is not the original consumer. Manufacturers cannot ensure that second-hand users receive safe products or adequate instructions and warnings. Finally, where the injured consumer uses the product for a purpose or in a manner other than the intended one, or where there were patent dangers that the user should have been aware of, it seems the user, not the manufacturer, should assume the risk of injury.

In sum, despite compelling interests in consumer safety and product innovation, holding manufacturers accountable for all injuries caused by their products is unjustifiably costly to society and unfair to manufacturers.

The speaker claims that our jobs greatly influence our personal interests, recreational activities and even appearance. While I agree that the personal lives of some people are largely determined by their work, in my view it would be a mistake to draw this conclusion generally. In my observation, the extent to which occupation influences personal life depends on (1) the nature of the work, and (2) how central the work is to one's sense of self.

On the one hand, consider my friends Steve and William. Steve works as a gardener, but after work he creates oil paintings of quality and poignancy. His leisure time is spent alternately at the sea, in the wilderness, and in dark cafes. William paints houses for a living, but on his own time he collects fine art and books in first edition, as well as reading voraciously in the area of American history. Their outside activities and appearance speak little about what Steve or William do for a living, because these men view their jobs as little more than a means of subsidizing the activities that manifest their true selves. At the same time, they have chosen jobs that need not spill over into their personal lives, so the nature of their jobs permits them to maintain a distinctive identity apart from their work.

On the other hand, consider my friend Shana—a business executive who lives and breathes her work. After work hours you can invariably find her at a restaurant or bar with colleagues, discussing work. Shana's wardrobe is primarily red—right off the dress-for-success page of a woman's magazine. For Shana, her job is clearly an expression of her self-concept. Also, by its nature it demands Shana's attention and time away from the workplace.

What has determined the influence of work on personal lives in these cases is the extent to which each person sees himself or herself in terms of work. Clearly, work is at the center of Shana's life, but not of either Steve's or William's. My sample is small; still, common sense and intuition tell me that the influence of work on one's personal life depends both on the nature of the work and on the extent to which the work serves as a manifestation of one's self-concept.

Issue No. 68   Workplace design and employee input

I agree that physical workspace can affect morale and productivity and that, as a result, employees should have a significant voice in how their work areas are designed. However, the speaker suggests that each employee should have full autonomy over his or her immediate workspace. I think this view is too extreme, for it ignores two important problems that allowing too much freedom over workspace can create.

On the one hand, I agree that some aspects of workspace design are best left to the individual preferences of each worker. Location of personal tools and materials, style and size of desk chair, and even desk lighting and decorative desk items, can each play an important role in a worker's comfort, psychological well-being, concentration, and efficiency. Moreover, these features involve highly subjective preferences, so it would be inappropriate for anyone but the worker to make such choices.

On the other hand, control over one's immediate workspace should not go unchecked, for two reasons. First, one employee's workspace design may inconvenience, annoy, or even offend nearby coworkers. For example, pornographic pinups may distract some coworkers and offend others, thereby impeding productivity, fostering ill-will and resentment, and increasing attrition—all to the detriment of the company. Admittedly, the consequences of most workspace choices would not be so far-reaching. Still, in my observation many people adhere, consciously or not, to the adage that one person's rights extend only so far as the next person's nose (or ears, or eyes). A second problem with affording too much workspace autonomy occurs when workspaces are not clearly delineated—by walls and doors—or when workers share an immediate workspace. In such cases, giving all workers concurrent authority would perpetuate conflict and undermine productivity.

In conclusion, although employees should have the freedom to arrange their work areas, this freedom is not absolute. Managers would be well-advised to arbitrate workspace disputes and, if needed, assume authority to make final decisions about workspace design.

Issue No. 69   **The ability to work well with other employees**

Whether the ability to work with others is more important than specific knowledge and technical competence depends on the specific job as well as the complexity of the job's technical aspects. In general, however, social skills are more critical than technical competence to the ultimate success of an organizational unit.

Admittedly, some level of technical competence and specific knowledge is needed to perform any job. Without some knowledge of the systems, procedures, and vocabulary used in one's department or division, an employee cannot communicate effectively with peers or contribute meaningfully to team goals. By the same token, however, nearly every job—even those in which technical ability would seem to be of paramount importance—calls for some skill in working with other employees. Computer programmers, for example, work in teams to develop products according to agreed-upon specifications and timelines. Scientists and researchers must collaborate to establish common goals and to coordinate efforts. Even teachers, who are autonomous in the classroom, must serve on committees and coordinate activities with administrators and other teachers.

Moreover, employees can generally learn technical skills and gain specific knowledge through on-the-job training and continuing education (depending on the complexity of the skills involved). Social skills, on the other hand, are more innate and not easily learned. They are, therefore, requisite skills that employees must possess at the outset if the organizational unit is to succeed.

In sum, specific knowledge does admittedly play a more critical role than social skills in some highly-technical jobs; nevertheless, the ability to work well with other employees is ultimately more important, since all jobs require this ability and since it is more difficult to learn social skills on the job.

Issue No. 70   Ethical constraints in creating and marketing products

The speaker asserts that in creating and marketing products, companies act ethically merely by not violating any laws. Although the speaker's position is not wholly insupportable, far more compelling arguments can be made for holding businesses to higher ethical standards than those required by the letter of the law.

On the one hand, two colorable arguments can be made for holding business only to legal standards of conduct. First, imposing a higher ethical duty can actual harm consumers in the long term. Compliance with high ethical standards can be costly for business, thereby lowering profits and, in turn, impeding a company's ability to create jobs (for consumers), keep prices low (for consumers), and so forth. Second, limited accountability is consistent with the "buyer beware" principle that permeates our laws of contracts and torts, as well as our notion in civil procedure that plaintiffs carry the burden of proving damage. In other words, the onus should be on consumers to protect themselves, not on companies to protect consumers.

On the other hand, several convincing arguments can be made for holding business to a higher ethical standard. First, in many cases government regulations that protect consumers lag behind advances in technology. A new marketing technique made possible by Internet technology may be unethical but nevertheless might not be proscribed by the letter of the laws which predated the Internet. Second, enforceability might not extend beyond geographic borders. Consider, for example, the case of "dumping." When products fail to comply with U.S. regulations, American companies frequently market—or "dump"— such products in third-world countries where consumer-protection laws are virtually nonexistent. Third, moral principles form the basis of government regulation and are, therefore, more fundamental than the law.

In the final analysis, while overburdening businesses with obligations to consumers may not be a good idea in the extreme, our regulatory system is not as effective as it should be. Therefore, businesses should adhere to a higher standard of ethics in creating and marketing products than what is required by the letter of the law.

Has commercialism become too widespread, particularly in schools, churches, and other places which traditionally have been safe havens from commercialism? If so, does the government have a responsibility to curb the problem? The answer to both questions, in my view, is no.

There is no evidence that commercialism is creeping into our churches. Admittedly, some commercial activity is present in our schools. Food service is increasing outsourced to fast-food chains; a plethora of goods and services is sold in college bookstores and advertised in their school newspapers; and students serve as walking billboards for the companies whose logos appear on clothing. However, this kind of commercialism does not interfere with school activities; to the contrary, in the first two cases they contribute to the efficient functioning of the organization. Outsourcing food service, for example, is a cost-cutting measure which provides additional funding for teaching materials, facilities, and teacher salaries.

I do agree that, in general, commercialism is becoming more widespread, and that one of the byproducts may be a decline in the quality of our culture. Electronic billboards now serve as backdrops for televised sporting events, and Web sites must sell advertising space to justify maintenance costs. Does this mean that government should step in and ban the sale of products in certain venues? No. This would require that government make ad hoc, and possibly arbitrary, decisions as to which products may be sold or advertised at which places and events. These are value judgments that are best left to individual schools, churches, and other organizations. Moreover, the expense of enforcing the regulations may well outweigh the cultural benefits, if any.

In sum, while commercialism is undeniably becoming more widespread, it is minimally intrusive and works to the net benefit of society. As a matter of public policy, therefore, government should not attempt to regulate the extent of commercialism.

Issue No. 72   **Effects of employee incentives**

Providing employee incentives can be a double-edged sword. On the one hand, the promise of bonuses or gifts can spur workers to higher achievement. On the other hand, incentives can create resentment and internal competitiveness that are damaging to morale and to the organization. Even so, I think a carefully designed incentive program can operate to the net benefit a company.

Incentive programs are counterproductive when the distribution of rewards appears to be personally biased, when the program recognizes just one kind among many important jobs in the organization, or when there are too few rewards available. For example, if a manager regularly rewards an employee who is perceived to be a favorite, coworkers will be resentful. Or if the company decides to recognize high sales, while ignoring an especially precise cost-assessment from the accounting department, the accountants may feel their work is not valued. Finally, if rewards are too few, some employees will become overly competitive, while others may simply stop trying.

However, incentive programs can be designed to avoid such pitfalls. First, the company must determine that it can provide sufficient rewards to motivate all employees. Then it must set, and follow, clear and non-arbitrary guidelines for achievement. Finally, management should provide appropriate incentives throughout the organization, thereby sending the message that all work is valued. Admittedly, even a thoughtfully designed incentive program cannot entirely prevent back-stabbing and unfair competitive tactics. But watchful management can quell much of this behavior, and the perpetrators usually show their true colors in time.

In sum, I think that the productivity inspired by thoughtful incentive programs will very likely outweigh any negative consequences. In the final analysis, then, I disagree with the speaker's recommendation against their use.

Issue No. 73   Following one's instincts

The advice to act naturally or follow one's instincts can, admittedly, be helpful advice for someone torn between difficult career or personal choices in life. In most situations, however, following this advice would neither be wise nor sensible. Following one's own instincts should be tempered by codes of behavior appropriate to the situation at hand.

First of all, doing what comes naturally often amounts to impulsive overreaction and irrational behavior, based on emotion. Everyone experiences impulses from time to time, such as hitting another person, quitting one's job, having an extramarital affair, and so forth. People who act however they please or say whatever is on their mind without thinking about consequences, especially without regard to social situation, may offend and alienate others. At the workplace, engaging in petty gossip, sexual harassment, or back-stabbing might be considered "natural"; yet such behavior can be destructive for the individuals at the receiving end as well as for the company. And in dealings with foreign business associates, what an American might find natural or instinctive, even if socially acceptable here, might be deeply insulting or confusing to somebody from another culture.

Second, doing what comes naturally is not necessarily in one's own best interests. The various behaviors cited above would also tend to be counterproductive for the person engaging in them. "Natural" behavior could prove deadly to one's career, since people who give little thought before they act cannot be trusted in a job that requires effective relationships with important clients, colleagues, and others.

Third, the speaker seems to suggest that you should be yourself, then act accordingly—in that order. But we define ourselves in large measure by our actions. Young adults especially lack a clear sense of self. How can you be yourself if you don't know who you are? Even for mature adults, the process of evolving one's concept of self is a perpetual one. In this respect, then, the speaker's recommendation does not make much sense.

In sum, one should not follow the speaker's advice universally or too literally. For unless a person's instincts are to follow standard rules of social and business etiquette, natural behavior can harm others as well as constrain one's own personal and professional growth.

Issue No. 74	Rule-breakers: the most memorable people

I strongly agree that rule-breakers are the most memorable people. By departing from the status quo, iconoclasts call attention to themselves, some providing conspicuous mirrors for society, others serving as our primary catalysts for progress.

In politics, for example, rule-breakers Mahatma Ghandi and Martin Luther King secured prominent places in history by challenging the status quo through civil disobedience. Renegades such as Ghengus Khan, Stalin, and Hussein, broke all the human-rights "rules," thereby leaving indelible marks in the historical record. And future generations will probably remember Nixon and Kennedy more clearly than Carter or Reagan, by way of their rule-breaking activities—specifically, Nixon's Watergate debacle and Kennedy's extra-marital trysts.

In the arts, mavericks such as Dali, Picasso, and Warhol, who break established rules of composition, ultimately emerge as the greatest artists, while the names of artists with superior technical skills are relegated to the footnotes of art-history textbooks. Our most influential popular musicians are the flagrant rule breakers—for example, be-bop musicians such as Charlie Parker and Thelonius Monk, who broke all the harmonic rules, and folk musician-poet Bob Dylan, who broke the rules for lyrics.

In the sciences, innovation and progress can only result from challenging conventional theories—i.e., by breaking rules. Newton and Einstein, for example, both refused to blindly accept what were perceived at their time as certain "rules" of physics. As a result, both men redefined those rules, and both men emerged as two of the most memorable figures in the field of physics.

In conclusion, it appears that the deepest positive and negative impressions appear on either side of the same iconoclastic coin. Those who leave the most memorable imprints in history do so by challenging norms, traditions, cherished values, and the general status quo—that is, by breaking the rules.

Issue No. 75   The motivating forces of self-interest and fear

The speaker claims that people are motivated only by fear and self-interest. This claim relies on the belief that human beings are essentially selfish, or egoistic. In my view, the speaker oversimplifies human nature, ignoring the important motivating force of altruism.

On the one hand, I agree that most of our actions result in large part from self-interest and from our survival instincts, such as fear. For example, our educational and vocational lives are to a great extent motivated by our interest in ensuring our own livelihood, safety, health, and so on. We might perpetuate bad personal relationships because we are insecure—or afraid—of what will happen to us if we change course. Even providing for our own children may to some extent be motivated by selfishness—satisfying a need for fulfillment or easing our fear that we will be alone in our old age.

On the other hand, to assert that all of our actions are essentially motivated by self-interest and fear is to overemphasize one aspect of human nature. Humans are also altruistic—that is, we act to benefit others, even though doing so may not in be in our own interest. The speaker might claim that altruistic acts are just egoistic ones in disguise—done to avoid unpleasant feelings of guilt, to give oneself pleasure, or to obligate another person. However, this counterargument suffers from three critical problems. First, some examples of altruism are difficult to describe in terms of self-interest alone. Consider the soldier who falls on a grenade to save his companions. It would be nonsensical to assert that this soldier is acting selfishly when he knows his action will certainly result in his own immediate death. Second, the argument offends our intuition that human motivation is far more complex. Third, it relies on a poor assumption; just because we feel good about helping others, it does not follow that the only reason we help is in order to feel good.

In sum, the speaker oversimplifies human nature. All human motivation cannot be reduced to fear and self-interest. We can also be motivated by altruism, and the pleasure we might take in helping others is not necessarily an indication that our actions are selfish.

Issue No. 76   Decision-making and effective leadership

I agree that decisiveness is one clear mark of an effective leader. However, the speaker goes further to make the dual claim that decision-making is the most difficult and the most important aspect of a leader's job. In my view, this additional claim amounts to an overstatement that fails to consider other aspects of a leader's job that are either difficult or important.

First of all, decisiveness is not necessarily the most difficult aspect of a leader's job. In fact, leaders rise to their positions typically because decisiveness comes easily or naturally to them. In this sense, the speaker's claim runs contrary to actual experience. Also, for some leaders the stress and the burden of their job pose more difficulties for them than the mere act of making decisions. For other leaders, balancing professional and personal life, or even time management in general, may be the most challenging aspect of the job, since leaders are typically very busy people.

Secondly, decisiveness is not necessarily the key factor in determining the quality of leadership. Decisiveness does not guarantee a good decision. An effective leader must also have wisdom, perspective, clear vision, judgment, and courage. Moreover, other factors such as trust and respect for others may be equally or more critical, since subordinates may not be willing to devote themselves to the plans and goals of a leader they mistrust or hold in low regard. Even the best decision will be of little value without the commitment of others to carry it out. Simply put, without someone to lead, a person cannot be a leader.

To sum up, I agree with the speaker only insofar as the ability to make decisions is a necessary ingredient of successful leadership. However, decision-making is not necessarily the most difficult aspect of every leader's job; nor is it necessarily the most important factor in determining the effectiveness of a leader.

I strongly agree that true genius is the ability to see beyond conventional modes of thinking and to suggest new and better ones. This definition properly sets genius apart from lesser instances of critical acumen, inventiveness or creativity. Under this definition, a true genius must successfully (1) challenge the assumptions underlying a current paradigm, and (2) supplant the old paradigm with a new, better, and more fruitful one.

This two-pronged standard for true genius is aptly illustrated by examining the scientific contribution of the 15th-century astronomer Copernicus. Prior to Copernicus, our view of the universe was governed by the Ptolemaic paradigm of a geocentric universe, according to which our earth was in a fixed position at the center of the universe, with other heavenly bodies revolving around it. Copernicus challenged this paradigm and its key assumptions by introducing a distinction between real motion and motion that is merely apparent. In doing so, he satisfied the first requirement of a true genius.

Had Copernicus managed to show only that the old view and its assumptions were problematic, we would not consider him a genius today. Copernicus went on, however, to develop a new paradigm; he claimed that the earth is rotating while hurtling rapidly through space, and that other heavenly bodies only appear to revolve around the earth. Moreover, he reasoned that his view about the earth's real motion could explain the apparent motion of the sun, stars and other planets around the earth. It turned out he was right; and his theories helped facilitate Galileo's empirical observations, Kepler's laws of planetary motion, and Newton's gravitational principle.

To sum up, I find the proposed definition of true genius incisive and accurate; and the example of Copernicus aptly points up the two required elements of true genius required by the definition.

Issue No. 78   **The historic value of older buildings**

The issue of whether to raze an old, historic building to make way for progress is a complex one, since it involves a conflict between our interest in preserving our culture, tradition, and history and a legitimate need to create practical facilities that serve current utilitarian purposes. In my view, the final judgment should depend on a case-by-case analysis of two key factors.

One key factor is the historic value of the building. An older building may be worth saving because it uniquely represents some bygone era. On the other hand, if several older buildings represent the era just as effectively, then the historic value of one building might be negligible. If the building figured centrally into the city's history as a municipal structure, the home of a founding family or other significant historical figure, or the location of important events, then its historic value would be greater than if its history was an unremarkable one.

The other key factor involves the specific utilitarian needs of the community and the relative costs and benefits of each alternative in light of those needs. For example, if the need is mainly for more office space, then an architecturally appropriate add-on or annex might serve just as well as a new building. On the other hand, an expensive retrofit may not be worthwhile if no amount of retrofitting would permit it to serve the desired function. Moreover, retrofitting might undermine the historic value of the old building by altering its aesthetic or architectural integrity.

In sum, neither modernization for its own sake nor indiscriminate preservation of old buildings should guide decisions in the controversies at issue. Instead, decisions should be made on a case-by-case basis, considering historic value, community need, and the comparative costs and benefits of each alternative.

This first part of this statement means that interpersonal—or social—skills can be marketed as part of a bundle of assets that one might tout to a prospective client, customer, or especially employer. Presumably, the extent and value of these skills can be gauged by one's previous experience with clients and customers or at jobs requiring a significant amount of teamwork and cooperation among workers—as measured by factors such as one's tenure in such a job and letters of reference from supervisors. While this claim seems plausible in the abstract, it ignores critical valuation problems. Furthermore, the claim that the ability to deal with people exceeds the value of all other commodities is an overgeneralization, since relative values depend on particular circumstances.

The first problem with this claim is that it is far more difficult to quantify the value of interpersonal skills, or other human qualities, than the value of commodities such as coffee or sugar, which can be measured, weighed, or otherwise examined prior to purchase. To a large extent, the ability to work with people is a quality whose true value can be determined only after it is purchased, then tried and tested for a period of time. Additionally, its value may vary depending on the idiosyncrasies of the job. For example, a technically-oriented programmer or researcher might function well with a team of like-minded workers, yet have trouble dealing with management or marketing personnel.

The second problem with this claim is that it overgeneralizes in asserting that the ability to work with people is "worth more than any other commodity." The relative value of this ability depends on the peculiarities of the job. In some jobs, especially sales, ambition and tenacity are more valuable. In other areas, such as research and development, technical skills and specific knowledge are paramount. Moreover, in some businesses, such as mining or oil-drilling, the value of raw materials and capital equipment might be far more important a commodity than the social skills, or most other skills, of employees—depending on the economic circumstances.

In sum, the ability to deal with people is purchasable only to a limited extent, since its full value cannot be determined prior to purchase. Moreover, its full value depends on the organizational unit as well as the nature of the business.

Issue No. 80   Our saving and borrowing habits

Whether an individual saves too little or borrows too much depends on the purpose and extent of either activity. While appropriate and prudent in some circumstances, either can be irresponsible in excess. The evidence suggests that, on balance, people today tend to borrow irresponsibly and are on the brink of saving irresponsibly as well.

Traditionally, saving is viewed as a virtue, while borrowing is considered a vice. However, just the opposite may be true under certain circumstances. Foregoing saving in favor of immediate spending may at times be well justified. A serious hobbyist, for example, may be justified in foregoing saving to spend money on a hobby that provides great joy and fulfillment—whether or not it also generates income. A relatively expensive automobile is justifiable if the additional expense provides added safety for the owner and his family. And foregoing saving is appropriate, and often necessary, for "rainy day" medical emergencies or unanticipated periods of unemployment. Borrowing can also be prudent—if the loan is affordable and applied toward a sound long-term investment.

Were saving and borrowing limited to these types of scenarios, I would aver that people today save and borrow responsibly. However, the evidence suggests otherwise. Americans now purchase on credit far more expensive automobiles, relative to income, than ever before—vehicles that are far more than what is needed for safe transportation. Excessive credit-card debt, another type of unjustifiable borrowing, is at record levels—and rising—among American households. Does the baby-boomers' current penchant for retirement investing compensate for these excesses? Probably not. This trend is fueled by unrealistic expectations of future returns; it may therefore, escalate to speculation and, at its height, widespread leveraging—i.e., borrowing. Such speculation is more suited to highly sophisticated investors who can well afford to lose their entire investment than to average Americans and their nest eggs.

In conclusion, while people seem to be saving aggressively today, their investment choices and concomitant high spending and borrowing levels call into question the assertion that we are indeed a "nation of savers."

Whether a conformist can achieve lasting success or "get rich" in business depends primarily on the type of business involved. Iconoclasts rise to the top in newer industries and in those where consumer demand is in constant flux. Conformists ultimately prevail, however, in traditional service industries ensconced in systems and regulations.

In consumer-driven industries, innovation, product differentiation, and creativity are crucial to lasting success. In the retail and media sectors, for example, unconventional products and advertising are necessary to catch the attention of consumers and to keep up with the vagaries of consumer tastes. Those who take an iconoclastic approach tend to recognize emerging trends and to rise above their peers. For example, Ted Turner's departure from the traditional format of the other television networks, and the responsiveness of Amazon.com to burgeoning Internet commerce, propelled these two giants to leadership positions in their industries. And in technology, where there are no conventional practices or ways of thinking to begin with, companies that fail to break away from last year's paradigm are soon left behind by the competition.

However, in traditional service industries—such as finance, accounting, insurance, legal services, and health care—lasting success and riches come not to non-conformists but rather to those who can deliver services most effectively within the confines of established practices, policies, and regulations. Of course, a clever idea for structuring a deal, or a creative legal maneuver, may play a role in winning smaller battles along the way. But such tactics are those of conformists who are playing by the same ground rules as their peers; winners are just better at the game.

In conclusion, while non-conformists tend to be the wildly successful players in technology-driven and consumer-driven industries, traditionalists are the winners in system-driven industries pervaded by policy, regulation, and bureaucracy.

The issue here is whether business and government are doing enough to help meet the needs and goals of women in the workplace. I agree with the speaker insofar as many employers can do more to accommodate the special needs of women in their role as mothers. However, it seems to me that business and government are doing their fair share otherwise for women in the workplace.

Women differ fundamentally from men in their child-bearing ability. Related to this ability is the maternal instinct—a desire to nurture that is far stronger for women than for men, generally speaking. At a minimum, then, businesses should acknowledge these fundamental differences and accommodate them so that a female employee's job and career are not jeopardized merely for fulfilling her instinctive role as a female. More and more businesses are providing maternal leave with full benefits, day-care facilities, and job-sharing programs to accommodate these special needs of women. In my observation, however, many businesses can do more in these respects.

However, beyond accommodating these fundamental differences, neither business nor government has a special duty to improve the status of women at the workplace. The government already has an obligation to enact and enforce anti-discrimination laws, and to provide legal means for seeking redress in cases of discrimination. Moreover, business and government both have a legal duty to abide by those laws by way of their hiring, salary, and job-promotion policies. Discharging this duty should, in my view, suffice to serve the special interests of women in the workplace. While many would argue that de facto double standards still run rampant and largely unchecked, this claim raises subjective perceptions about fairness that can neither be confirmed nor dispelled with certainty.

In sum, business and government can always do more to accommodate women in their special role as mothers. Otherwise, insofar as they are adhering to our current anti-discrimination laws, business and government are discharging their duty to help meet the needs and goals of women at the workplace.

Issue No. 83   How buildings shape us

I believe this statement should be interpreted broadly—to mean that we are influenced by the exterior shape of buildings, as well as by the arrangement of multiple buildings and by a building's various architectural and aesthetic elements. While I doubt that buildings determine our character or basic personality traits, I agree that they can greatly influence our attitudes, moods, and even life styles.

On the structural and multi-structural scales, the arrangement of numerous buildings can shape us in profound ways. High-density commercial districts with numerous skyscrapers might result in stressful commuting, short tempers, a feeling of dehumanization, and so on. A "campus" arrangement of smaller, scattered buildings can promote health, well-being, and stress reduction by requiring frequent brisk outdoor jaunts. Buildings with multiple floors can also "shape" us, literally, by requiring exercise up and down stairs.

As for floor plans and internal space, physical arrangement of workspaces can shape workers' attitudes toward work and toward one another. Sitting in small, gray cubicles lined up in militaristic rows is demoralizing, leaving workers with the feeling that they are little more than impersonal cogs of some office machine. But creative design of workspaces in varied arrangements can create feelings of uniqueness and importance in each employee. Workspace relationships that suggest some sort of hierarchy may breed competitiveness among coworkers, and may encourage a more bureaucratic approach to work.

Finally, as for aesthetic elements, the amount of light and location of windows in a building can shape us in significant psychological ways. For most people, daily tasks are more enjoyable in settings with plenty of natural light and at least some natural scenery. Choice of colors can influence our mood, concentration, and efficiency. Numerous psychological studies show that different colors influence behavior, attitudes, and emotions in distinctly different ways. Yellow enhances appetite, blue has a tranquilizing effect, and gray is the color of choice for companies who want their workers to be subservient.

In sum, our buildings, the space around them and the space within them, can affect us in important ways that influence our outlook on life, relationships with coworkers, and even physical health and well-being.

Issue No. 84   **Informing customers about products and services**

Requiring businesses to provide complete product information to customers promotes various consumer interests, but at the same time imposes burdens on businesses, government, and taxpayers. On balance, the burdens outweigh the benefits, at least in most cases.

A threshold problem with disclosure requirements is that of determining what constitutes "complete" information. Admittedly, legislating disclosure requirements clarifies the duties of business and the rights of consumers. Yet determining what requirements are fair in all cases is problematic. Should it suffice to list ingredients, instructions, and intended uses, or should customers also be informed of precise specifications, potential risks, and results of tests measuring a product's effectiveness vis-a-vis competing products? A closely related problem is that determining and enforcing disclosure standards necessarily involves government regulation, thereby adding to the ultimate cost to the consumer by way of higher taxes. Finally, failure to comply may result in regulatory fines, a cost that may either have a chilling effect on product innovation or be passed on to the customers in the form of higher prices. Either result operates to the detriment of the consumer, the very party whom the regulations are designed to protect.

These burdens must be weighed against the interest in protecting consumers against fraud and undue health and safety hazards. To assume that businesses will voluntarily disclose negative product information ignores the fact that businesses are motivated by profit, not by public interest concerns. However, consumers today have ready access to many consumer-protection resources, and may not need the protection of government regulation. Although health and safety concerns are especially compelling in the case of products that are inherently dangerous—power tools, recreational equipment, and the like—or new and relatively untested products, especially pharmaceuticals, narrow exceptions can always be carved out for these products.

In conclusion, while stringent disclosure requirements may be appropriate for certain products, businesses and consumers alike are generally better off without the burdens imposed by requiring that businesses provide complete product information to all customers.

Advertising is clearly the most influential art form in this century. It is therefore tempting to think it is also the most important. However, great artistic achievement is determined by criteria beyond mere influence. And when examined against these criteria, the genre of advertising does not measure up as truly important.

To begin with, great art inspires us to look at the human situation from new perspectives. For example, early impressionist paintings challenge our thinking about visual perception and about the nature of the reality we assume we see. Other works, like Rodin's "The Thinker," capture for our reflection the essential value of human rationality. In stark contrast, advertising encourages people not to think or reflect at all, but simply to spend.

In addition, the significance of great artistic achievement transcends time, even when it reflects a particular age. Yet advertising, by its very nature, is transient; in an eye-blink, today's hot image or slogan is yesterday's news. Of course, the timelessness of a work cannot be determined in its own time. Still, it's hard to imagine even the most powerful advertisement living beyond its current ad campaign.

Admittedly, one ad—Andy Warhol's painting of the Campbell Soup can—has achieved timelessness. But notice the irony; the packaging or advertising image was banal until it was elevated above mere graphic design to high art. The lesson here is that advertising, in itself, probably will not achieve great importance as art. But taken up by the artist as content in a larger commentary on society, it can become transcendent.

In sum, artists will no doubt continue to comment on advertising and on the materialistic values it reflects and promotes. But the ads themselves, however influential in marketing terms, fail to fulfill all the criteria for important art.

Issue No. 86   Advertising—appeal to emotion vs. reason

There are two traditional advertising tactics for promoting a product, event, candidate, or point of view. One is to provide reasons; the other is to bypass reasons altogether and appeal strictly to emotion. Considered in isolation, emotional appeals are far more effective. But many of the most influential ads combine slim reasons with powerful appeals to emotion.

To appreciate the power of emotional appeals we need only consider the promotion of sodas, beer, cigarettes, cosmetics and so on. This advertising is the most successful in the industry; and it trades almost exclusively on the manipulation of our desires, fears and senses of humor. In fact, it wouldn't make sense to offer up arguments, because there really aren't any good reasons for consuming such products.

Even so, some of these products are advertised with at least superficial reasoning. For instance, in the promotion of facial moisturizers it has become popular to use the image of a youthful woman with fresh, unlined skin along with the claim that the product "can reduce the signs of aging." This is indeed a reason, but a carefully couched one that never really states that product users will look younger. Still, countless middle-aged women will pay twice as much for products that add this claim to the expected image of youthfulness that trades on their fears of growing old.

One of the most clever and ironic combined uses of reason and emotion is seen in the old Volvo slogan, "Volvo, the car for people who think." The suggested reason for buying the car is obvious: it is the intelligent choice. But the emotional snare is equally clear; the ad appeals to one's desire to be included in the group of intelligent, thoughtful people.

In conclusion, I agree that appeals to emotion are more powerful tools than arguments or reasoning for promoting products. It is no coincidence that advertising agencies hire professional psychologists, but not logicians. Still, in my view the most influential advertisements mix in a bit of reasoning as well.

Issue No. 87   Technology and adjusting to job obsolescence

As technology and changing social needs render more and more jobs obsolete, who is responsible for helping displaced workers adjust? While individuals have primary responsibility for learning new skills and finding work, both industry and government have some obligation to provide them the means of doing so.

I agree that individuals must assume primary responsibility for adjusting to job obsolescence, especially since our educational system has been preparing us for it. For decades, our schools have been counseling young people to expect and prepare for numerous major career changes during their lives. And concerned educators have recognized and responded to this eventuality with a broader base of practical and theoretical coursework that affords students the flexibility to move from one career to another.

However, industry should bear some of the responsibility as well. It is industry, after all, that determines the particular directions technological progress and subsequent social change will take. And since industry is mainly responsible for worker displacement, it has a duty to help displaced workers adjust—through such means as on-site training programs and stipends for further education.

Government should also assume some of the responsibility, since it is partly government money that fuels technological progress in industry. Moreover, government should help because it can help—for example, by ensuring that grants and federally insured student loans are available to those who must retool in order to find new work. Government can also help by observing and recording trends in worker displacement and in job opportunities, and by providing this information to individuals so that they can make prudent decisions about their own further education and job searches.

In conclusion, while individuals should be prepared for future job changes, both government and industry shoulder obligations to provide training programs, funding and information that will help displaced workers successfully retool and find new employment.

Issue No. 88   Accepting blame for hateful actions and words

The issue at hand is whether each generation is blameworthy for the hateful words and actions of some of its members, and for the failure of others to denounce those hateful words and actions. In my view, it does not make clear sense to hold a vague abstraction like a generation responsible for anything. Nevertheless, each person has a duty to resist hateful words and actions, and to speak out against them.

Admittedly, up to a point we have no legal obligation to resist hateful words. Given our First Amendment right of free speech, we are entitled to say whatever hateful things we wish, as long as our words do not harass, slander, libel, incite to riot, or otherwise cause significant harm. Even so, this legal entitlement does not absolve us of deeper moral duties. For example, all persons are morally bound not to harm others, and to be helpful where it is important and within our capacity. The rhetoric of hate violates both these duties by promoting attitudes and social climates in which those who are hated are refused help and often harmed.

Not so clear is the issue of whether we also have a moral duty to denounce the hateful rhetoric and conduct of others. I believe we do, for silence is perceived as tacit approval or at least indifference. Seen this way, silence helps foster hateful attitudes and related harm. In other words, not speaking out is just another way to fail in our obligations to be helpful and not harmful. Moreover, as individuals we are able to speak out against hateful words and actions, in a variety of ways. By teaching tolerance to our children, for example, we can help them understand and appreciate differences among people, and therefore understand that hate-based responses to difference are simply wrong.

In sum, while it makes no sense to hold a generation responsible for anything as a group, I agree that every individual bears responsibility for speaking out against hateful words and behavior, as well as for resisting them.

Issue No. 89   **Studying history: a waste of time?**

The speaker suggests that studying history is a waste of time because it distracts us from current challenges. Posed this way, the question carries the assumption that the study of history has no bearing on present problems or their possible solutions. On the contrary, history can provide examples, perspectives and insights that are directly relevant to contemporary challenges.

One way that studying history can help us face new challenges is by showing us inspirational examples of success. For instance, we can learn from the experience of the great inventor Thomas Edison that sometimes a series of apparent failures is really a precursor to success. Also consider the journey of Lewis and Clark into the Northwest Territory. Understanding the motivations needed to overcome adversities they faced can help to inspire modern-day explorers and scientists.

Studying history can also help us avoid repeating mistakes. For instance, we can learn from the failure of Prohibition during the 1930s that it can be a mistake to legislate morality. And future generations might learn from the 1997 indictment of the tobacco industry that it is bad policy to trade off the well-being of consumers in order to secure profits.

Finally, the study of history is important because we cannot fully appreciate our present challenges without understanding their historical antecedents. Consider the issue of whether California should be officially bilingual. The treaty that transferred California from Mexico to the United States stipulated that California must embrace both Spanish and English as official languages. Those who view the current bilingual debate as purely a contemporary issue might bring to the debate a more enlightened viewpoint by appreciating this historical fact and the events that led to the treaty.

In sum, though the past might seem distant, it is far from irrelevant. Studying history can inspire us to achievement, help us avoid costly mistakes, and help us simply appreciate that in most cases we've been down this road before.

Issue No. 90   **Should products be made to last?**

This topic raises the issue of whether, on balance, consumers are damaged or benefited by quality-cutting production methods. Indisputably, many consumer products today are not made to last. Nevertheless, consumers themselves sanction this practice, and they are its ultimate beneficiaries—in terms of lower prices, more choices, and a stronger economy.

Common sense tells us that sacrificing quality results in a net benefit to consumers and to the overall economy. Cutting production corners not only allows a business to reduce a product's retail price, it compels the business to do so, since its competitors will find innovative ways of capturing its market share otherwise. Lower prices stimulate sales, which in turn generate healthy economic activity. Observation also strongly supports this claim. One need only look at successful budget retail stores such as Walmart as evidence that many—and perhaps most— consumers indeed tend to value price over quality.

Do low-quality products waste natural resources? On balance, probably not. Admittedly, to the extent that a product wears out sooner, more materials are needed for replacement units. Yet cheaper materials are often synthetics, which conserve natural resources, as in the case of synthetic clothing, dyes and inks, and wood substitutes and composites. Moreover, many synthetics and composites are now actually safer and more durable than their natural counterparts—especially in the area of construction materials.

Do lower-quality products waste human resources? If by "waste" we mean "use up unnecessarily," the answer is no. Many lower-quality products are machine-made ones that conserve, not waste, human labor—for example, machine-stitched or dyed clothing and machine-tooled furniture. Moreover, other machine-made products are actually higher in quality than their man-made counterparts, such as those requiring a precision and consistency that only machines can provide. Finally, many cheaply-made products are manufactured and assembled by the lower-cost Asian and Central American labor force—a legion for whom the alternative is unemployment and poverty. In these cases, producing lower-quality products does not "waste" human resources; to the contrary, it creates productive jobs.

In the final analysis, cost-cutting production methods benefit consumers, both in the short-term through lower prices and in the long run by way of economic vitality and increased competition. The claim that producing low-quality products wastes natural and human resources is specious at best.

PART 3

Sample Responses to the *Real* **Analysis-of-an-Argument** Questions

PART 3 includes sample responses to all 90 Analysis-of-an-Argument questions. The responses are numbered sequentially from 1 to 90, corresponding to the sequence of questions in the ETS question "bank." (See the *Appendix* for details about downloading the questions via the GMAC Web site.) As you study these responses, keep these facts in mind:

- These essays are *not* actual responses by GMAT test-takers; they are responses that *we* wrote. And they are not, of course, "the" answers; there is no one "correct" response to any AWA question.

- These essays were written under timed conditions. However, we did go back and fine-tune them to make them better models for you to study. So don't be concerned if your essays aren't as polished as these. Be realistic about what you can produce in 30 minutes.

- These essays are intended to provide you with substantive, organizational, and stylistic ideas for composing your Argument essay; but they are *not* for copying word-for-word. Be forewarned: GMAT graders will be on the lookout for plagiarism.

- The AWA question to which each essay responds is referenced by number *and* by a brief identifying phrase (in the shaded area above the response). We've included these phrases to help you match each response to its corresponding AWA question. These phrases are not substitutes for or summaries of the official questions. Be sure to obtain and read the actual questions as well!

Argument No. **1**	Increasing efficiency at Olympic Foods

Citing facts drawn from the color-film processing industry that indicate a downward trend in the costs of film processing over a 24-year period, the author argues that Olympic Foods will likewise be able to minimize costs and thus maximize profits in the future. In support of this conclusion the author cites the general principle that "as organizations learn how to do things better, they become more efficient." This principle, coupled with the fact that Olympic Foods has had 25 years of experience in the food processing industry leads to the author's rosy prediction. This argument is unconvincing because it suffers from two critical flaws.

First, the author's forecast of minimal costs and maximum profits rests on the gratuitous assumption that Olympic Foods' "long experience" has taught it how to do things better. There is, however, no guarantee that this is the case, nor does the author cite any evidence to support this assumption. Just as likely, Olympic Foods has learned nothing from its 25 years in the food-processing business. Lacking this assumption, the expectation of increased efficiency is entirely unfounded.

Second, it is highly doubtful that the facts drawn from the color-film processing industry are applicable to the food processing industry. Differences between the two industries clearly outweigh the similarities, thus making the analogy highly suspect. For example, problems of spoilage, contamination, and timely transportation all affect the food industry but are virtually absent in the film-processing industry. Problems such as these might present insurmountable obstacles that prevent lowering food processing costs in the future.

As it stands the author's argument is not compelling. To strengthen the conclusion that Olympic Foods will enjoy minimal costs and maximum profits in the future, the author would have to provide evidence that the company has learned how to do things better as a result of its 25 years of experience. Supporting examples drawn from industries more similar to the food-processing industry would further substantiate the author's view.

Argument No. 2   Centralization and profitability

In this argument the author concludes that the Apogee Company should close down field offices and conduct all its operations from a single, centralized location because the company had been more profitable in the past when all its operations were in one location. For a couple of reasons, this argument is not very convincing.

First, the author assumes that centralization would improve profitability by cutting costs and streamlining supervision of employees. This assumption is never supported with any data or projections. Moreover, the assumption fails to take into account cost increases and inefficiency that could result from centralization. For instance, company representatives would have to travel to do business in areas formerly served by a field office, creating travel costs and loss of critical time. In short, this assumption must be supported with a thorough cost-benefit analysis of centralization versus other possible cost-cutting and/or profit-enhancing strategies.

Second, the only reason offered by the author is the claim that Apogee was more profitable when it had operated from a single, centralized location. But is centralization the only difference relevant to greater past profitability? It is entirely possible that management has become lax regarding any number of factors that can affect the bottom line—such as inferior products, careless product pricing, inefficient production, poor employee expense account monitoring, ineffective advertising, sloppy buying policies and other wasteful spending. Unless the author can rule out other factors relevant to diminishing profits, this argument commits the fallacy of assuming that just because one event (decreasing profits) follows another (decentralization), the second event has been caused by the first.

In conclusion, this is a weak argument. To strengthen the conclusion that Apogee should close field offices and centralize, this author must provide a thorough cost-benefit analysis of available alternatives and rule out factors other than decentralization that might be affecting current profits negatively.

Argument No. 3   Arts funding

In this argument the author concludes that the city should allocate some of its arts funding to public television. The conclusion is based on two facts: (1) attendance at the city's art museum has increased proportionally with increases in visual-arts program viewing on public television, and (2) public television is being threatened by severe cuts in corporate funding. While this argument is somewhat convincing, a few concerns need to be addressed.

To begin with, the argument depends on the assumption that increased exposure to the visual arts on television, mainly public television, has caused a similar increase in local art-museum attendance. However, just because increased art-museum attendance can be statistically correlated with similar increases in television viewing of visual-arts programs, this does not necessarily mean that the increased television viewing of arts is the cause of the rise in museum attendance.

Moreover, perhaps there are other factors relevant to increased interest in the local art museum; for instance, maybe a new director had procured more interesting, exciting acquisitions and exhibits during the period when museum attendance increased. In addition, the author could be overlooking a common cause of both increases. It is possible that some larger social or cultural phenomenon is responsible for greater public interest in both television arts programming and municipal art museums.

To be fair, however, we must recognize that the author's assumption is a special case of a more general one that television viewing affects people's attitudes and behavior. Common sense and observation tells me that this is indeed the case. After all, advertisers spend billions of dollars on television ad time because they trust this assumption as well.

In conclusion, I am somewhat persuaded by this author's line of reasoning. The argument would be strengthened if the author were to consider and rule out other significant factors that might have caused the increase in visits to the local art museum.

Argument No. 4   Falling revenues and manufacturing delays

In response to a coincidence between falling revenues and delays in manufacturing, the report recommends replacing the manager of the purchasing department. The grounds for this action are twofold. First, the delays are traced to poor planning in purchasing metals. Second, the purchasing manager's lack of knowledge of the properties of metals is thought to be the cause of the poor planning. It is further recommended that the position of purchasing manager be filled by a scientist from the research division and that the current purchasing manager be reassigned to the sales department. In support of this latter recommendation, the report states that the current purchasing manager's background in general business, psychology, and sociology equip him for this new assignment. The recommendations advanced in the report are questionable for two reasons.

To begin with, the report fails to establish a causal connection between the falling revenues of the company and the delays in manufacturing. The mere fact that falling revenues coincide with delays in manufacturing is insufficient to conclude that the delays caused the decline in revenue. Without compelling evidence to support the causal connection between these two events, the report's recommendations are not worthy of consideration.

Second, a central assumption of the report is that knowledge of the properties of metals is necessary for planning in purchasing metals. No evidence is stated in the report to support this crucial assumption. Moreover, it is not obvious that such knowledge would be required to perform this task. Since planning is essentially a logistical function, it is doubtful that in-depth knowledge of the properties of metals would be helpful in accomplishing this task.

In conclusion, this is a weak argument. To strengthen the recommendation that the manager of the purchasing department be replaced, the author would have to demonstrate that the falling revenues were a result of the delays in manufacturing. Additionally, the author would have to show that knowledge of the properties of metals is a prerequisite for planning in purchasing metals.

Argument No. 5   Increasing newspaper circulation

A newspaper publisher is recommending that the price of its paper, The Mercury, be reduced below the price of a competing newspaper, The Bugle. This recommendation is in response to a severe decline in circulation of The Mercury during the 5-year period following the introduction of The Bugle. The publisher's line of reasoning is that lowering the price of The Mercury will increase its readership, thereby increasing profits because a wider readership attracts more advertisers. This line of reasoning is problematic in two critical respects.

While it is clear that increased circulation would make the paper more attractive to potential advertisers, it is not obvious that lowering the subscription price is the most effective way to gain new readers. The publisher assumes that price is the only factor that caused the decline in readership. But no evidence is given to support this claim. Moreover, given that The Mercury was the established local paper, it is unlikely that such a mass exodus of its readers would be explained by subscription price alone.

There are many other factors that might account for a decline in The Mercury's popularity. For instance, readers might be displeased with the extent and accuracy of its news reporting, or the balance of local to other news coverage. Moreover, it is possible The Mercury has recently changed editors, giving the paper a locally unpopular political perspective. Or perhaps readers are unhappy with the paper's format, the timeliness of its feature articles, its comics or advice columns, the extent and accuracy of its local event calendar, or its rate of errors.

In conclusion, this argument is weak because it depends on an oversimplified assumption about the causal connection between the price of the paper and its popularity. To strengthen the argument, the author must identify and explore relevant factors beyond cost before concluding that lowering subscription prices will increase circulation and, thereby, increase advertising revenues.

Argument No. 6   Locating a business in the city of Helios

In this argument corporations are urged to consider the city of Helios when seeking a new location or new business opportunities. In support of this recommendation the author points out that Helios is the industrial center of the region, provides most of the region's manufacturing jobs, and enjoys a lower than average unemployment rate. Moreover, it is argued, efforts are currently underway to expand the economic base of the city by attracting companies that focus on research and development of innovative technologies. This argument is problematic for two reasons.

To begin with, it is questionable whether the available labor pool in Helios could support all types of corporations. Given that Helios has attracted mainly industrial and manufacturing companies in the past, it is unlikely that the local pool of prospective employees would be suitable for corporations of other types. For example, the needs of research and development companies would not be met by a labor force trained in manufacturing skills. For this reason, it is unlikely that Helios will be successful in its attempt to attract companies that focus on research and development of innovative technologies.

Another problem with the available work force is its size. Due to the lower than average unemployment rate in Helios, corporations that require large numbers of workers would not find Helios attractive. The fact that few persons are out of work suggests that new corporations will have to either attract new workers to Helios or pay the existing workers higher wages in order to lure them away from their current jobs. Neither of these alternatives seems enticing to companies seeking to relocate.

In conclusion, the author has not succeeded in providing compelling reasons for selecting Helios as the site for a company wishing to relocate. In fact, the reasons offered function better as reasons for not relocating to Helios. Nor has the author provided compelling reasons for companies seeking new business opportunities to choose Helios.

Argument No. 7   Aspartame vs. sugar

In this argument the author concludes that people trying to lose weight are better off consuming sugar than the artificial sweetener aspartame. In support of this conclusion the author argues that aspartame can cause weight gain by triggering food cravings, whereas sugar actually enhances the body's ability to burn fat. Neither of these reasons provides sufficient support for the conclusion.

The first reason—that aspartame encourages food cravings—is supported by research findings that high levels of aspartame deplete the brain chemical responsible for registering a sense of being sated, or full. But the author's generalization based on this research is unreliable. The research was based on a sample in which large amounts of aspartame were administered; however, the author applies the research findings to a target population that includes all aspartame users, many of whom would probably not consume high levels of the artificial sweetener.

The second reason—that sugar enhances the body's ability to burn fat—is based on studies in which experimental groups, whose members consumed sugar after at least 45 minutes of continuous exercise, showed increased rates of fat burning. The author's general claim, however, applies to all dieters who use sugar instead of aspartame, not just to those who use sugar after long periods of exercise. Once again, the author's generalization is unreliable because it is based on a sample that clearly does not represent all dieters,

In conclusion, each of the studies cited by the author bases its findings on evidence that does not represent dieters in general; for this reason, neither premise of this argument is a reliable generalization. Consequently, I am not convinced that dieters are better off consuming sugar instead of aspartame.

Argument No. 8   Worker interest in management issues

Based upon a survey among workers that indicates a high level of interest in the topics of corporate restructuring and redesign of benefits programs, the author concludes that workers are not apathetic about management issues. Specifically, it is argued that since 79 percent of the 1200 workers who responded to survey expressed interest in these topics, the notion that workers are apathetic about management issues is incorrect. The reasoning in this argument is problematic in several respects.

First, the statistics cited in the editorial may be misleading because the total number of workers employed by the corporation is not specified. For example, if the corporation employs 2000 workers, the fact that 79 percent of the nearly 1200 respondents showed interest in these topics provides strong support for the conclusion. On the other hand, if the corporation employs 200,000 workers, the conclusion is much weaker.

Another problem with the argument is that the respondents' views are not necessarily representative of the views of the work force in general. For example, because the survey has to do with apathy, it makes sense that only less apathetic workers would respond to it, thereby distorting the overall picture of apathy among the work force. Without knowing how the survey was conducted, it is impossible to assess whether or not this is the case.

A third problem with the argument is that it makes a hasty generalization about the types of issues workers are interested in. It accords with common sense that workers would be interested in corporate restructuring and redesign of benefits programs, since these issues affect workers very directly. However, it is unfair to assume that workers would be similarly interested in other management issues— ones that do not affect them or affect them less directly.

In conclusion, this argument is not convincing as it stands. To strengthen it, the author would have to show that the respondents account for a significant and representative portion of all workers. Additionally, the author must provide evidence of workers' interest other management topics—not just those that affect workers directly.

Argument No. 9   **Consumer trends**

Based on an expected increase in the number of middle-aged people during the next decade, the author predicts that retail sales at department stores will increase significantly over the next ten years. To bolster this prediction, the author cites statistics showing that middle-aged people devote a much higher percentage of their retail expenditure to department-store services and products than younger consumers do. Since the number of middle-aged consumers is on the rise and since they spend more than younger people on department-store goods and services, the author further recommends that department stores begin to adjust their inventories to capitalize on this trend. Specifically, it is recommended that department stores increase their inventory of products aimed at middle-aged consumers and decrease their inventory of products aimed at younger consumers. This argument is problematic for a two reasons.

First, an increase in the number of middle-aged people does not necessarily portend an overall increase in department-store sales. It does so only on the assumption that other population groups will remain relatively constant. For example, if the expected increase in the number of middle-aged people is offset by an equally significant decrease in the number of younger people, there would be little or no net gain in sales.

Second, in recommending that department stores replace products intended to attract younger consumers with products more suitable to middle-aged consumers, the author assumes that the number of younger consumers will not also increase. Since a sizable increase in the population of younger consumers could conceivably offset the difference in the retail expenditure patterns of younger and middle-aged consumers, it would be unwise to make the recommended inventory adjustment lacking evidence to support this assumption.

In conclusion, this argument is unacceptable. To strengthen the argument the author would have to provide evidence that the population of younger consumers will remain relatively constant over the next decade.

Argument No. 10   Students protest funding cuts

The conclusion in this argument is that the state legislature need not consider the views of protesting students. To support this conclusion, the author points out that only 200 of the 12,000 students traveled to the state capitol to voice their concerns about proposed cuts in college programs. Since the remaining students did not take part in this protest, the author concludes they are not interested in this issue. The reasoning in this argument is flawed for two reasons.

First, the author assumes that because only one-tenth of the students took part in the protest, these students' views are unrepresentative of the entire student body. This assumption is unwarranted. If it turns out, for example, that the protesting students were randomly selected from the entire student body, their views would reflect the views of the entire college. Without information regarding the way in which the protesting students were selected, it is presumptuous to conclude that their opinions fail to reflect the opinions of their colleagues.

Second, the author cites the fact that the remaining 12,000 students stayed on campus or left for winter break as evidence that they are not concerned about their education. One obvious rejoinder to this line of reasoning is that the students who did not participate did so with the knowledge that their concerns would be expressed by the protesting students. In any case, the author has failed to demonstrate a logical connection between the students' alleged lack of concern and the fact that they either stayed on campus or left for winter break. Without this connection, the conclusion reached by the author that the remaining 12,000 students are not concerned about their education is unacceptable.

As it stands the argument is not well-reasoned. To make it logically acceptable, the author would have to demonstrate that the protesting students had some characteristic in common that biases their views, thereby nullifying their protest as representative of the entire college.

Argument No. 11   **Choosing a mayor**

The recommendation endorsed in this argument is that residents of San Perdito vote current mayor Montoya out of office, and re-elect former mayor Varro. The reasons cited are that during Montoya's four years in office the population has decreased while unemployment has increased, whereas during Varro's term unemployment declined while the population grew. This argument involves the sort of gross oversimplification and emotional appeal typical of political rhetoric; for this reason it is unconvincing.

First of all, the author assumes that the Montoya administration caused the unemployment in San Perdito as well as its population loss. The line of reasoning is that because Montoya was elected before the rise in unemployment and the decline in population, the former event caused the latter. But this is fallacious reasoning unless other possible causal explanations have been considered and ruled out. For example, perhaps a statewide or nationwide recession is the cause of these events. Or perhaps the current economic downturn is part of a larger picture of economic cycles and trends, and has nothing to do with who happens to be mayor. Yet another possibility is that Varro enjoyed a period of economic stability and Varro's own administration set the stage for the unemployment and the decline in population the city is now experiencing under Montoya.

Secondly, job availability and the economic health of one's community are issues that affect people emotionally. The argument at hand might have been intentionally oversimplified for the specific purpose of angering citizens of San Perdito, and thereby turning them against the incumbent mayor. Arguments that bypass relevant, complex reasoning in favor of stirring up emotions do nothing to establish their conclusions; they are also unfair to the parties involved.

In conclusion, I would not cast my vote for Varro on the basis of this weak argument. The author must provide support for the assumption that Mayor Montoya has caused San Perdito's poor economy. Moreover, such support would have to involve examining and eliminating other possible causal factors. Only with more convincing evidence could this argument become more than just an emotional appeal.

Argument No. 12   Advertising grocery items

The conclusion of this argument is that advertising the reduced price of selected grocery items in the Daily Gazette will result in increased sales overall. To support this claim, the author cites an informal poll conducted by sales clerks when customers purchased advertised items. Each time one or more of the advertised items was sold, the clerks asked whether the customer had read the ad. It turned out that two-thirds of 200 shoppers questioned said that they had read the ad. In addition, of those who reported reading the ad, more than half spent over $100 in the store. This argument is unconvincing for two reasons.

To begin with, the author's line of reasoning is that the advertisement was the cause of the purchase of the sale items. However, while the poll establishes a correlation between reading the ad and purchasing sale items, and also indicates a correlation, though less significantly, between reading the ad and buying non-sale items, it does not establish a general causal relationship between these events. To establish this relationship, other factors that could bring about this result must be considered and eliminated. For example, if the four days during which the poll was conducted preceded Thanksgiving and the advertised items were traditional foodstuffs associated with this holiday, then the results of the poll would be extremely biased and unreliable.

Moreover, the author assumes that the poll indicates that advertising certain sale items will cause a general increase in sales. But the poll does not even address the issue of increased overall sales; it informs us mainly that, of the people who purchased sales items, more had read the ad than not. A much clearer indicator of the ad's effectiveness would be a comparison of overall sales on days the ad ran with overall sales on otherwise similar days when the ad did not run.

In sum, this argument is defective mainly because the poll does not support the conclusion that sales in general will increase when reduced-price products are advertised in the Daily Gazette. To strengthen the argument, the author must, at the very least, provide comparisons of overall sales reports as described above.

Argument No. 13   **Radio advertising**

In an attempt to sell radio advertising time, this ad claims that radio advertising will make businesses more profitable. The evidence cited is a ten percent increase in business that the Cumquat Cafe has experienced in the year during which it advertised on the local radio station. This argument is unconvincing because two questionable assumptions must be made for the stated evidence to support the author's conclusion.

The first assumption is that radio advertising alone has caused the increase in business at the Cumquat Cafe. This assumption is questionable because it overlooks a number of other factors that might have contributed to the Cumquat's success. For example, the Cumquat might have changed owners or chefs; it might have launched a coupon ad campaign in the local print media; or it might have changed or updated the menu. Yet another possibility is that a local competitor went out of business. These are just a few of the factors that could help explain the Cumquat's growth. Because the author fails to eliminate these possibilities, the assumption in question need not be accepted.

Even if it is granted that radio advertising is responsible for the Cumquat's success, another assumption must be made before we can conclude that radio advertising will result in increased profits for businesses in general. We must also assume that what is true of the Cumquat will likewise be true of most other businesses. But there are all kinds of important differences between cafes and other businesses that could affect how radio audiences react to their advertising. We cannot safely assume that because a small restaurant has benefited from radio advertising, that any and all local businesses will similarly benefit.

In conclusion, it would be imprudent for a business to invest in radio advertising solely on the basis of the evidence presented. To strengthen the conclusion, it must be established that radio advertising was the principal cause of increased business at the Cumquat. Once this is shown, it must be determined that the business in question is sufficiently like the Cumquat, and so can expect similar returns from investment in radio ad time.

Argument No. 14   Interactive computer instruction

The editorial recommends that the school board of Nova High spend a greater portion of available funds on the purchase of additional computers and adopt interactive computer instruction throughout the curriculum. Two reasons are offered in support of this recommendation. First, the introduction of interactive computer instruction in three academic subjects was immediately followed by a decline in the school dropout rate. Second, impressive achievements in college were experienced by last year's graduates. This argument is unconvincing for two reasons.

To begin with, this argument is a classic instance of "after this, therefore because of this" reasoning. The mere fact that the introduction of interactive computer instruction preceded the impressive performance of recent graduates and the decline in the dropout rate is insufficient to conclude that it was the cause of these events. Many other factors could bring about these same results. For example, the school may have implemented counseling and training programs that better meet the needs of students who might otherwise leave school to take jobs. In addition, the school may have introduced programs to better prepare students for college.

Secondly, the author assumes that the impressive achievements of last year's graduates bear some relation to the introduction of interactive computer instruction at Nova High. However, no evidence is offered to support this assumption. Lacking evidence that links the achievements of the recent graduates to the interactive instruction, it is presumptuous to suggest that the computer instruction was in some way responsible for the students' impressive performance.

In conclusion, the recommendation that Nova High spend a greater portion of available funds on the purchase of additional computers and adopt interactive computer instruction throughout the curriculum is ill-founded. To strengthen this recommendation the author would have to demonstrate that the decline in the dropout rate and the impressive performance of recent graduates came about as a result of the use of computer-interactive instruction. All that has been shown so far is a correlation between these events.

Argument No. 15	Adams for governor

This political advertisement recommends re-electing governor Adams because he has a proven leadership role in improving the state's economy. In support of this reason the author cites these statistics: in the past year, most state workers' wages have gone up; 5,000 new jobs have been created; and six corporations have located in the state. Another reason offered for re-electing Adams is a recent poll indicating most respondents believe the state economy would continue to improve if he were re-elected. Finally, the author claims that rival Zebulon would harm the state's economy because he disagrees with Adams' fiscal policies. This argument is fraught with vague, oversimplified and unwarranted claims.

To begin with, the statistics are intended to support the main claim that the state is economically better off with Adams as governor. But these statistics are vague and oversimplified, and thus may distort the state's overall economic picture. For example, state workers' pay raises may have been minuscule and may not have kept up with cost of living or with pay for state workers in other states. Moreover, the 5,000 new jobs may have been too few to bring state unemployment rates down significantly; at the same time, many jobs may have been lost. Finally, the poll indicates that six new corporations located in the state, but fails to indicate if any left.

Next, the poll cited by the author is described in the vaguest possible terms. The ad does not indicate who conducted the poll, who responded, or how the poll was conducted. Until these questions are answered, the survey results are worthless as evidence for public opinion about Adams or his economic policies.

Finally, while we have only vague and possibly distorted evidence that the state is better off with Adams, we have absolutely no evidence that it would be worse off with Zebulon. Given that the state economy is good now, none of the author's reasons establishes that Adams is the cause of this nor do they establish that the state wouldn't be even better off with someone else in office.

In conclusion, this argument is weak. To strengthen the argument, the author must provide additional information about the adequacy of state workers' pay raises, the effect of the 5,000 jobs on the state's employment picture, the overall growth of corporations in the state, and other features of the state economy. Also, the author must support the claims that Adams' actions have caused any economic improvement and that in the future Adams will impart more economic benefit than would Zebulon.

Argument No. 16   **The job market for college-level instructors**

Demographic trends that indicate an increase in the number of college-aged people over the next ten years lead the author to predict an improved job market for all people seeking college-level teaching positions in their academic disciplines. Moreover, the author argues that since Waymarsh University students with advanced degrees had an especially difficult time finding teaching jobs in the past, these trends portend better times ahead for Waymarsh graduates. This argument is problematic in three important respects.

First, the author assumes that an increase in the number of college-aged people over the next decade will necessarily result in an increase in the number of people who attend college during this period. While this is a reasonable assumption, it is by no means a certainty. For example, a world war or economic depression in the next decade would certainly nullify this expectation.

Second, even if we grant the preceding assumption, we must also consider the additional assumption that increased university enrollments will lead to an increase in teaching positions in all fields. However, it might turn out that some teaching specialties are in greater demand than others in the future, resulting in a disproportionate number of teaching positions available in various fields. Consequently, persons trained in some fields might find it more difficult, if not impossible, to find teaching jobs in the future.

Finally, little can be foretold regarding the employability of Waymarsh graduates in the future based on the information provided in the argument. Lacking information about the reasons Waymarsh graduates had an especially difficult time finding teaching jobs, it is difficult to assess their prospects for the future. It is probable, however, that since Waymarsh has had an especially hard time placing graduates in the past, the mere fact that more jobs are available will not, by itself, ensure that Waymarsh graduates will have an easier time finding teaching jobs during the next decade.

In conclusion, this argument is unconvincing. To strengthen the argument, the author must provide evidence that the only major trend in the next decade will be an increase in the number of people reaching college age. Regarding the future prospects for Waymarsh graduates, the author must provide evidence that there were no idiosyncratic reasons that prevented them from finding jobs in the past.

Argument No. 17   Recommending one acid-relief product over another

This ad recommends non-prescription Acid-Ease over non-prescription Pepticaid for relief of excess stomach acid. The only reason offered is that doctors have written 76 million more prescriptions for the full-strength prescription form of Acid-Ease than for full-strength Pepticaid. While this reason is relevant, and provides some grounds for preferring Acid-Ease over Pepticaid, it is insufficient as it stands because it depends on three unwarranted assumptions.

The first assumption is that the prescription form of Acid-Ease is more popular among doctors. But this might not be the case, even though doctors have written 76 million more prescriptions for Acid-Ease. Acid-Ease may have been available for several more years than Pepticaid; and in the years when both products were available, Pepticaid might have actually been prescribed more often than Acid-Ease.

The second assumption is that doctors prefer the prescription form of Acid-Ease for the reason that it is in fact more effective at relieving excess stomach acid. However, doctors may have preferred Acid-Ease for reasons other than its effectiveness. Perhaps Acid-Ease is produced by a larger, more familiar drug company or by one that distributes more free samples. For that matter, the medical community may have simply been mistaken in thinking that Acid-Ease was more effective. In short, the number of prescriptions by itself is not conclusive as to whether one product is actually better than another.

The third assumption is that the milder non-prescription forms of Acid-Ease and Pepticaid will be analogous to the full-strength prescription forms of each. But this might not be the case. Suppose for the moment that the greater effectiveness of prescription Acid-Ease has been established; even so, the non-prescription form might not measure up to non-prescription Pepticaid. This fact must be established independently.

In conclusion, this ad does not provide enough support for its recommending non-prescription Acid-Ease over non-prescription Pepticaid. To strengthen its argument, the promoter of Acid-Ease would have to show that (1) the comparison between the number of prescriptions is based on the same time period; (2) its effectiveness is the main reason more doctors have prescribed it, and (3) the comparative effectiveness of the two non-prescription forms is analogous to that of the prescription forms.

Argument No. 18   Ensuring ethical behavior

In this argument, the head of a government department concludes that the department does not need to strengthen either its ethics regulations or its enforcement mechanisms in order to encourage ethical behavior by companies with which it does business. The first reason given is that businesses have agreed to follow the department's existing code of ethics. The second reason is that the existing code is relevant to the current business environment. This argument is unacceptable for several reasons.

The sole support for the claim that stronger enforcement mechanisms are unnecessary comes from the assumption that companies will simply keep their promises to follow the existing code. But, since the department head clearly refers to rules violations by these same businesses within the past year, his faith in their word is obviously misplaced. Moreover, it is commonly understood that effective rules carry with them methods of enforcement and penalties for violations.

To show that a strengthened code is unnecessary, the department head claims that the existing code of ethics is relevant. In partial clarification of the vague term "relevant," we are told that the existing code was approved in direct response to violations occurring in the past year. If the full significance of being relevant is that the code responds to last year's violations, then the department head must assume that those violations will be representative of all the kinds of ethics problems that concern the department. This is unlikely; in addition, thinking so produces an oddly short-sighted idea of relevance.

Such a narrow conception of the relevance of an ethics code points up its weakness. The strength of an ethics code lies in its capacity to cover many different instances of the general kinds of behavior thought to be unethical—to cover not only last year's specific violations, but those of previous years and years to come. Yet this author explicitly rejects a comprehensive code, preferring the existing code because it is "relevant" and "not in abstract anticipation of potential violations."

In sum, this argument is naive, vague and poorly reasoned. The department head has not given careful thought to the connection between rules and their enforcement, to what makes an ethics code relevant, or to how comprehensiveness strengthens a code. In the final analysis, he adopts a backwards view that a history of violations should determine rules of ethics, rather than the other way around.

Argument No. 19   More restaurants for Spiessa

Recent social changes in the country of Spiessa lead the author to predict a continued surge in growth of that country's restaurant industry. Rising personal incomes, additional leisure time, an increase in single-person households, and greater interest in gourmet food are cited as the main reasons for this optimistic outlook. All of these factors are indeed relevant to growth in the restaurant industry; so the prediction appears reasonable on its face. However, three questionable assumptions operative in this argument bear close examination.

The first dubious assumption is that the supply of restaurants in Spiessa will continue to grow at the same rate as in the recent past. However, even in the most favorable conditions and the best of economic times there are just so many restaurants that a given population can accommodate and sustain. It is possible that the demand for restaurants has already been met by the unprecedented growth of the past decade, in which case the recent social changes will have little impact on the growth of the restaurant industry.

A second assumption is that the economic and social circumstances cited by the author will actually result in more people eating out at restaurants. This assumption is unwarranted, however. For example, increased leisure time may just as likely result in more people spending more time cooking gourmet meals in their own homes. Also, single people may actually be more likely than married people to eat at home than to go out for meals. Finally, people may choose to spend their additional income in other ways—on expensive cars, travel, or larger homes.

A third poor assumption is that, even assuming people in Spiessa will choose to spend more time and money eating out, no extrinsic factors will stifle this demand. This assumption is unwarranted. Any number of extrinsic factors—such as a downturn in the general economy or significant layoffs at Spiessa's largest businesses—may stall the current restaurant surge. Moreover, the argument fails to specify the "social changes" that have led to the current economic boom. If it turns out these changes are politically driven, then the surge may very well reverse if political power changes hands.

In conclusion, this argument unfairly assumes a predictable future course for both supply and demand. To strengthen the argument, the author must at the very least show that demand for new restaurants has not yet been exhausted, that Spiessa can accommodate new restaurants well into the future, and that the people of Spiessa actually want to eat out more.

In this argument the author concludes that drinking Saluda Natural Spring Water (SNSW) is preferable to drinking tap water. Three reasons are offered in support of this conclusion: SNSW contains several of the minerals necessary for good health, it is completely free of bacteria, and residents of Saluda—the town where it is bottled—are hospitalized less frequently than the national average. This argument is unconvincing because it relies on a variety of dubious assumptions.

The first questionable assumption underlying this argument that tap water does not contain the minerals in question and is not completely free of bacteria. This assumption is not supported in the argument. If tap water is found to contain the same minerals and to be free of bacteria, the author's conclusion is substantially undermined.

A second assumption of the argument is that the water residents of Saluda drink is the same as SNSW. Lacking evidence to the contrary, it is possible that Saluda is not the source of the bottled water but is merely the place where SNSW is bottled. No evidence is offered in the argument to dispute this possibility.

Finally, it is assumed without argument that the reason residents are hospitalized less frequently than the national average is that they drink SNSW. Again, no evidence is offered to support this assumption. Perhaps the residents are hospitalized less frequently because they are younger than the national average, because they are all vegetarians, or because they exercise daily. That is, there might be other reasons than the one cited to account for this disparity.

In conclusion, this is an unconvincing argument. To strengthen the conclusion that SNSW is more healthful than tap water, the author must provide evidence that tap water contains harmful bacteria not found in SNSW. Moreover, the author must demonstrate that the residents of Saluda regularly drink the same water as SNSW and that this is why they are hospitalized less frequently than the national average.

The conclusion of this editorial is that the government should lower property taxes for railroad companies. The first reason given is that railroads spend billions per year maintaining and upgrading their facilities. The second reason is that shipping goods by rail is cost-effective and environmentally sound. This argument is unconvincing for several reasons.

First of all, the argument depends upon a misleading comparison between railroad and truck company expenditures. Although trucking companies do not pay property tax on roads they use, they do pay such taxes on the yards, warehouses and maintenance facilities they own. And while trucking companies pay only a portion of road maintenance costs, this is because they are not sole users of public roads. Railroad companies shoulder the entire burden of maintenance and taxes on their own facilities and tracks; but they distribute these costs to other users through usage fees.

In addition, the author assumes that property taxes should be structured to provide incentives for cost-effective and environmentally beneficial business practices. This assumption is questionable because property taxes are normally structured to reflect the value of property. Moreover, the author seems to think that cost-effectiveness and environmental soundness are equally relevant to the question of tax relief. However, these are separate considerations. The environmental soundness of a practice might be relevant in determining tax structuring, but society does not compensate a business for its cost-efficiency.

Splitting the issues of cost-efficiency and environmental impact highlights an ambiguity in the claim that railway shipping is more appropriate. On the one hand, it may be appropriate, or prudent, for me to ship furniture by rail because it is cost-effective; on the other hand, it might be appropriate, or socially correct, to encourage more railway shipping because it is environmentally sound. The argument thus trades on an equivocation between social correctness on the one hand, and personal or business prudence on the other.

In sum, this argument is a confusion of weak comparisons, mixed issues and equivocal claims. I would not accept the conclusion without first determining: (1) the factors relevant to tax structure, (2) whether specific tax benefits should accrue to property as well as to income and capital gains taxes, (3) whether railway shipping really does provide greater social benefits, and (4) whether it is correct to motivate more railway shipping on this basis.

Argument No. 22   Drug enforcement

The conclusion in this argument is that increased vigilance by drug enforcement authorities has resulted in an increase in the illegal use of cocaine. The author reaches this conclusion on the grounds that drug traffickers have responded to increased enforcement efforts by switching from bulkier and riskier drugs to cocaine. Presumably, the author's reasoning is that the increased enforcement efforts inadvertently brought about an increase in the supply of cocaine which, in turn, brought about the observed increase in the illegal use of cocaine. This line of reasoning is problematic in two important respects.

In the first place, the author has engaged in "after this, therefore because of this" reasoning. The only reason offered for believing that the increased vigilance caused the increase in cocaine use is the fact that the former preceded the latter. No additional evidence linking the two events is offered in the argument, thus leaving open the possibility that the two events are not causally related but merely correlated. This in turn leaves open the possibility that factors other than the one cited are responsible for the increase in cocaine use.

In the second place, the author assumes that an increase in the supply of cocaine is sufficient to bring about an increase in its use. While this is a tempting assumption, it is a problematic one. The presumption required to substantiate this view is that drug users are not particular about which drugs they use, so that if marijuana and heroin are not available, they will switch to whatever drug is available—cocaine in this case. The assumption does not seem reasonable on its face. Marijuana, heroin, and cocaine are not alike in their effects on users; nor are they alike in the manner in which they are ingested or in their addictive properties. The view that drug users' choice of drugs is simply a function of supply overlooks these important differences.

In conclusion, the author has failed to establish a causal link between increased enforcement efforts and the observed increase in illegal cocaine use. While the enforcement activities may have been a contributing factor, to show a clear causal connection the author must examine and rule out various other factors.

Argument No. 23

Funding for Einstein High School

This speaker draws the conclusion that there is no need to substantially increase funding for Einstein High School. To support this conclusion, the speaker claims that Einstein has improved its educational efficiency over the past 20 years, even though funding levels have remained relatively constant. His evidence is that two-thirds of Einstein's graduates now go on to college, whereas 20 years ago only half of its students did so. This argument suffers from several critical problems.

To begin with, we must establish the meaning of the vague concept "educational efficiency." If the term is synonymous with the rate of graduation to college, then the statistics cited would strongly support the argument. But, normally we are interested in something more than just the numbers of students who go on to college from a high school; we also want to know how well the school has prepared students for a successful college experience—that is, whether the school has provided a good secondary education. Thus, for the speaker the term "educational efficiency" must essentially carry the same meaning as "educational quality."

Given this clarification, one of the speaker's assumptions is that the rate of graduation to college has increased because Einstein is doing a better job of educating its students. However, the fact that more Einstein graduates now go on to college might simply reflect a general trend. And the general trend might have less to do with improved secondary education than with the reality that a college degree is now the standard of entry into most desirable jobs.

But even if the quality of education at Einstein had improved, would this be a compelling reason to deny Einstein additional funding? I don't think so. It is possible that the school has managed to deliver better education in spite of meager funding. Teachers may be dipping into their own pockets for supplies and other resources necessary for doing their job well. Perhaps the quality of education at Einstein would improve even more with additional financial support.

In sum, this argument does not establish the conclusion that additional funding for Einstein is unnecessary. To do so, the speaker would have to provide evidence that the quality of education at Einstein has improved. This could be done by examining student assessment scores or by tracking students through their college careers to see how many successfully graduate and find jobs. In addition, the speaker would also have to show that Einstein is doing a good job with adequate financial support, and not merely in spite of insufficient funding.

Argument No. 24   Improving customer service

The customer-service division of Mammon Savings and Loan recommends that the best way for the bank to attract new customers and differentiate itself from its competitors is to improve its service to customers—specifically, by reducing waiting time in teller lines, opening for business 30 minutes earlier, and closing an hour later. These improvements, it is argued, will give the bank the edge over its competitors and make it appear more customer-friendly. For the most part this recommendation is well-reasoned; a few concerns must be addressed, however.

First, the author assumes that Mammon's competitors are similar to Mammon in all respects other than the ones listed. In fact, Mammon's competitors may be more conveniently located to customers, or offer other services or products on more attractive terms than Mammon. If so, Mammon may not gain the edge it seeks merely by enhancing certain services.

Secondly, the author assumes that the proposed improvements will sufficiently distinguish Mammon from its competitors. This is not necessarily the case. Mammon's competitors may already offer, or may plan to offer, essentially the same customer-service features as those Mammon proposes for itself. If so, Mammon may not gain the edge it seeks merely by enhancing these services.

Thirdly, the author assumes that Mammon can offer these improved services without sacrificing any other current features that attract customers. In fact, Mammon may have to cut back other services or offer accounts on less attractive terms, all to compensate for the additional costs associated with the proposed improvements. By rendering its other features less attractive to customers, Mammon may not attain the competitive edge it seeks.

In conclusion, Mammon's plan for attracting new customers and differentiating itself from its competitors is only modestly convincing. While improvements in customer service generally tend to enhance competitiveness, it is questionable whether the specific improvements advocated in the recommendation are broad enough to be effective.

Argument No. 25   The quality of life in City L

The author concludes that City L has good schools, affordable housing, friendly people, flourishing arts and a safe environment. To support this claim the author cites an annual survey that ranks cities according to quality of life. Two years ago City L was listed 14th in this survey. As it stands this argument is unconvincing.

First, the author fails to indicate what individual characteristics of cities were used as criteria for the ranking. To the extent that the criteria used in the survey were the same as the features listed by the author in the conclusion, the conclusion would be warranted. On the other hand, if the survey employed entirely different criteria—for example, outdoor recreational opportunities or educational achievement levels of adult residents—then the author's conclusion would be wholly unwarranted.

Secondly, the author provides no indication of how each characteristic was weighted in the ranking. For example, City L may have far and away the most flourishing arts scene among the cities surveyed, but it may have poor schools, unfriendly people, and an unsafe environment. The extent to which the survey accurately reflects City L's overall quality of life in this case would depend largely on the relative weight placed on the arts as a factor affecting quality of life.

Thirdly, the author fails to indicate how many cities were included in the survey. The more cities included in the survey, the stronger the argument—and vice versa. For example, if 2,000 cities were surveyed, then City L would rank in the top one percent in terms of quality of life. On the other hand, if only 14 cities were surveyed then City L would rank last.

Finally, the author's conclusion depends on the questionable assumption that the conditions listed by the author have remained unchanged in City L since the survey was conducted two years ago. Admittedly, had ten years elapsed the argument would be even weaker. Yet two years is sufficient time for a significant change in the overall economy, the city's fiscal policies, its financial condition, or its political climate. Any of these factors can affect the quality of schools, the extent to which art is flourishing, or the cost of housing.

In conclusion, the author does not adequately support the conclusion. To strengthen the argument, the author must show that the criteria used in the survey were the same as the features listed in the conclusion and were weighted in a way that does not distort the picture in City L. To better assess the argument, we would also need more information about the cities included in the survey, as well as what changes in City L have occurred during the past two years.

Argument No. 26	Checking purchasing invoices

In this argument a member of a financial management and consulting firm reasons that since Windfall Ltd. increased its net gains by checking 10 percent of its purchasing invoices for errors, it would be a good idea to advise the firm's clients to institute a policy of checking all purchasing invoices for errors. Two potential benefits are foreseen from this recommendation: it could help the firm's clients increase their net gains, and it could help the firm land the Windfall account. The member's argument is unconvincing for a couple of reasons.

The main problem with the argument is that the conclusion is based upon insufficient evidence. The fact that some of Windfall's purchasing invoices contained errors might simply be attributable to the sloppy accounting practices of Windfall's suppliers. Thus, rather than indicating a general problem, the invoice errors might simply be indicative of a problem that is specific to Windfall Ltd. In other words, the evidence drawn from Windfall's experience is insufficient to support the conclusion that all purchasing invoices are subject to similar errors.

Secondly, the evidence offered in the argument suggests only that companies purchasing from the same suppliers that Windfall purchases from are likely to experience similar problems. If the firm's clients do not purchase from Windfall's suppliers, checking for errors might turn out to be a monumental waste of time.

In conclusion, the author's argument fails to provide good grounds for instituting the policy of routinely checking purchasing invoices for errors. To strengthen the conclusion the author would have to provide evidence that this is a widespread problem. Specifically, what is required are additional instances of purchasing invoices containing errors that are drawn from various companies.

Argument No. 27   Movie violence and the crime rate

Based upon a correlation between increases in movie violence and crime rates in cities, the author argues that to combat crime in cities we must either censor movies that contain violence or prohibit people who are under 21 years of age from viewing them. The author further argues that because legislators failed to pass a bill calling for these alternatives, they are not concerned with the problem of crime in our cities. The author's reasoning is unconvincing, since it suffers from two critical problems.

To begin with, the author's solution to the problem rests on the claim that portrayals of violence in movies are the cause of crime in the cities. However, the evidence offered is insufficient to support this claim. A mere positive correlation between movie violence and city crime rates does not necessarily prove a causal relationship. In addition, all other prospective causes of city crime such as poverty or unemployment must be ruled out. As it stands, the author's solution to the problem is based upon an oversimplified analysis of the issue.

Another problem with the argument is that the author's solution assumes that only persons under 21 years of age are adversely affected by movie violence. Ultimately, this means that the author is committed to the view that, for the most part, the perpetrators of crime in cities are juveniles under 21. Lacking evidence to support this view, the author's solution cannot be taken seriously.

In conclusion, the best explanation of the failure of the bill calling for the actions proposed in this argument is that most legislators were capable of recognizing the simplistic analysis of the problem upon which these actions are based. Rather than providing a demonstration of a lack of concern about this issue, the legislators' votes reveal an understanding of the complexities of this problem and an unwillingness to accept simple solutions.

| Argument No. 28 | Increasing use of shuttle buses |

The author concludes that the local transit company must either reduce fares for the shuttle buses that transport people to their subway stations or increase parking fees at the stations. The reasons offered to support this conclusion are that commuter use of the subway train is exceeding the transit company's expectations, while commuter use of the shuttle buses is below projected volume. This argument is unconvincing because the author oversimplifies the problem and its solutions in a number of ways.

To begin with, by concluding that the transit company must either reduce shuttle fares or increase parking fees, the author assumes that these are the only available solutions to the problem of limited shuttle use. However, it is possible that other factors—such as inconvenient shuttle routing and/or scheduling, safety concerns, or an increase in carpools—contribute to the problem. If so, adjusting fares or parking fees would might not solve the problem.

In addition, the author assumes that reducing shuttle fees and increasing parking fees are mutually exclusive alternatives. However, the author provides no reason for imposing an either/or choice. Adjusting both shuttle fares and parking fees might produce better results. Moreover, if the author is wrong in the assumption that parking fees and shuttle fees are the only possible causes of the problem, then the most effective solution might include a complex of policy changes—for example, in shuttle fares, parking fees, rerouting, and rescheduling.

In conclusion, this argument is weak because the author oversimplifies both the problem and its possible solutions. To strengthen the argument the author must examine all factors that might account for the shuttle's unpopularity. Additionally, the author should consider all possible solutions to determine which combination would bring about the greatest increase in shuttle use.

Argument No. 29   Organic farming

This speaker argues that farmers who invested in organic farming equipment should resume synthetic farming because it is financially unwise to continue organic farming. The speaker cites studies showing that farmers who switched to organic farming last year had lower crop yields. Based on these studies, the speaker concludes that the relatively inexpensive investment in organic farming equipment cannot justify continuing to farm organically. The speaker also claims that continuing to farm organically is financially unwise because it is motivated by environmental, not economic, concerns. The argument suffers from three problems.

One problem with this reasoning involves the vague comparative claim that farmers who switched to organic farming last year had lower crop yields. We are not informed whether the survey compared last year's organic crop yields with yields from previous years or with those from synthetic farms. Moreover, the author provides no evidence about how the survey was conducted. Lacking more information about the survey, we cannot accept the speaker's conclusion.

Secondly, the speaker assumes that the low crop yields for first-time organic farmers last year are representative of crop yields for organic farmers overall. However, more experienced organic farmers might have had much better crop yields last year. Also, the first-time organic farmers might improve their own crop yields in future years. Moreover, last year's yield may have been unusually low due to poor weather or other factors, and thus not indicative of future yields.

Finally, in asserting that organic farming is financially unwise because it is motivated by environmental instead of economic concerns, the speaker unfairly assumes that a practice cannot be both environmentally and economically beneficial. It is possible that, in the long run, practices that help protect the environment will also result in greater economic benefits. For instance, organic farming methods may better protect soil from depletion of the elements that contribute to healthy crops, providing an economic benefit in the long run.

In conclusion, the speaker's argument is poorly supported and is short-sighted. To better evaluate the argument, we would need more information about the how the survey was conducted, especially about the comparison the survey makes. To strengthen the argument, the speaker must present evidence that last years' crop yields from first-time organic farmers are representative of yields among organic farms in general. The author must also provide evidence that environmentally sound practices cannot be economically beneficial as well.

Argument No. 30   Investments and our aging population

In this argument prudent investors are advised to stop investing in hotels and invest instead in hospitals and nursing homes. The author cites two related trends—an aging population and a decline in hotel occupancy—as grounds for this advice. To illustrate these trends, the author refers to another region of the country, where 20 percent of the population is over 65 years old and where occupancy rates in resort hotels have declined significantly during the past six months. This argument is unconvincing in a couple of important respects.

In the first place, the author provides no evidence to support the claim that the population as a whole is aging and that the hotel occupancy rate in general is declining. The example cited, while suggestive of these trends, is insufficient to warrant their truth because there is no reason to believe that data drawn from this unnamed region is representative of the entire country. For example, if the region from which the data was gathered was Florida, it would clearly be unrepresentative. The reason for this is obvious. Florida is populated by a disproportionate number of retired people over 65 years old and is a very popular vacation destination during the winter months. Moreover, resort hotel occupancy in Florida typically declines significantly during the summer months.

In the second place, the author has provided no evidence to support the claim that the decline in hotel occupancy is related to the aging of the population. The author appears to believe that the decrease in occupancy rates at resort hotels is somehow caused by the increase in the number of people over age 65. However, the example cited by the author establishes only that these two trends are correlated; it does not establish that the decline in hotel occupancy is due to an increase in the number of people over the age of 65.

In conclusion, the author's investment advice is not based on sound reasoning. To strengthen the conclusion, the author must show that the trends were not restricted to a particular region of the country. The author must also show that the cause of the decline in hotel occupancy is the increase in the number of people over 65.

Argument No. 31   Trends in coffee and cola consumption

In this argument a consulting firm recommends the transfer of investments from Cola Loca to Early Bird Coffee because, during the next 20 years, coffee demand will increase while cola demand will decrease. This prediction is based on the expectation that the number of older adults will significantly increase over the next 20 years, together with statistics, reportedly stable for the past 40 years, indicating that coffee consumption increases with age while cola consumption declines with increasing age. For three reasons, this financial advice may not be sound.

First, the argument assumes that relative supply conditions will remain unchanged over the next twenty years. However, the supply and cost of cola and coffee beans, as well as other costs of doing business as a producer of coffee or cola, may fluctuate greatly over a long time period. These factors may affect comparative prices of coffee and cola, which in turn may affect comparative demand and the value of investments in coffee and cola companies. Without considering other factors that contribute to the value of a coffee or cola company, the firm cannot justify its recommendation.

Secondly, the argument fails to account for the timing of the increase in coffee consumption. Perhaps the population will age dramatically during the next five years, then remain relatively flat over the following 15 years. Or perhaps most of the increase in average age will occur toward the end of the 20-year period. An investor has more opportunity to profit over the short and long term in the first scenario than in the second, assuming the investor can switch investments along the way. If the second scenario reflects the facts, the firm's recommendation would be ill-founded.

Finally, the firm unjustifiably relies on the studies that correlate coffee and cola consumption with age. The firm does not provide evidence to confirm the reliability of the studies. Moreover, while the phrase "studies suggest" may appear to lend credibility to these claims, the phrase is vague enough to actually render the claims worthless, in the absence of any information about them.

In conclusion, the firm should not transfer investments from Cola Loca to Early Bird Coffee on the basis of this argument. To better evaluate the recommendation, we would need more information about the study upon which it relies. We would also need more detailed projections of population trends during the next 20 years.

Argument No. 32   **Better ambulance service**

In this argument the author concludes that West Cambria can increase revenues and provide better care to accident victims by disbanding the volunteer ambulance service and hiring a commercial one. The author reasons that this change would yield additional revenues because service fees could be imposed for ambulance use. The author also reasons that the city would provide better service to accident victims because a commercial service would respond more quickly to accidents than a volunteer service would. The author's argument is flawed in two respects.

To begin with, the author's plan for raising revenue for West Cambria is questionable. Unless the service fees are considerable or the accident rate is extremely high, it is unlikely that significant revenues will be raised by charging a fee for ambulance use. Consequently, revenue generation is not a good reason to disband the volunteer service and hire a commercial service.

Next, the author's belief that better patient care would be provided by a commercial ambulance service than by a volunteer service is based on insufficient evidence. The fact that the commercial service in East Cambria has a lower average response time than the volunteer service in West Cambria is insufficient evidence for the claim that this will be the case for all commercial services. Moreover, the author's recommendation depends upon the assumption that response time to an accident is the only factor that influences patient care. Other pertinent factors—such as ambulance-crew proficiency and training, and emergency equipment—are not considered.

In conclusion, this argument is unconvincing. To strengthen the argument the author would have to show that substantial revenue for the town could be raised by charging service fees for ambulance use. Additionally, the author would have to provide more evidence to support the claim that commercial ambulance services provide better patient care than volunteer services.

Argument No. 33   Employee benefits at Perks Company

The author of Perks Company's business plan recommends that funds currently spent on the employee benefits package be redirected to either upgrade plant machinery or build an additional plant. The author reasons that offering employees a generous package of benefits and incentives year after year is no longer cost-effective given current high unemployment rates, and that Perks can attract and keep good employees without such benefits and incentives. While this argument has some merit, its line of reasoning requires close examination.

To begin with, the author relies on the reasoning that it is unnecessary to pay relatively high wages during periods of high unemployment because the market will supply many good employees at lower rates of pay. While this reasoning may be sound in a general sense, the particular industry that Perks is involved in may not be representative of unemployment levels generally. It is possible that relatively few unemployed people have the type of qualifications that match job openings at Perks. If this is the case, the claim that it is easier now to attract good employees at lower wages is ill-founded.

Secondly, the argument relies on the assumption that the cost-effectiveness of a wage policy is determined solely by whatever wages a market can currently bear. This assumption overlooks the peripheral costs of reducing or eliminating benefits. For example, employee morale is likely to decline if Perks eliminates benefits; as a result, some employees could become less productive, and others might quit. Even if Perks can readily replace those employees, training costs and lower productivity associated with high turnover may outweigh any advantages of redirecting funds to plant construction. Moreover, because the recommended reduction in benefits is intended to fund the retrofitting of an entire plant or the building of a new one, the reduction would presumably be a sizable one; consequently, the turnover costs associated with the reduction might be very high indeed.

In conclusion, this argument is not convincing, since it unfairly assumes that a broad employment statistic applies to one specific industry, and since it ignores the disadvantages of implementing the plan. Accordingly, I would suspend judgment about the recommendation until the author shows that unemployment in Perks' industry is high and until the author produces a thorough cost-benefit analysis of the proposed plan.

Argument No. 34   Promoting a credit-card service

In this argument the author concludes that the Easy Credit Company would gain several advantages over its competitors by donating a portion of its profits to a well-known environmental organization in exchange for the use of the organization's logo on their credit card. The author reaches this conclusion on the basis of a recent poll that shows widespread public concern about environmental issues. Among the advantages of this policy, the author foresees an increase in credit card use by existing customers, the ability to charge higher interest rates, and the ability to attract new customers. While the author's argument has some merit, it suffers from two critical problems.

To begin with, the author assumes that the environmental organization whose logo is sought is concerned with the same environmental issues about which the poll shows widespread concern. However, the author provides no evidence that this is the case. It is possible that very few credit-card users are concerned about the issues that are the organization's areas of concern; if so, then it is unlikely that the organization's logo would attract much business for the Easy Credit Company.

Next, the author assumes that the public's concern about environmental issues will result in its taking steps to do something about the problem—in this case, to use the Easy Credit Company credit card. This assumption is unsupported and runs contrary to experience. Also, it is more reasonable to assume that people who are concerned about a particular cause will choose a more direct means of expressing their concern.

In conclusion, the author's argument is unconvincing as it stands. To strengthen the argument, the author must show a positive link between the environmental issues about which the public has expressed concern and the issues with which this particular environmental organization is concerned. In addition, the author must provide evidence to support the assumption that concern about a problem will cause people to do something about the problem.

Argument No. 35   **Improving Fern Valley University**

The financial-planning office at Fern Valley University concludes that it is necessary to initiate a fund-raising campaign among alumni that will enable the university to expand the range of subjects it offers and increase the size of its library facilities. Its argument is based on a five-year decline in enrollments and admission applications, together with the claim that students cite poor teaching and inadequate library resources as their chief sources of dissatisfaction with Fern Valley. The conclusion of the financial-planning office is not strongly supported by the reasons given.

To begin with, this argument depends on the assumption that providing a greater range of subjects and a larger library will alleviate the students' chief sources of dissatisfaction. However, the students have not complained about inadequate course offerings or about the size of the library; their complaint is that the existing courses are poorly taught and that library resources are inadequate. Offering more kinds of classes does not improve teaching quality, and increasing a library's size does nothing to enhance its holdings, or resources. Accordingly, the recommendation does not bear directly on the problem as stated.

Secondly, the proposal unfairly assumes that the recent enrollment and application decline was caused by poor teaching and inadequate library resources. It is equally possible that all colleges, regardless of teaching quality and library resources, have experienced similar declines. These declines may have been due to unrelated factors, such as unfavorable economic conditions, or an increase in high-paying computer jobs not requiring a college education.

Thirdly, the author provides no support for the claim that students are dissatisfied with the teaching and library resources at Fern Valley. It is possible that the claim is based on hearsay or on scant anecdotal evidence. Without more information about the basis of the claim, we cannot be sure that the financial-planning office is addressing the real problems.

In conclusion, the advice of the financial planning office is not well supported. To strengthen the argument, the planning office must provide evidence that students are dissatisfied with the range of subjects and with the library's size, and that this dissatisfaction is the cause of the recent decline in enrollment and the number of admission applications. To better assess the argument as it stands, we would need to know whether the students' attitudes were measured in a reliable, scientific manner.

Argument No. 36	Foreign language instruction

This newsletter article claims that Professor Taylor's foreign-language program at Jones University is a model of foreign language instruction. This conclusion is based on a study in which foreign language tests were given to students at 25 other universities. The study shows that first-year language students at Jones speak more fluently after just 10 to 20 weeks in the program than do 90 percent of foreign-language majors at other colleges at graduation. Despite these impressive statistics, I am unconvinced by this argument for two reasons.

To begin with, the assumption here is that students from Professor Taylor's program have learned more than foreign language students at other universities. However, we are not given enough information about the study to be sure that this comparison is reliable. For example, the article does not tell us whether the foreign language students at Jones were given the tests; it only reports that the tests in question were "given to students at 25 other colleges." If Jones students were not tested, then no basis exists for comparing them to students at the other universities. In addition, the article does not indicate whether students at all the universities, including Jones, were given the same tests. If not, then again no basis exists for the comparison.

Furthermore, we cannot tell from this article whether the universities in the study, or their students, are comparable in other ways. For instance, Jones might be a prestigious university that draws its students from the top echelon of high school graduates, while the other universities are lower-ranked schools with more lenient admission requirements. In this event, the study wouldn't tell us much about Professor Taylor's program, for the proficiency of his students might be a function of their superior talent and intelligence.

In conclusion, the statistics cited in the article offer little support for the claim about Taylor's program. To strengthen the argument, the author must show that the universities in the study, including Jones, were comparable in other ways, that their foreign language students were tested identically, and that Taylor's program was the only important difference between students tested at Jones and those tested at the other universities.

Argument No. 37   Motorcycle X

The author rejects the claim that the loud engine noise of American-made Motorcycle X appeals to the manufacturer's customers and explains why they are not attracted to quieter, foreign-made imitations. The author's rejection is based on two reasons. First, the author points out that foreign cars tend to be quieter than similar American-made cars, yet they sell just as well. Secondly, the author claims that ads for Motorcycle X do not emphasize its engine noise; instead, the ads highlight its durability and sleek lines, and employ voice-overs of rock music rather than engine roar. In my view, these reasons do not establish that the quieter engines of the foreign imitations fail to account for their lack of appeal.

To begin with, the first reason rests on the assumption that what automobile customers find appealing is analogous to what motorcycle customers find appealing. This assumption is weak, since although there are points of comparison between automobiles and motorcycles, there are many dissimilarities as well. For example, head room, smooth ride, and quiet engines are usually desirable qualities in a car. However, head room is not a consideration for motorcycle customers; and many motorcycle riders specifically want an exciting, challenging ride, not a smooth one. The same may be true of engine noise; it is possible that motorcyclists like what loud engine noise adds to the experience of motorcycle riding.

The author's second reason is also problematic. Although the engine noise of Motorcycle X is not explicitly touted in advertisements, it does not necessarily follow that engine noise is not an important selling feature. Because Motorcycle X has been manufactured in the U.S. for over 70 years, its reputation for engine noise is probably already well known and need not be advertised. Moreover, the advertisers might use rock music on Motorcycle X ad soundtracks for the specific purpose of suggesting, or even simulating, its loud engine noise.

In conclusion, this author has not provided convincing reasons for rejecting the claim that quieter engines make foreign-made motorcycles less popular. The author's analogy involving foreign car sales is weak, and the claim about Motorcycle X advertisements misses the purpose of including rock music in the ads.

Argument No. 38   Campus-housing occupancy

The author of this article argues that, to reverse declining revenues from campus housing rentals, campus housing officials should decrease the number of available housing units and reduce rent prices on the units. The author's line of reasoning is that fewer available units will limit supply while lower rents will increase demand, thereby improving overall occupancy rates, and that the resulting increase in occupancy rates will, in turn, boost revenues for the campus. This reasoning is unconvincing for several reasons.

To begin with, the author assumes that boosting occupancy rates will improve revenues. All other factors remaining unchanged, this would be the case. However, the author proposes reducing both the supply of units and their rental prices. Both of these actions would tend to reduce revenues. The author provides no evidence that the revenue-enhancing effect of a higher occupancy rate will exceed the revenue-decreasing effect of reduced supply and price. Without such evidence, the argument is unconvincing.

Secondly, the author assumes that lowering rents will lead to higher revenues by increasing demand. However, it is possible that demand would decrease, depending on the extent of the rent reduction as well as other factors—such as overall enrollment and the supply and relative cost of off-campus housing. Moreover, even if demand increases by lowering rents, revenues will not necessarily increase as a result. Other factors, such as maintenance and other costs of providing campus housing units and the reduced supply of rental units might contribute to a net decrease in revenue.

Thirdly, in asserting that lowering rental rates will increase demand, the author assumes that current rental rates are causing low demand. However, low demand for student housing could be a function of other factors. For instance, the student housing units may be old and poorly maintained. Perhaps students find the campus housing rules oppressive, and therefore prefer to live off-campus; or perhaps enrollments are down generally, affecting campus housing occupancy.

In conclusion, the author of this editorial has not argued effectively for a decrease in the number of available campus housing units and a reduction in rental rates for those units. To strengthen the argument, the author must show that a rent reduction will actually increase demand, and that the revenue-enhancing effect of greater demand will outweigh the revenue-reducing effect of a smaller supply and of lower rental rates.

Argument No. 39   Baggage-handling procedures

The conclusion in this Avia Airlines memorandum is that a review of the airline's baggage-handling procedures will not further its goal of maintaining or increasing the number of Avia passengers. The author's line of reasoning is that the great majority of Avia passengers are happy with baggage handling at the airline because only one percent of passengers who traveled on Avia last year filed a complaint about Avia's procedures. This argument is problematic in two important respects.

First, the argument turns on the assumption that the 99 percent of Avia passengers who did not complain were happy with the airline's baggage-handling procedures. However, the author provides no evidence to support this assumption. The fact that, on the average, 9 out of 1000 passengers took the time and effort to formally complain indicates nothing about the experiences or attitudes of the remaining 991. It is possible that many passengers were displeased but too busy to formally complain, while others had no opinion at all. Lacking more complete information about passengers' attitudes, we cannot assume that the great majority of passengers who did not complain were happy.

Secondly, in the absence of information about the number of passengers per flight and about the complaint records of competing airlines, the statistics presented in the memorandum might distort the seriousness of the problem. Given that most modern aircraft carry as many as 300 to 500 passengers, it is possible that Avia received as many as 4 or 5 complaints per flight. The author unfairly trivializes this record. Moreover, the author fails to compare Avia's record with those of its competitors. It is possible that a particular competitor received virtually no baggage-handling complaints last year. If so, Avia's one percent complaint rate might be significant enough to motivate customers to switch to another airline.

In conclusion, the author has failed to demonstrate that a review of the baggage-handling procedures at Avia Airlines is not needed to maintain or increase the number of Avia's passengers. To strengthen the argument, the author must at the very least provide affirmative evidence that most Avia passengers last year were indeed happy with baggage-handling procedures. To better evaluate the argument, we would need more information about the numbers of Avia passengers per flight last year and about the baggage-handling records of Avia's competitors.

Argument No. 40   Overcoming a trade deficit

The author of this article argues that the country of Sacchar can best solve its current trade deficit problem by lowering the price of its main export, sugar. The line of reasoning is that this action would make Sacchar more competitive with other sugar-exporting countries, thereby increasing sales of Sacchar's sugar abroad and, in turn, substantially reducing the trade-deficit. This line of reasoning is unconvincing for a couple of reasons.

In the first place, this argument is based on an oversimplified analysis of the trade deficit problem Sacchar currently faces. A trade-deficit occurs when a country spends more on imports than it earns from exports. The author's argument relies on the assumption that earnings from imports will remain constant. However, the author provides no evidence that substantiates this assumption. It is possible that revenues from imports will increase dramatically in the near future; if so, the course of action proposed by the author might be unnecessary to solve Sacchar's trade deficit problem. Conversely, it is possible that revenues from imports are likely to decrease dramatically in the near future. To the extent that this is the case, lowering sugar prices may have a negligible countervailing effect, depending on the demand for Sacchar's sugar.

In the second place, increasing sales by lowering the price of sugar will not yield an increase in income unless the increase in sales is sufficient to overcome the loss in income due to the lower price. This raises three questions the author fails to address. First, will a price decrease in fact stimulate demand? Second, is demand sufficient to meet the increase in supply? Third, can Sacchar increase the sugar production sufficiently to overcome the deficit? In the absence of answers to these questions, we cannot assess the author's proposal.

In conclusion, the author provides an incomplete analysis of the problem and, as a result, provides a questionable solution. To better evaluate the proposal, we would need to know how revenues from imports are likely to change in the future. To strengthen the argument, the author must provide evidence that demand is sufficient to meet the proposed increase in supply, and that Sacchar has sufficient resources to accommodate the increase.

Argument No. 41   Home security systems

The author of this article warns that stronger laws are needed to protect new kinds of home security systems from being copied and sold by imitators in order to prevent an eventual loss of manufacturing jobs within the industry. This conclusion is based on the following chain of reasoning: With the protection of stronger laws, manufacturers will naturally invest in the development of new home security products and production technologies, whereas without such protection, manufacturers will cut back on investment. If manufacturers cut back on investment, then a decline in product quality and marketability, as well as in production efficiency, will result. This, in turn, will cause the predicted loss of industry jobs. This line of reasoning is unconvincing for several reasons.

To begin with, the author assumes that existing copyright, patent and trade secret laws are inadequate to protect home security system design. But the author never explains why these laws don't offer sufficient protection, nor does he offer any evidence to show that this is the case.

Secondly, the argument depends on the twin assumptions that stronger legal protection will encourage manufacturers to invest in home security-system production, while the absence of strong legal protection will have the opposite effect. The author fails to provide any evidence or reasons for accepting these assumptions about cause-and-effect connections between the law and what happens in the marketplace.

Moreover, both of these assumptions can be challenged. It is possible that stronger protections would not greatly affect industry investment or jobs overall, but would instead help to determine which companies invested heavily and, therefore, provided the jobs. For instance, a less-restricted market might foster investment and competition among smaller companies, whereas stronger legal protections might encourage market domination by fewer, larger companies.

In conclusion, I do not find this argument compelling. The author must provide evidence that home security system designs are not being adequately protected by current patent, copyright or trade secret laws. The author must also provide an argument for the assumptions that stronger laws will create more industry jobs overall, while the absence of stronger laws will result in fewer industry jobs.

Argument No. 42   Postage-stamp prices

The author concludes that a postage-stamp price increase is needed to reduce the deterioration of the postal service. The author reasons that raising the price of stamps will accomplish this goal because it will generate more revenue, thereby eliminating the strain on the system. The author further reasons that a price increase will also reduce the volume of mail, thereby improving the morale of postal workers. The reasoning in this argument is problematic in three respects.

The main problem with the argument is the author's mistaken assumption that eliminating strain on the system and improving employee morale are mutually achievable by way of an increase in stamp prices. A price increase will generate more revenue only if the volume of mail remains constant or increases. But, if the volume of mail increases or remains constant, worker morale will not be improved. On the other hand, if the price increase reduces the volume of mail, revenues may decrease, and the strain on the system will not be eliminated. Consequently, eliminating the strain on the system and improving the morale of the workers cannot both be achieved by simply raising the price of postage stamps.

Secondly, the author's conclusion that the proposed price increase is necessary to reduce deterioration of the postal service relies on the assumption that no other action would achieve the same result. However, the author provides no evidence to substantiate this assumption. It is possible, for example, that careful cost-cutting measures that do not decrease worker morale might achieve the same goal. It is also possible that other revenue-enhancing measures that do not undermine employee morale are available.

Thirdly, the author unfairly assumes that reducing mail volume and increasing revenues will improve employee morale. This is not necessarily the case. It is possible that employee morale is materially improved only by other means, and that additional revenues will not be used in ways that improve morale. It is also possible that a decrease in mail volume will result in a reduction of the size of the labor force, regardless of revenues, which in turn might undermine morale.

In conclusion, the author's proposed solution to the problem of the deterioration of the postal service will not work. Raising postage-stamp prices cannot bring about both of the outcomes the author identifies as being necessary to solve the problem. Before we can accept the argument, the author must modify the proposal accordingly and must provide more information about the relationship between employee morale and mail volume.

Argument No. 43   **Hospital care**

In this argument the author concludes that university hospitals provide no better care than private or community hospitals. The author bases this conclusion on the following claims about university hospitals: the ones in this region employ 15 percent fewer doctors; they have a 20 percent lower success rate in treating patients; they pay their staffs less money; they make less profit than community hospitals; and they utilize doctors who divide their time between teaching, research and treating patients. This argument is unconvincing for several reasons.

The most egregious reasoning error in the argument is the author's use of evidence pertaining to university hospitals in this region as the basis for a generalization about all university hospitals. The underlying assumption operative in this inference is that university hospitals in this region are representative of all university hospitals. No evidence is offered to support this gratuitous assumption.

Secondly, the only relevant reason offered in support of the claim that the quality of care is lower in university hospitals than it is at other hospitals is the fact that university hospitals have a lower success rate in treating patients. But this reason is not sufficient to reach the conclusion in question unless it can be shown that the patients treated in both types of hospitals suffered from similar types of maladies. For example, if university hospitals routinely treat patients suffering from rare diseases whereas other hospitals treat only those who suffer from known diseases and illnesses, the difference in success rates would not be indicative of the quality of care received.

Finally, the author assumes that the number of doctors a hospital employs, its success rate in treating patients, the amount it pays its staff, and the profits it earns are all reliable indicators of the quality of care it delivers. No evidence is offered to support this assumption nor is it obvious that any of these factors is linked to the quality of care delivered to patients. Moreover, the fact that doctors in university hospitals divide their time among many tasks fails to demonstrate that they do a poorer job of treating patients than doctors at other kinds of hospitals. In fact, it is highly likely that they do a better job because they are more knowledgeable than other doctors due to their teaching and research.

In conclusion, the author's argument is unconvincing. To strengthen the argument the author would have to demonstrate that university hospitals in this region are representative of all university hospitals, as well as establishing a causal link between the various factors cited and the quality of care delivered to patients.

| Argument No. 44 | One-stop shopping at Megamart |

The management of the Megamart grocery store concludes that adding new departments and services is the surest way to increase profits over the next couple of years. They are led to this conclusion because of a 20 percent increase in total sales, realized after the addition of a pharmacy section to the grocery store. On the basis of this experience, they concluded that the convenience of one-stop shopping was the main concern of their customers. The management's argument is faulty in several respects.

In the first place, the management assumes that the increase in total sales was due to the addition of the pharmacy section. However, the only evidence offered to support this conclusion is the fact that the addition of the pharmacy preceded the increase in sales. But the mere fact that the pharmacy section was added before the increase occurred is insufficient grounds to conclude that it was responsible for the increase. Many other factors could bring about this same result. Lacking a detailed analysis of the source of the sales increase, it would be sheer folly to attribute the increase to the addition of the pharmacy section.

In the second place, even if it were the case that the increase in total sales was due to the addition of the pharmacy section, this fact alone is insufficient to support the claim that adding additional departments will increase sales even further. It is quite possible that the addition of the pharmacy section increased sales simply because there was no other pharmacy in the vicinity. The additional proposed departments and services, on the other hand, might be well represented in the area and their addition might have no impact whatsoever on the profits of the store. In other words, there may be relevant differences between the pharmacy section and the additional proposed sections that preclude them from having a similar effect on the sales of the store.

In conclusion, the management's argument is not well-reasoned. To strengthen the conclusion, the management must provide additional evidence linking the addition of the pharmacy section to the increase in total sales. It must also show that there are no exceptional reasons for the sales increase due to the pharmacy section that would not apply to the other proposed additions.

Argument No. 45   Maximizing movie profits

In this argument the author concludes that paying Robin Good several million dollars to star in the movie "3003" is the most likely way for the movie's producers to maximize their profits. The author's line of reasoning is that because Robin has been paid similar amounts of money to work in other films that were financially successful, it is likely that "3003" will also be financially successful if Robin stars in it. This argument is unconvincing in two important respects.

The main problem with this argument involves the author's assumption that the financial success of the other films was due entirely to Robin Good's participation. If this were the case, it would certainly make good sense to pay Robin handsomely to star in "3003." However, the author offers no evidence to support this contention.

Moreover, there are many factors that could account for the financial success of the movies in which Robin previously appeared, other than the mere fact that Robin appeared in them. For example, their financial success might have been due to the photography, the plot of the story, the director, or any combination of these. Lacking a more detailed analysis of the reasons for the success of these other movies, it is folly to presume that their financial success was entirely due to Robin's participation.

In conclusion, this is a weak argument. To strengthen the conclusion that hiring Robin is the best way for the producers of "3003" to maximize their profits, the author would have to provide evidence that the financial success of the movies Robin previously worked in resulted solely from the fact that Robin starred in them.

Argument No. 46 — Employee theft

In this argument the directors of a security- and safety-consulting service conclude that the use of photo identification badges should be recommended to all of their clients as a means to prevent employee theft. Their conclusion is based on a study revealing that ten of their previous clients who use photo identification badges have had no incidents of employee theft over the past six-year period. The directors' recommendation is problematic in several respects.

In the first place, the directors' argument is based on the assumption that the reason for the lack of employee theft in the ten companies was the fact that their employees wear photo identification badges. However, the evidence revealed in their research establishes only a positive correlation between the lack of theft and the requirement to wear badges; it does not establish a causal connection between them. Other factors, such as the use of surveillance cameras or spot checks of employees' briefcases and purses could be responsible for lack of employee theft within the ten companies analyzed.

In the second place, the directors assume that employee theft is a problem that is common among their clients and about which their clients are equally concerned. However, for some of their clients this might not be a problem at all. For example, companies that sell services are much less likely to be concerned about employee theft than those who sell products. Moreover, those that sell small products would be more concerned about theft than those that sell large products. Consequently, even if wearing badges reduces employee theft, it might not be necessary for all of the firm's clients to follow this practice.

In conclusion, the director's recommendation is not well supported. To strengthen the conclusion they must establish a causal relation between the wearing of identification badges and the absence of employee theft. They also must establish that the firm's clients are sufficiently similar to all profit from this practice.

Argument No. 47   **Location and business success**

In this argument the author concludes that Cumquat Cafe was correct in its decision to move to a new location. In support of this assessment the author points out that while the Cafe has been in business for two years at its new location, three businesses have failed at its previous location. The author's line of reasoning is that the cause of the failure of the three businesses is the fact that they all occupied the same location. This argument is problematic in two important respects.

In the first place, no evidence has been offered to support the assumption that the reason the three businesses failed was their location. While location is an important contributing factor to a business' success or failure, it is not the only such factor. Many other reasons—poor business practices, lack of advertising, or poor customer service—could just as likely account for their lack of success. Lacking a detailed analysis of the reasons these businesses failed, it would be foolish to attribute their failure to their location.

In the second place, while location may have been a factor which contributed to the failure of these businesses, the reason may not have been the location itself but rather the suitability of the business to the location. For example, a pet-grooming shop or a tanning salon located in a downtown metropolitan business district is unlikely to succeed simply because this type of business is obviously unsuitable to the location. On the other hand, a bank in the same location might be extremely successful simply because of its suitability to the location.

In conclusion, the author's argument is unconvincing. To strengthen the conclusion, the author would have to evaluate other possible causes of the failure of the three businesses, then in each case eliminate all possible causes except location.

Argument No. 48   Private vs. public ownership of Croesus Company

Based upon the profitability of the Croesus Company and the fact that it was recently converted from public to private ownership, the author concludes that private ownership is better for businesses than public ownership. I find this argument unconvincing in two respects.

In the first place, the evidence the author provides is insufficient to support the conclusion drawn from it. One example is rarely sufficient to establish a general conclusion. Unless it can be shown that Croesus Company is representative of all companies that have converted from public to private ownership, the conclusion that all companies would be more profitable under private ownership is completely unwarranted. In fact, in the face of such limited evidence it is fallacious to draw any conclusion at all.

In the second place, the author assumes that the reason for Croesus' profitability was its conversion from public to private ownership. This assumption, however, is not supported in the argument. In the absence of evidence to support this assumption many other explanations for Croesus Company's profitability are possible. For example, its success may be due to the fact that Croesus has few competitors or because the product or service it provides is unique, or because it has an exceptionally skilled management team.

In conclusion, this argument is unconvincing. To strengthen the conclusion, additional examples of successful companies that converted from public to private ownership are required. Additionally, the author would have to show that the reason for the success of these companies was the fact that they were privately owned.

Argument No. 49   Recycling newspaper

This editorial begins with the impressive statistic that five-million trees could be saved every year if the morning edition of the nation's largest newspaper were collected and rendered into pulp that the newspaper could reuse. But then the author goes on to conclude that this kind of recycling is unnecessary because the newspaper maintains its own forests to ensure an uninterrupted supply of paper. This argument is seriously flawed by two unwarranted assumptions.

The first assumption is that the only reason to recycle the newspaper is to ensure a continuous supply of paper. The author reasons that since this need is currently met by the forests that the newspaper maintains, recycling is unnecessary. This reasoning is extremely shortsighted. Not only does the author fail to see the ecological advantages of preserving the trees, he also fails to see the obvious economic advantages of doing this. Moreover, using recycled paper is the best way to ensure a continuous paper supply because, unlike the forest, paper is a reusable resource.

The second assumption is that only the newspaper would have an interest in the pulp processed from its recycled morning edition. This is probably not the case, however, given the enormous market for recycled paper—for books, packaging, other newspapers, and so on. Moreover, there is no direct connection between the newspaper that is recycled and those companies that find uses for the products of recycling. Accordingly, contrary to the author's assumption, there may be a great interest, indeed a need, for pulp from recycling the newspaper in question.

In conclusion, the author's claim that recycling the newspaper is unnecessary is ill-founded. To strengthen the argument the author would have to show that there are no other compelling reasons to recycle the newspaper besides the one cited in the editorial.

Argument No. 50   Key to success for a rock musical group

The new manager of the rock group Zapped believes that name recognition is the key to attaining financial success for the group. To increase name recognition the manager recommends that Zapped diversify its commercial enterprises. The grounds for this recommendation is an analogy with Zonked, a much better-known rock group that plays the same kind of music as Zapped. According to the manager, the main reason Zonked is better known than Zapped is that Zonked participates in several promotional enterprises in addition to concerts and albums. The manager's recommendation is questionable for two reasons.

In the first place, the author assumes that the only relevant difference between Zapped and Zonked is that Zonked has greater name recognition than Zapped. If this were the case, the manager's recommendation would be apt. However, the fact that the two rock groups play the same kind of music leaves open the question of whether their performance of this music is comparable. If Zonked's performance is sufficiently better than Zapped's, this could go a long way toward explaining why Zonked is much better known.

In the second place, the author assumes that name recognition is all that is required for financial success. While name recognition is an important element in determining the success or failure of any enterprise, it is hardly the only element required. Other factors are equally important. In the case of rock bands, factors such as musical talent, showmanship, and repertoire play a significant role in determining the financial success of the group. If Zonked is superior to Zapped in these areas, this difference could account for Zonked's financial success.

In conclusion, the manager's argument is unconvincing. To strengthen the argument the author would have to show that Zapped and Zonked are alike in all relevant ways except name recognition.

Argument No. 51   Red meat and fatty foods

The author of an article about lifestyle trends concludes that, in general, people are not as concerned as they were a decade ago with regulating their intake of red meat and fatty cheeses. As evidence, the author cites the fact that a wide selection of high-fat cheeses is now available at a long-established grocery store, Heart's Delight, which specializes in organic fruits and vegetables and whole grains. The author further points out that the owners of the vegetarian restaurant next door, Good Earth Cafe, now make only a modest living while the owners of the new House of Beef across the street are millionaires. This argument is unconvincing.

To begin with, the argument relies on the assumption that the dietary habits and attitudes of customers at these three businesses will reflect those of people generally. But the three businesses, all located in the same area of a single community, just might serve a clientele whose diets differ greatly from the diets of people in other areas of the community, or in other communities. The generalization that the author draws from this biased sample cannot be considered reliable.

In addition, trends at these three businesses do not necessarily reflect the dietary habits and attitudes of their customers in the way the author claims. For example, we are not informed about how well the high-fat cheeses at Heart's Delight are selling relative to lowfat and nonfat alternatives. Similarly, it is possible that at House of Beef menu items other than red meat—such as chicken, fish, or salad bar—are just as popular as red meat among the restaurant's patrons.

Finally, the author assumes that the financial conditions of the owners of the two restaurants were caused by a general lack of concern with regulating red meat and fatty-cheese intake. However, it is equally possible that the lackluster financial success of Good Earth was caused by mismanagement or increasing overhead costs. Furthermore, it is possible that House of Beef is generating little business, but its owners were already millionaires before they opened this restaurant or are making their money in other concurrent business endeavors.

In conclusion, the author's evidence is too weak to support any conclusion about general dietary trends. Before we can accept the conclusion, the author must provide evidence from a representative sample of food-service businesses, and must clearly show that sales of red meat and fatty cheeses are increasing relative to sales of lowfat alternatives. The author must also provide evidence that the financial conditions of the owners of the two restaurants were actually caused by a general waning concern with regulating fat intake.

Argument No. 52   **Oak City's new shopping mall**

In this editorial the author rebukes Oak City for allowing the construction of a new downtown shopping mall. Citing a number of problems that have occurred since the building of the mall, the author concludes that the residents of Oak City have not benefited from the mall and that Oak City exercised poor judgment in allowing the mall to be built. Among the problems cited by the author are the closure of local businesses, lack of parking in the downtown area, and increased trash and litter in a city park near the mall. Moreover, the author argues that profits derived from sales are not benefiting Oak City because the owner of the mall lives in another city. The author's argument is problematic in several respects.

In the first place, the author assumes that addition of the new mall is the cause of the various problems cited. The only evidence offered to support this claim is that the construction of the mall occurred before these problems manifested themselves. However, this evidence is insufficient to establish the claim in question. A chronological relationship is only one of the indicators of a causal relationship between two events.

In the second place, the author has focused only on negative effects the mall has had on the city. A more detailed analysis of the situation might reveal that the positive benefits for the city far outweigh the problems on which the author focuses. For example, new jobs might have been created for the residents of Oak City, and tax revenues might have been increased for the city. Lacking a more comprehensive analysis of the impact of the mall on Oak City, it is presumptuous on the part of the author to conclude that Oak City's decision to allow the mall to be built was incorrect.

In conclusion, the author's argument is unconvincing. To strengthen the argument the author would have to demonstrate that the construction of the mall caused the various problems mentioned. The author would also have to show that the negative effects of the project outweighed the positive effects.

Argument No. 53   A shortage of engineers

An editorial in a weekly news magazine warns that we must quickly increase funding for education in order to remain economically competitive in the world marketplace. The line of reasoning is that the nation will soon face a shortage of engineers because engineers have come from universities, and that our university-age population is shrinking. Moreover, decreasing enrollments in high schools clearly show that this drop in university-age students will continue throughout the decade. The author's argument is not convincing because it is based on several questionable assumptions.

First, the author assumes that because our university-age population is shrinking, university enrollments will likewise shrink. But even if the number of university-age students is dropping, it is possible that a greater proportion of those students will enter universities. If this percentage were sufficiently large, university enrollments could remain relatively stable. Moreover, even if overall university enrollments did drop, we must further assume that the number of engineering students would likewise drop. However, decreases in overall enrollments do no necessarily result in proportional enrollment decreases in each field of study. If demand for engineers were high, then a larger percentage of university students might study to become engineers, in which case engineering enrollments could increase or remain constant, while those in other major fields of study would drop disproportionately.

An additional assumption is that economic success in the world marketplace depends on the number of engineers produced by our universities. This assumption is simplistic. Professionals in other fields—such as agriculture, banking, and business—may contribute equally to our global success. The author does not explain why the predicted shortage of engineers is more critical than shortages in other fields that might result from shrinking university enrollments. Nor does the author demonstrate that providing more funds for education will correct the predicted shortage of engineers. Even if all of the previous assumptions are accepted, no connection between increased funding and the desired enrollment increase has been established.

In conclusion, the author has failed to make a convincing case for increased funding for education. Before we accept the conclusion, the author must provide evidence that we face a critical shortage of engineers, and that increased funding will have direct bearing on correcting this shortage. As it stands, both these claims rest on unwarranted assumptions.

Argument No. 54   Citrus fruit

In this editorial the author argues for the imposition of strict pricing regulations in order to prevent citrus growers from continued inflation of prices of citrus fruit. The need for such regulation is supported by the author's contention that citrus growers have been unnecessarily raising prices of citrus fruit in the past. The evidence for this allegation is the fact that the price of lemons has increased from 15 cents per pound to over a dollar per pound during the preceding 11-year period, even though weather conditions have been favorable to citrus production in all but one of those years. This argument is flawed in two important respects.

First and foremost, the author assumes that the only factor that influences the price of citrus fruit is the weather. Other factors—such as monetary inflation, increased distribution and labor costs, or alterations in supply and demand conditions—are ignored as possible sources for the increase. The charge that citrus growers have unnecessarily raised prices can be sustained only if these and other possible factors can be completely ruled out as contributing to the price increases. Since the author fails to address these factors, the recommendation calling for strict pricing regulations can be dismissed out-of-hand as frivolous.

Second, the author assumes that the only way to combat increased prices is through government intervention. In a free-enterprise system many other means of affecting the pricing of goods are available. For example, boycotting a product and thereby influencing supply and demand conditions of the commodity is an effective means of influencing the price of the product. In a free market economy the government should consider regulating prices only when all other means to rectify the problem have been exhausted.

In conclusion, the author's argument is unconvincing. To strengthen the argument the author would have to show that the only factor influencing the price increases is the growers' desire for increased profits.

Argument No. 55   A new brand of coffee

This company memorandum recommends that Excelsior conduct a temporary sales promotion for its new brand of coffee that includes offering free samples, price reductions, and discount coupons. This recommendation is based on the fact that Superior, the leading coffee company, used just such a promotion to introduce the newest brand in its line of coffees. This argument is unconvincing because it relies on three questionable assumptions.

First of all, the argument rests on the assumption that a promotional strategy that works for one company will work for another. However, Excelsior and Superior may not be sufficiently similar to warrant this assumption. Promotional techniques that work for a leader with established name recognition for its brand of coffees may be ineffective for a company with no similar name recognition new to the brand coffee market. Accordingly, Excelsior might be better advised to employ some other strategy, such as a media advertising plan, to first attain broad name recognition.

The argument also depends on the assumption that Excelsior can afford a promotional plan similar to Superior's. However, free samples, price reductions, and discounts all reduce profits and may actually result in temporary losses. While a leading company with other profitable products in the same line can absorb a temporary loss, for a fledgling competitor this strategy might be very risky and may even result in business failure.

Finally, the argument relies on the assumption that Superior's promotional campaign for its newest coffee was successful. However, the memo provides no evidence that this was the case. It is possible that the promotion was entirely ineffective, and that Superior remains the leader in its field despite this small failure. If so, Excelsior may be ill-advised to follow Superior's promotional strategy.

In conclusion, the two companies are too dissimilar to justify the recommendation that Excelsior model its promotional strategy on Superior's. To strengthen the argument, the author of the memo must establish that Excelsior has sufficient operating capital to launch the recommended sales campaign, and that this strategy would be more effective than another strategy, such as using extensive media advertising.

Argument No. 56   **Health-club usage**

Because Healthy Heart fitness centers experienced no significant increase in member usage as a result of building a new indoor pool, the author cautions other health club managers against installing new features as a means of increasing member usage. Instead, they are advised to lower membership fees. This argument is flawed in two critical respects.

First, the conclusion that installing new features at fitness centers will not increase member usage is based on too small a sample to be reliable. The only evidence offered in support of this conclusion is the fact that Healthy Heart fitness center did not experience an increase. Unless it can be shown that Healthy Heart is typical of all fitness centers, the fact that it experienced no increase in member usage is not grounds for concluding that all fitness centers will experience similar results.

Second, the author fails to consider other possible reasons why building an indoor pool failed to increase Healthy Heart's member usage. Perhaps Healthy Heart's members are primarily interested in body-building rather than cardiovascular exercise, or perhaps they prefer racquetball; or perhaps they just don't like swimming. Reasons such as these would help to explain why the addition of a new indoor pool failed to increase member usage. The author's failure to investigate or even consider other possible explanations for Healthy Heart's poor results renders the conclusion based upon them highly suspect.

In conclusion, the author's argument is not convincing. To strengthen the argument it would be necessary to show that Healthy Heart fitness center is typical of all fitness centers. Additionally, the author would have to show that other possible reasons for the lack of increase in member usage could be eliminated.

Argument No. 57   Safety codes for public buildings

The conclusion of this argument is that technological innovation as well as the evolution of architectural styles and design will be minimized in the future. The author's line of reasoning is that the imposition of strict safety codes on public buildings inhibits the evolution of architectural styles and design, because they discourage technological innovation within the building industry. Furthermore, the strictness of the codes governing public buildings discourages technological innovation because the surest way for architects and builders to pass the codes is to construct buildings that use the same materials and methods that are currently allowed. This argument is unconvincing for two reasons.

In the first place, the author's conclusion goes beyond the evidence presented. The evidence cited pertains only to the construction of public buildings, yet the author draws a conclusion about the building industry as a whole. Technological innovation and architectural experimentation in style and design in the construction of private buildings is not precluded by the reasons cited. Consequently, in the absence of evidence that similar problems beset the construction of privately owned buildings, the author's conclusion is not warranted.

In the second place, it is not evident that the strict safety codes governing public buildings will have the effects predicted by the author. Architectural styles and design are not dictated solely by the materials or the methods employed in construction. Consequently, it is premature to conclude that little evolution in style and design will occur because the materials and methods will likely remain the same. Moreover, technological innovation is not restricted to the use of new materials and methods. Significant technological innovation can be achieved by applying existing methods to new situations and by finding new uses for familiar materials.

In conclusion, the author has failed to make the case for the claim that technological innovation as well as the evolution of architectural styles and design will be minimized in the future. To strengthen the argument the author would have to show that similar safety code restrictions impede the evolution of the design and the innovation of new technologies in the construction of private buildings. Additionally, the author must show that materials and methods are the prime determinants of architectural style and design.

Argument No. 58   **Billboard advertising**

In an advertising experiment, Big Board, Inc. displayed the name and picture of a little-known athlete on several of its local billboards over a 3-month period. Because the experiment increased recognition of the athlete's name, Big Boards now argues that local companies will increase their sales if they advertise their products on Big Board's billboards. This argument is unconvincing for two important reasons.

The main problem with this argument is that the advertising experiment with the athlete shows only that name recognition can be increased by billboard advertising; it does not show that product sales can be increased by this form of advertising. Name recognition, while admittedly an important aspect of a product's selling potential, is not the only reason merchandise sells. Affordability, quality, and desirability are equally, if not more, important features a product must possess in order to sell. To suggest, as Big Board's campaign does, that name recognition alone is sufficient to increase sales is simply ludicrous.

Another problem with the argument is that while the first survey—in which only five percent of 15,000 randomly-selected residents could name the athlete—seems reliable, the results of the second survey are questionable on two grounds. First, the argument provides no information regarding how many residents were polled in the second survey or how they were selected. Secondly, the argument does not indicate the total number of respondents to the second survey. In the absence of this information about the second survey, it is impossible to determine the significance of its results.

In conclusion, Big Board's argument is not convincing. To strengthen the argument, Big Board must provide additional information regarding the manner in which the second survey was conducted. It must also provide additional evidence that an increase in name recognition will result in an increase in sales.

Argument No. 59   Regulating copper mining

The author contends that it makes good sense to reduce funding for mining regulation, because regulatory problems with overmining and pollution will be solved when scientists learn how to create large amounts of copper from other chemical elements. One reason the author gives for this conclusion is that the problem of overmining will be quickly eliminated when the amount of potentially available copper is no longer limited by the quantity of actual copper deposits. Another reason given is that pollution problems created by production of synthetic copper substitutes will be eliminated when manufacturers no longer depend on substitutes. This argument is weak because the conclusion goes beyond the scope of the premises and because the argument relies on questionable assumptions.

To begin with, the wording of the conclusion suggests that funding for mining regulation generally should be reduced, yet the premises are about copper mining only. There are many mined resources other than copper; advances in copper synthesis technology will in all likelihood have no bearing on whether regulation of other kinds of mining should be changed.

Furthermore, the argument depends on the assumption that copper mining will slow down once copper can be chemically synthesized. However, the author provides no evidence to substantiate this assumption. Moreover, it is entirely possible that copper mining will remain less expensive than copper synthesis. If so, there will be no incentives, outside of regulatory ones, to slow down copper mining. In a word, the problem of overmining will remain.

Finally, the argument relies on the assumption that synthesizing copper will not create the same kind of pollution problems as those resulting from the synthesis of copper substitutes. However, the author provides no evidence to substantiate this assumption. Without such evidence, we cannot accept the premise that pollution problems will be eliminated by switching from producing copper substitutes to producing copper itself.

In conclusion, I am not convinced on the basis of this argument that the time has come to cut funding for the regulation of mining in general, or even for the regulation of copper mining in particular. To strengthen the argument, the author must restrict the scope of the conclusion to copper mining rather than to mining in general. The author must also provide support for the two assumptions underlying the argument.

Argument No. 60	**Scientists and affordable day care**

This editorial argues that, since career advancement for scientists typically requires 60 to 80 hours of work per week, affordable all-day child care must be made available to scientists of both genders if they are to advance in their fields. Moreover, the editorial urges that requirements for career advancement be made more flexible to insure that pre-school children can spend a significant amount of time each day with a parent. This argument is problematic in two crucial respects.

The major problem with the view expressed in the article is that inconsistent recommendations are endorsed in the argument. On the one hand, scientists are urged to put their children in all-day child-care facilities in order to advance their careers. On the other hand, they are encouraged to spend a significant amount of time each day with their children. Obviously, scientists cannot be expected to adhere to both of these recommendations.

Another problem is that the recommendations are based on the assumption that all, or at least most, scientists have young or preschool-age children. But the editorial provides no evidence to support this assumption, nor is this assumption very likely to be true. Since, childless scientists or scientists whose children are old enough to take care of themselves will have no need for the services advocated in this article, it is doubtful that these recommendations will receive much widespread support.

In conclusion, this argument is unconvincing. To strengthen it, the author must show that most scientists have preschool children and consequently are in need of the recommended services. Additionally, the author must address and resolve the apparent conflict between the recommendations.

Argument No. 61   Employee lay-offs

A director of Beta Company suggests that Beta can improve its competitive position by hiring a significant number of former Alpha Company employees who have recently retired or been laid off. The director's reasoning is that because Alpha manufactures some products similar to Beta's, former Alpha employees would be experienced and need little training, could provide valuable information about Alpha's successful methods, and would be particularly motivated to compete against Alpha. The director's argument is problematic in several respects.

First of all, the argument presupposes that Alpha's methods are successful. This is not necessarily the case. To the contrary, the fact that Alpha has laid off 15 percent of its employees in every division and at every level suggests that Alpha's methods may have been unsuccessful and that downsizing was necessary for the company to minimize financial losses.

Secondly, the director assumes that the former Alpha employees hired by Beta will be well-trained and valuable. During a typical lay-off, however, the best and most experienced employees are typically the last to be laid off. By following the director's advice, Beta would probably be hiring Alpha's least efficient and least experienced employees—that is, those who would be least valuable to Beta.

Thirdly, the author assumes that Alpha and Beta are sufficiently similar so that former Alpha employees could provide special value for Beta. However, we are informed only that Beta manufactures "some products similar to Alpha's." It is possible that former Alpha employees have experience with only a small segment of Beta's product line, and thus have little inside information of any value to Beta.

Finally, the claim that former Alpha employees would be motivated to compete against Alpha is partially unwarranted. While many of those who were laid off may be so motivated, those who retired early from Alpha probably departed on good terms with Alpha, and would in any event be unmotivated to reenter the work force.

In conclusion, the argument fails to provide key facts needed to assess it. To better evaluate the director's suggestion, we would need more information about why Alpha reduced its work force, what type of workers left Alpha and under what circumstances, and how similar Alpha's range of products is to Beta's.

Argument No. 62   **Exercise machines**

In this argument the author concludes that the new community fitness center should be equipped with the state-of-the-art exercise machines featured in Powerflex magazine. In support of this recommendation two reasons are offered: (1) Powerflex contains pictures of bodybuilders using such machines, and (2) Powerflex is a popular magazine, as evidenced by the fact that it frequently sells out at the local newsstand. This argument is questionable on two counts.

First, a major implication of the argument is that the bodybuilders pictured using the machines in Powerflex magazine reached their state of fitness as a result of using these machines. The only evidence offered to support this contention, however, is the pictures in the magazine. It is possible that the bodybuilders pictured use different equipment for their workouts and are merely posing with the machines for advertising purposes.

Second, the author assumes that machines that are suitable for bodybuilding will also be suitable to help maximize the fitness levels of the town's residents. This assumption is highly questionable. Machines designed to increase muscle development are significantly different from those designed to increase cardiovascular fitness. Consequently, it is unlikely that the machines pictured in the magazine will be of much use to help maximize the fitness levels of the town's residents.

In conclusion, this argument is unconvincing. To strengthen the argument the author would have to show that the bodybuilders pictured using the exercise machines actually used the machines to reach their level of muscle development. Additionally, the author would have to show that the machines were suitable for increasing the fitness levels of the persons using them.

Argument No. 63   Evaluating a business relocation

According to this newspaper article, the Cumquat Cafe made a mistake by relocating one year ago. The author supports this claim by pointing out that Cumquat is doing about the same volume of business as before it moved, while RoboWrench plumbing supply outlet, which took over Cumquat's old location, is apparently "doing better" because its owners plan to open a new outlet in a nearby city. This argument suffers from several critical flaws.

To begin with, the two businesses are too dissimilar for meaningful comparison. Cumquat's old location may simply have been better suited to hardware, plumbing, and home improvement businesses than to cafes and restaurants. The article's claim that Cumquat made a mistake in moving fails to take this possibility into account.

Secondly, the article's claim that RoboWrench is "doing better" since it took over Cumquat's old location is too vague to be meaningful. The author fails to provide a second term of this comparison. We are not informed whether RoboWrench is doing better than before it moved, better than other plumbing stores, or better than Cumquat. This uninformative comparison is worthless as evidence from which to judge the wisdom of Cumquat's decision to relocate.

Thirdly, the claim that RoboWrench is doing better is unwarranted by the evidence. The mere fact that RoboWrench plans to open a new store in a nearby city does not by itself establish that business is good. It is possible that the purpose of this plan is to compensate for lackluster business at the current location. Or perhaps the RoboWrench owners are simply exercising poor business judgment.

Finally, the claim that Cumquat made a mistake in moving may be too hasty, since the conclusion is based on only one year's business at the new location. Moreover, given the time it ordinarily takes for a business to develop a new customer base in a new location, the fact that Cumquat's volume of business is about the same as before it moved tends to show that the move was a good decision, not a mistake.

In conclusion, the claim that Cumquat's move was a mistake is ill-founded, since it is based on both poor and incomplete comparisons as well as on a premature conclusion. To better assess the argument, we need to know what the author is comparing RoboWrench's performance to; we also need more information about the extent of RoboWrench's success at this location and why its owners are opening a new store.

Argument No. 64	An employee survey at Company X

The Director of Human Resources concludes that most employees at Company X feel that the improvement most needed at the company has been satisfactorily addressed. Two reasons are offered in support of this conclusion. First, a survey of employees showed that the issue respondents were most concerned about was employee-management communication. Second, the company has since instituted regular voluntary sessions for employees and management designed to improve communication. The director's argument is questionable for two reasons.

To begin with, the validity of the survey is doubtful. Lacking information about the number of employees surveyed and the number of respondents, it is impossible to assess the validity of the results. For example, if 200 employees were surveyed but only two responded, the conclusion that most of the employees ranked employee-management communication as the most pressing issue would be highly suspect. Because the argument offers no evidence that would rule out interpretations such as this, the survey results are insufficient to support the author's conclusion.

Furthermore, even if the survey accurately ranks certain issues according to level of employee concern, the highest-ranked issue in the survey might not be the issue about which employees are most concerned. Why? The improvement most needed from the point of view of the employees might not have appeared as one of the choices on the survey. For example, if the list of improvements presented on the survey was created by management rather than by the employees, then the issues of greatest concern to the employees might not be included on the list. Lacking information about how the survey was prepared, it is impossible to assess its reliability. Consequently, any conclusion based on it is highly questionable.

In conclusion, the director's conclusion is not well-founded. To strengthen the argument, additional information regarding the way in which the employee survey was prepared and conducted is required.

Argument No. 65   Determining the cause of and cure for low profits

In this memorandum, the vice president of Road Food suggests that the company motivate its advertising agency to perform better by basing the agency's pay on the Road Food's profits. In support of this suggestion, the vice president points out that although Road Food initially thought the ad agency was following company recommendations, competitor Street Eats earned higher profits last year. The vice president also notes that Street Eats has fewer restaurants than Road Food, and that Road Food spent nearly as much money on advertising as Street Eats did. This argument is unconvincing, since it relies on dubious assumptions and comparisons.

First, the vice president assumes that the ad campaign caused the low profits. However, the vice president ignores many other factors that contribute to profitability. In particular, the fact that Road Food has been spending less advertising money per restaurant than Street Eats suggests that its unwillingness to spend more may be the main reason for disappointing profits.

Second, the author implies that the ad agency failed to implement Road Food's guidelines, and that this failure was the reason for disappointing profits. However, it is equally possible that the ad agency faithfully followed all suggestions from Road Food, and that those suggestions were the cause of the disappointing profits. In this respect, the author unfairly shifts blame from Road Food to the ad agency.

Third, the author's comparison between Road Food and Street Eats is less relevant than a comparison between Road Food's own profits prior to its latest ad campaign and its profits during this campaign. Comparing its own profits during these time periods would more accurately reflect the ad agency's effectiveness than comparing profits of two different companies.

Finally, the author assumes that the ad agency will be more motivated if its fee is based on Road Food profits. However, the author does not support this claim. In fact, given that Road Food's profits have been lower than expected, it is just as likely that the ad agency would be less motivated by the suggested fee structure than by some other fee structure.

In conclusion, the argument is unconvincing as it stands. To strengthen it, the vice president must provide evidence that the ad campaign caused last year's disappointing profits, and must examine and rule out other factors that may have contributed to disappointing profits.

Argument No. 66   Obesity among dogs

In this argument the makers of Cerebus dog food recommend their reduced-calorie product as the best way for dog owners to help their obese dogs lose weight. Their reasoning in support of this recommendation is simple. To begin with, they point out that the best way to treat obesity in humans is by a reduced-calorie diet that is high in fiber and carbohydrates but low in fat. Second, they indicate that reduced-calorie Cerebus dog food is high in fiber and carbohydrates but low in fat. The conclusion drawn from this information is that Cerebus dog food is the best way to treat obesity in dogs. This argument is unconvincing for a couple of reasons.

In the first place, the makers of Cerebus dog food assume that the cause of obesity in dogs is the same as the cause in humans. Given the vast differences between the exercise patterns and basic diets of humans and dogs, this assumption is highly dubious. Lacking evidence to support this claim, the argument is unacceptable.

In the second place, the author assumes that the gastrointestinal systems of dogs and humans are sufficiently similar to ensure that treatment that is effective on humans will be equally effective on dogs. Again, this is a highly dubious assumption due to the obvious physiological differences between humans and dogs. Since no evidence has been offered to support this assumption, it too can be rejected.

In conclusion, this argument is unconvincing. To strengthen the argument evidence is required to substantiate the assumption that dogs and humans are sufficiently similar in both their diets and their physiology to warrant similar treatment.

Argument No. 67   **Airline on-time rates**

A travel magazine article claims that Speedee Airlines is the best choice for today's business traveler. To support this claim, the author points out that Speedee has ranked first in terms of on-time arrival rate since the airline industry began requiring airlines to report their on-time rates. The claim is also based on the assertion that "Speedee now offers more flights to more destinations than ever before." This argument suffers from several critical flaws.

First of all, the claim relies on a couple of unwarranted assumptions. One assumption is that on-time rates, number of flights, and destination choices are the only features of airline service that determine how a particular airline would rank overall for a business traveler. However, the author of this article ignores other factors such as fare prices and discounts, safety record, baggage-handling, and in-flight amenities. Another assumption is that Speedee's overall on-time record affects business and non-business travelers equally. However, this is not necessarily the case. Speedee may have a poorer record for commuter flights, which are popular among business travelers, than for other flights. If so, the conclusion that Speedee is the best choice for the business traveler would be seriously undermined.

Secondly, the author's claim that "Speedee now offers more flights to more destinations than ever before" is too vague to be meaningful. We are not informed how many flights or how many destinations were previously offered or how many are offered now. Moreover, the article makes no comparison with other airlines regarding these features. Without these comparisons, the claim is worthless as a reason for choosing Speedee over another airline.

Thirdly, the article fails to indicate how long ago the industry began requiring airlines to report on-time rates. If the requirement was imposed recently, then the brief reporting period may be insufficient to show that the airlines' relative on-time performance will continue in the future. Moreover, the article fails to provide evidence that all airlines, regardless of on-time record, actually reported, or that the reports are accurate.

In conclusion, the article's claim that Speedee is the best choice for the business traveler is unsubstantiated and may be too hasty. To better evaluate the article's claim, we need more information about Speedee's other features that contribute to its overall appeal, about its on-time record for commuter flights specifically, and about the integrity and length of the reporting upon which the ranking was based.

Argument No. 68   Investing in solar energy

In this argument the planning department of an investment firm reaches the conclusion that the firm should encourage investment in Solario—a new manufacturer of solar-powered products. The basis for this recommendation is the expectation that solar energy will soon become more cost efficient and attractive than other forms of energy. This expectation is based on recent declines in the cost of equipment used to convert solar energy into electricity and on new technologies that are being developed for this purpose. An additional reason given in support of this recommendation is that Solario's chief executive was a member of the financial planning team for a company that has shown remarkable growth since its recent incorporation. While this argument has some merit, there are a few assumptions that deserve attention.

In the first place, the author assumes that the previous business experience of Solario's chief executive will be an asset in the development of the new company. While this may be the case, the fact that the two companies deal in vastly different products is cause for some concern. The executive's expertise in the software-engineering business will not necessarily be applicable to the solar-powered products business.

In the second place, the author assumes that the major impediment to the use of solar-powered products is the cost of solar energy and that, given a choice, consumers would prefer products powered by solar energy over those powered by energy derived from coal or oil. On the face of it, this assumption seems acceptable; but it may be that there are other factors besides cost that make solar energy less desirable than other forms of energy.

In conclusion, this argument is convincing. To strengthen the argument additional evidence indicating consumer preference for solar-powered products over products powered by conventional forms of energy would be desirable.

Argument No. 69   Marketing air filters

The company's marketing department recommends discontinuing a deluxe air filter and concentrating advertising efforts on an economy filter, which requires replacement more often than the deluxe model. This recommendation is based on reports showing that sales of economy filters, and company profits, have dropped significantly since the company began manufacturing and marketing the deluxe filter six months ago. The marketing department's argument is specious in three important respects.

First, the marketing department assumes that if the company discontinues the new deluxe air filter, customers will resume buying its economy filter. This assumption may not be correct. Customers who prefer the deluxe model may do so because it requires replacement less often. Thus, instead of buying the company's economy filters again, these customers may just as likely turn to a competitor for a product similar to the deluxe model. In this event, the result would be lower profits.

Secondly, the marketing department fails to recognize alternative strategies that might enhance profits more than discontinuing the deluxe filter would. It is possible that lowering the price of the economy model, raising the price of the deluxe model, or both, may actually maximize profits. A lower-priced economy filter might lure customers from competing products and retain current customers. At the same time, buyers of the deluxe model may place a premium value on its convenience and may be willing to pay an even higher price for the filter.

Thirdly, the marketing department unfairly assumes that the availability of its deluxe filter is the cause of decreasing profits. It is equally possible that other factors, such as increased competition or supply prices, or decreased demand for these kinds of filters generally, are responsible for the decrease in profits. If so, discontinuing the deluxe filter may not serve to maximize, or even enhance, the company's profits.

In conclusion, the department's argument for discontinuing the deluxe filter is weak because the department has not considered the possible adverse consequences of doing so, or the alternatives to doing so. Moreover, the department has failed to establish a clear causal connection between the availability of the deluxe filter and decreasing profits. To strengthen its argument, the department must consider and rule out pricing adjustments as a better strategy to maximize profits, and must provide better evidence that the deluxe filter is the cause of the decrease in profits.

Argument No. 70   Hair loss and shampoo

The president of the company that produces Glabrous Shampoo argues against removing the ingredient HR2 from the shampoo even though a scientific study claims that prolonged use of HR2 can contribute to hair loss. Three reasons are cited as the basis for this decision. First, it is argued that since the scientific study involved only 500 subjects, it can be disregarded. Second, none of Glabrous' customers have complained of problems during the past year. And, finally, Glabrous' competitors use more HR2 per bottle than Glabrous. The president's decision is problematic in several respects.

To begin with, the fact that the scientific study on HR2 involved only 500 subjects is insufficient grounds to dismiss the results of that study. If the subjects for the study were randomly chosen and represent a diverse cross section of the population of shampoo users, the results will be reliable regardless of the number of participants.

Next, the scientific study determined that prolonged use could contribute to hair loss. While "prolonged use" was not defined in the memorandum, the fact that none of Glabrous' customers have complained of problems during the past year is not a reliable reason to believe that problems will not arise in the future.

Finally, the fact that Glabrous' competitors use more HR2 in their products than Glabrous uses is irrelevant to the question of whether Glabrous should remove HR2 from its product. Moreover, rather than providing a reason for not removing the compound, this fact serves better as a reason for doing so. By removing HR2 from its product Glabrous could gain an edge over its competitors.

In conclusion, the reasoning in this argument is not convincing. To strengthen the argument the author would have to show that the study was biased or was based on too small a sample to yield reliable results.

Argument No. 71   **Medical-helicopter accidents**

The author of this editorial concludes that the guidelines for training pilots and maintaining equipment in the medical-helicopter industry are ineffective, even though they are far more stringent than those in other airline industries. To support this conclusion, the author cites statistics showing that the rate of medical-helicopter accidents is much higher than the rate of accidents for non-medical helicopters or commercial airliners. This argument is problematic in three critical respects.

The first problem with the argument is that it rests on the unstated assumption that accidents involving medical helicopters have been due to inadequate pilot training or equipment maintenance. However, the author fails to acknowledge and rule out other possible causes of such accidents. In fact, common sense tells us that medical-helicopter accidents are most likely to result from the exigent circumstances and dangerous flying and landing conditions which typify medical emergencies where helicopters are required to gain access to victims.

A second, and related, problem is that the author unfairly compares the accident rate of medical helicopters with the accident rate for non-emergency aircraft. Medical helicopters are almost invariably deployed during emergencies to dangerous flying locales, whereas other types of aircraft are not. Consequently, medical-helicopter accidents will in all likelihood occur far more frequently than other aircraft accidents, regardless of pilot training or equipment maintenance.

A third problem with the argument is that the statistical evidence upon which it relies is too vague to be informative. The statistics concerning aircraft accidents may have been based on all types of accidents, whether minor or major. The statistics would be more meaningful if we knew that the accidents to which they refer were all of comparable severity. For all we know, the rate of casualty-causing accidents for medical helicopters is actually lower than for other aircraft. Additionally, we are not told the time period of the survey. An old survey or one that covered only a brief time period would be poor evidence in support of the author's claim.

In conclusion, the author's evidence does little to support the conclusion. To be persuasive, the author must at the very least acknowledge and rule out other possible causes of accidents that are unique to the medical-helicopter industry. In any event, a more effective argument would be based on a statistical comparison of accident rates under differing sets of training and maintenance guidelines within the medical-helicopter industry, not among different aircraft industries.

Argument No. 72   Department-store sales

Based upon sales reports over a three-month period that indicate an increase in profits for stores that sell products for the home and a decrease in profits for clothing stores, the business manager of a department store concludes that consumers are choosing to purchase home furnishings rather than clothing. On the basis of this conclusion, the manager recommends a reduction in the size of the clothing department and an increase in the size of the home-furnishings department. This recommendation is problematic in two critical respects.

In the first place, the author's conclusion that consumers are choosing to buy products for their homes instead of clothing is based upon too small a sample. Data gathered from a three-month period is insufficient to establish the conclusion drawn from it. It is quite possible that the three-month period chosen is idiosyncratic and not representative of entire year's sales. If so, reducing the size of the clothing departments and enlarging the home-furnishings departments may be a costly mistake.

In the second place, the data collected during the three month period may be biased. The fact that the data reflects sales in local stores is cause for concern. It is possible that the sales trend in a particular location is not representative of sales in other regions. For example, sales of clothing in Florida during the winter months are likely to be quite different from sales of clothing in Alaska during the same period.

In conclusion, this argument is not persuasive as it stands. A more convincing argument must provide additional sales data, collected at different periods of the year and at different locations, that substantiates the trend in question.

Argument No. 73   Rural vs. urban crime

The author of this editorial asserts that trespassing, vandalism, and theft associated with stealing fruit from farms is a trivial problem and, as a result, enacting laws to protect farm- and land-owners from these crimes is a waste of lawmakers' time. In support of this claim, the author points out only that the nation's cities are plagued by far more serious problems of violence and crime. To the extent that this author has provided any argument at all, it is a poor one.

First of all, the author unfairly assumes that if lawmakers are taking rural crime issues seriously, then they cannot be taking urban crime issues seriously. The author is presenting a false dilemma by imposing an either-or choice between two courses of action that need not be mutually exclusive. It is equally possible that legislators can address both areas of concern concurrently.

Secondly, the argument relies on the assumption that the legislators in question have the opportunity to address urban crime problems. However, we are not told whether this legislature's jurisdiction encompasses both rural and urban areas. If it encompasses only rural areas, then the author's implicit conclusion that the legislators in this region should instead be addressing urban crime problems would be completely undermined.

Finally, the author unfairly trivializes the severity of rural crime by simply comparing it with urban crime. While trespassing, vandalism, and fruit-stealing may seem minor peccadilloes, especially compared to violent urban crimes, these rural crimes might nevertheless result in serious financial damage to farm owners, depending on the frequency and extent of the violations. The author fails to provide evidence for the claim that these rural crimes are trivial. Instead, the author attempts to call attention to a more dramatic but potentially irrelevant problem.

In conclusion, the argument is weak. It potentially distorts the alternatives available to legislators in the region, as well as deflecting attention from the problem at hand. To better evaluate it, we would need more information about the geographical scope of this legislature's jurisdiction and about the extent of the fruit-stealing problem in the region.

Argument No. 74 — A nationwide labor shortage

In this argument the author predicts a nationwide labor shortage in the near future. The basis for this prediction is an increasing demand for highly skilled workers, especially in technical and professional fields, coupled with a slow-growing labor force and a government proposal to cut funds for aid to education. At first glance, the author's argument appears to be somewhat convincing; but further reflection reveals that it is based on some dubious assumptions.

In the first place, the author assumes that the present labor force is immobile and that the demand for highly skilled workers will have to be met by workers who are entering the labor market for the first time. Recent American history, however, shows that this assumption is entirely unfounded. At the beginning of the Industrial Revolution most Americans were farm workers, but by the end of that revolution most had become factory workers. Thus, even though the labor pool remained relatively constant during this period, the number of farm workers decreased and the number of factory workers increased. This example clearly demonstrates the mobility of the labor force.

In the second place, the author assumes that the government proposal to cut funds for aid to education will have a significant negative impact on the ability to train workers in technical and professional fields. The fact is, however, that the percentage of students who rely on government aid for their education is relatively small, so the effect of such cuts would be negligible.

In conclusion, this argument is unconvincing. To strengthen the argument the author would have to show that the present work force was relatively static and that the proposed cuts in educational aid would have a deleterious effect on the numbers of highly skilled workers available to enter the work force in the future.

Argument No. 75   Allocating money for bridge repair

The author of this government agency memorandum argues that the government should not spend any money this year fixing the bridge that crosses the Styx River, given the limited resources available for building and repair of roads and bridges. The author reasons that this bridge is less important than others because it is located near a city with a weakening economy, and because the city's small population is unlikely to contribute enough tax revenue to justify fixing their bridge. This argument is unconvincing for four reasons.

First of all, the author unfairly assumes that the importance of a bridge is determined solely by the economic condition of nearby cities. This assumption overlooks other criteria for determining a bridge's importance—such as the number of commuters using the bridge, the role of the bridge in local emergencies and disasters, and the impact that bridge closure would have on the economies of nearby cities. Without accounting for these other potential factors, the author fails to provide a convincing argument that the Styx River bridge is unimportant.

Secondly, the author fails to provide any evidence that other bridges are more important than the Styx River bridge. Without such evidence, we cannot accept the author's conclusion that no government funds should be directed toward maintaining the Styx River bridge.

Thirdly, the fact that the nearby city has a weakening economy does not prove that the city will not contribute significantly to tax revenues. Perhaps tax revenues are based on property taxes, which are not related directly to economic conditions. If so, and if property values and taxes are high in this nearby city, then the city would contribute significantly to tax revenues, and the bridge would be important to maintain those property values and the revenues they generate.

Finally, the author assumes that a city should receive government services commensurate with the tax dollars it contributes. Substantiating this assumption requires examining the proper duty of government. However, the author provides no such examination. Accordingly, this assumption is simply an unproven claim.

In conclusion, this editorial fails to substantiate its claim that the Styx River bridge is not important enough for the government to spend tax dollars to maintain and repair it. To strengthen the argument, the author must account for other factors that also determine a bridge's importance, and must compare the importance of this bridge relative to other bridges.

Argument No. 76   A movie sequel based on a book series

In this argument the author reasons that a sequel to a popular movie will be profitable because the original movie was profitable and because books based on the characters of the movie are consistently bestsellers. This argument is unconvincing for several reasons.

In the first place, a great deal of empirical evidence shows that sequels are often not as profitable as the original movie. For example, none of the "Superman" movie sequels even approached the success of the original movie. Accordingly, the mere fact that the first movie was successful does not guarantee that movies based upon it will also be profitable.

In the second place, a movie's financial success is a function of many elements in addition to well-liked characters. Admittedly, the fact that the books based on the characters of the original film are bestsellers bodes well for the movie's commercial prospects. However, unless the original cast and production team are involved in making the sequel, there is a good chance it will not be financially successful.

Finally, another important element in creating a successful movie is the script. The transformation of a popular book into a popular movie script is a difficult process. Examples of best-selling books that were not made into successful movies are commonplace. Obviously, the success of the sequel that Vista is planning will depend in great part on the screenwriter's ability to capture the elements of the story that make the books popular. Since the difficulties inherent in this process make it hard to predict whether the result will be a success or a failure, the conclusion that the sequel will be profitable is presumptuous.

In conclusion, this is an unconvincing argument. To strengthen the argument, it would be necessary to provide assurances that the original cast and production team will be involved in the project and that the script will capture and develop the particular elements responsible for the books' popularity.

Argument No. 77   Agricultural technology

The conclusion of this letter is that consumers are not truly benefiting from advances in agricultural technology. The author concedes that, on the average, consumers are spending a decreasing proportion of their income on food. But the author contends that this would happen without advances in agricultural technology. The author reasons that demand for food does not rise in proportion with real income, so as real income rises, consumers will spend a decreasing portion of their income on food. This argument turns on a number of dubious assumptions.

First of all, while asserting that real incomes are rising, the author provides no evidence to support this assertion; moreover, it might be false. Even if salaries and wages go up, this fact may not indicate that real income has increased proportionally. Real income takes into account any effect inflation might have on the relative value of the dollar. It is possible that, when salaries and wages are adjusted for inflation, what appear to be increases in real income are actually decreases.

In addition, the author assumes that increases in real income explain why, on the average, consumers are now spending a decreasing proportion of their income on food. But no evidence is provided to show that this explanation is correct. Moreover, the author fails to consider and rule out other factors that might account for proportional decreases in spending on food.

Finally, the entire argument turns on the assumption that benefits to consumers from advances in agricultural technology are all economic ones—specifically, ones reflected in food prices. The author ignores other likely benefits of agricultural technology that affect food prices only indirectly or not at all. Such likely benefits include increased quality of food as it reaches the market and greater availability of basic food items. Moreover, the author cannot adequately assess the benefits of agricultural technology solely on the basis of current food prices because those prices are a function of more than just the technology that brings the food to market.

In conclusion, this letter has provided little support for the claim that consumers are not really benefiting from advances in agricultural technology. A stronger argument would account for the benefits of technology other than the current price of food, and would account for other factors that affect food prices. To better evaluate the argument, we would need more information about whether real incomes are actually rising and whether this alone explains why consumers now spend a proportionately smaller amount of income on food.

Argument No. 78	Funding city services

In this editorial the author argues that improvements to existing city services as well as new services should be paid for by developers rather than taxpayers. In support of this opinion, the author points out that developers can make large profits from building projects, and that these projects increase the demand for city services and raise the city's expenses. I disagree with the author's opinion for two reasons.

First, the fact that developers stand to make profits from their projects is not a good reason to require them to pay more than their fair share of the costs of services. In fact, to require them to do this in order to win approval of their projects is tantamount to bribery. City officials would find it difficult to justify a policy that endorsed this practice. Moreover, the adoption of such a practice would discourage the development of new buildings in the city.

Second, the increase in demand for city services as well as the increase in the city's expenses will most likely be offset by the tax revenues these projects generate. Consequently, unless the author can demonstrate that the city will incur expenses that are not covered by the increased revenues from these projects, the author's concern about these issues is unfounded.

In conclusion, I find the author's reasoning on this issue unconvincing. To strengthen the argument the author would have to show that the city would be harmed financially by approving new building projects.

Argument No. 79   **Trash disposal—incinerators vs. landfills**

This newspaper editorial concludes that our city should build a plant for burning trash in order to avoid the serious health threats associated with many landfills. The author adds that an incinerator could offer economic benefits as well, since incinerators can be adapted to generate small amounts of electricity for other uses, and since ash residue from some kinds of trash can be used as a soil conditioner. Even if these claims are true, the author's argument is unconvincing in three important respects.

To begin with, the author fails to consider health threats posed by incinerating trash. It is possible, for example, that respiratory problems resulting from the air pollution caused by burning trash might be so extensive that they would outweigh the health risks associated with landfills. If so, the author's conclusion that switching to incineration would be more salutary for public health would be seriously undermined.

Secondly, the author assumes that discontinuing landfill operations would abate the heath threats they now pose. However, this is not necessarily the case. It is possible that irreversible environmental damage to subterranean water supplies, for example, has already occurred. In this event, changing from landfills to incinerators might not avoid or abate serious public health problems.

Thirdly, the author's implicit claim that incinerators are economically advantageous to landfills is poorly supported. Only two small economic benefits of incineration are mentioned, while the costs associated with either burning trash or switching refuse disposal systems are ignored. In all likelihood, such costs would be significant, and may very well outweigh the economic benefits.

In conclusion, the author's argument provides inadequate justification for switching from one disposal system to the other. As it stands, the argument takes into account only a limited number of benefits from the change, while addressing none of its costs. To better evaluate the argument, we must first examine all the health risks posed by each refuse disposal system, and conduct a thorough cost-benefit analysis of each system, accounting for the cost of the new system, the cost of the changeover itself, and the expected costs to the community of health problems resulting from each system.

Argument No. 80	Workplace safety and wages

In this editorial the author argues that it makes financial sense for employers to make the workplace safer. In support of this claim the author reasons that since wages paid to employees should increase as the risk of physical injury increases, the converse should be true as well. Hence, by decreasing the risk of injury, employers could decrease the wages paid to workers and thereby save money. This argument is unconvincing for two reasons.

To begin with, the author assumes that because companies would agree that as risk of injury increases wages should also increase, they would also agree that as risk decreases wages should also decrease accordingly. This is tantamount to the assumption that risk of injury is the primary factor that determines workers' wages. It is obvious that few employers, and even fewer employees, would agree that this is the case. To adopt this position one would have to disregard education, experience, and skill as equally important factors in determining the wages paid to workers.

Secondly, the author's reasoning suggests that the only benefit of a safer workplace is the savings employers could realize from lower wages. This is obviously not true. The costs associated with accidents on the job could far outweigh any savings that could be realized by paying workers lower wages.

In conclusion, the author's argument is unconvincing. Risk of injury is an important factor to consider in determining the wages paid to workers but is not the only such factor. Furthermore, there are far better reasons for employers to make the workplace safer than the one presented by the author.

Argument No. 81   Adopting a code of ethics

This company memorandum suggests that, in lieu of adopting an official code of ethics, the company should conduct a publicity campaign that stresses the importance of promoting certain societal interests. The reason for the suggestion is that an official code of ethics might harm the company in the public eye because a competing company received unfavorable publicity for violating its own ethics code. This argument is unconvincing, since it depends on several unwarranted assumptions as well as arguing against its own conclusion.

First of all, the author unfairly assumes that the two companies are sufficiently similar to ensure the same consequences of adopting an ethics code for this company as for its competitor. The competitor may have adopted an entirely different code from the one this company might adopt—perhaps with unrealistic standards not embraced by any other companies. Perhaps the competitor's violation was extremely egregious, amounting to an aberration among businesses of its type; or perhaps one notorious executive is solely responsible for the competitor's violation. Any of these scenarios, if true, would show that the two companies are dissimilar in ways relevant to the likelihood that this company will experience similar violations and similar publicity if it adopts any ethics code.

Secondly, the author unfairly assumes that the competitor was damaged by its code violation and the resulting publicity more than it would have been had it not violated its code. Just as likely, however, the violation was necessary to ensure a certain level of profitability or to protect other important interests. Without knowing the extent and nature of the damage resulting from the bad publicity or the reason for the violation, we cannot accept the author's conclusion.

Thirdly, the author's proposal is inconsistent with the author's conclusion about the consequences of adopting an ethics code. The author suggests that, instead of adopting an ethics code, this company should stress "the importance of protecting the environment and assisting charitable organizations." This proposal is tantamount to adopting an ethics code. In this sense, the author suggests going against his own advice that the company should not adopt such a code.

In conclusion, differences between this company and its competitor may undermine the author's conclusion that this company should not adopt an ethics code. To better evaluate the argument, we need more information about the nature of the competitor's ethics code and about the nature and extent of the violation. To strengthen the argument, the author must accord his advice with his conclusion that the company should not adopt an ethics code.

Argument No. 82   Opinion polls and election outcomes

In this editorial the author asserts that opinion polls are little better than random guesses in predicting outcomes of presidential elections. The author's basis for this assertion is that opinion polls measure only the preferences of voters at the time of the poll and that many voters change their preferences several time before voting—some remaining undecided until the moment they cast their vote. The author's reasoning is unconvincing in two critical respects.

First of all, the predictions based on random guessing are such that the greater the number of candidates, the less likely the prediction will be correct. The reason for this is obvious: random guessing, in order to be random, requires that no outside information be allowed to influence the guess. Predictions based on opinion polls, on the other hand, will differ considerably from those based on random guesses simply because outside information will influence the result. For example, in a four person race, random guessing would yield the correct prediction 25 percent of the time, whereas the percentage of correct predictions based on opinion polls would be much higher. The reason for this disparity is simple. Opinion polls enable us to narrow the choices. That is, opinion polls serve to reduce the number of viable candidates in the voter's mind and thereby increase the likelihood that the prediction based on them will be correct.

In addition, while it is true that many voters change their minds several times before voting, and that some remain undecided until entering the voting booth, this is not true of everyone. Moreover, people who do change their minds frequently or wait until the last moment to decide have typically narrowed their choice to a few candidates.

In conclusion, the author is mistaken in believing that random guessing would be as reliable as opinion polls in predicting the outcomes of presidential elections.

Argument No. 83   Changing speed limits

This editorial asserts that West Cambria should not change its highway speed limits because such changes adversely affect driver alertness and are therefore dangerous. To support this claim, the editorial cites statistics indicating that whenever East Cambria changed its speed limits, an average of 3 percent more automobile accidents occurred during the week after the change than during the week preceding it, even when the speed limit was lowered. As it stands, this argument suffers from three critical flaws.

First, it is unlikely that the brief one-week periods under comparison are representative of longer time periods. A difference of only 3 percent during one particular week can easily be accounted for by other factors, such as heavy holiday traffic or bad weather, or by problems with reporting or sampling. Had the editorial indicated that several speed-limit changes in East Cambria contributed to the statistic, the argument would be more convincing; but for all we know, the statistic is based on only one such change. In any event, a one-week period is too brief to be representative because it is likely that accidents will occur more frequently immediately following the change, while people adjust to the new limit, than over the longer term when drivers have become accustomed to the change.

Secondly, the editorial fails to acknowledge possible differences in the types of accidents occurring before and after the change. It is possible that the accidents during the week before the change all involved fatalities, while those during the week after the change were minor fender-benders. If so, even though 3 percent more accidents occurred after the change, the author's argument that changing the speed limit increases danger for drivers would be seriously weakened.

Thirdly, the editorial fails to take into account possible differences between East and West Cambria that are relevant to how drivers react to speed-limit changes. Factors such as the condition of roads, average age and typical driving habits of residents, and weather patterns, would probably affect how well or how quickly drivers adapt to speed-limit changes. Thus, changing speed limits in East Cambria might be more dangerous than changing them in West Cambria.

In conclusion, the statistical evidence cited to support the argument is insignificant and probably unrepresentative. To better evaluate the argument, we need to know how many speed-limit changes contributed to the statistic and when the speed-limit changes were made. Finally, to strengthen the argument the author should show that East and West Cambria would be similarly affected by speed-limit changes.

Argument No. 84   **Health and retirement benefits**

The vice president of Nostrum argues that implementing an increase in health and retirement benefits for employees is not a good idea at this time. His main line of reasoning is that an increase in benefits is both financially unjustified and unnecessary—financially unjustified because last year's profits were lower than the preceding year's, and unnecessary because Nostrum's chief competitor offers lower benefits to its employees and because a recent Nostrum employee survey indicated that two-thirds of the respondents viewed the current benefits package favorably. While the argument has some merit, it is not completely convincing.

Admittedly, the vice president's reasoning linking employee benefits with company profits seems reasonable on its face. Companies that are not profitable are ill-advised to take on additional costs such as increased employee benefits. However, the fact that Nostrum's profits last year were lower than the preceding year does not imply that Nostrum is experiencing financial difficulties that preclude it from increasing employee benefits at this time. Perhaps the previous year's profits were extremely high whereas last year's profits, albeit lower, were sufficient to fund an increase in the benefits package without threatening the company's bottom line.

Also, the fact that Nostrum's chief competitor provides lower benefits to its employees is not a good reason for Nostrum to deny an increase to its employees. Employee loyalty is an important asset to any company, and providing good pay and good benefits are among the best ways to acquire it. Nostrum would be well advised to insure that its employees have little reason to seek employment elsewhere, and especially from its chief competitor.

Finally, one can infer from the survey's results that a full one-third of the respondents may have viewed the current benefits package unfavorably. If so, such widespread dissatisfaction would weaken the vice president's argument. Lacking more specific information about how these other employees responded, it is impossible to assess the reliability of the survey's results or to make an informed recommendation.

In conclusion, the vice president's argument against implementing a benefits increase is unconvincing. To strengthen the argument, he must provide evidence that the increase in benefits would have a negative impact on the company's overall profitability. Additionally, he must provide more information about the manner in which the survey was conducted before we can determine the degree of employee satisfaction with the current benefits.

Argument No. 85   Television advertising strategies

This article concludes that businesses using commercial television to promote their products will achieve the greatest advertising success by sponsoring only highly-rated programs—preferably, programs resembling the highly-rated non-commercial programs on public channels. Supporting this claim is a recent study indicating that many programs judged by viewers to be high in quality appeared on non-commercial networks, and that the most popular shows on commercial television are typically sponsored by the best-selling products. This argument is weak because it depends on three questionable assumptions.

The first of these assumptions is that non-commercial public television programs judged by viewers to be high in quality are also popular. However, the study cited by the author concerns viewer attitudes about the "high quality" of programs on non-commercial public television, not about their popularity. A program might rate highly as to quality but not in terms of popularity. Thus, the author unfairly assumes that highly-rated public television programs are necessarily widely viewed, or popular.

The argument also assumes that programs resembling popular non-commercial programs will also be popular on commercial television. However, the audiences for the two types of programs differ significantly in their tastes. For example, a symphony series may be popular on public television but not as a prime-time network show, because public-television viewers tend to be more interested than commercial-television viewers in the arts and higher culture. Thus, a popular program in one venue may be decidedly unpopular in the other.

A third assumption is that products become best-sellers as a result of their being advertised on popular programs. While this may be true in some cases, it is equally possible that only companies with products that are already best-sellers can afford the higher ad rates that popular shows demand. Accordingly, a lesser-known product from a company on a smaller budget might be better off running repeated—but less expensive—ads on less popular shows than by running just one or two costly ads on a top-rated show.

In conclusion, the results of the cited study do not support the author's conclusion. To better evaluate the argument, we need to know the intended meaning of the phrase "highly-rated." To strengthen the argument, the author must limit his conclusion by acknowledging that popularity in public television might not translate to popularity in commercial television, and that the best advertising strategy for companies with best-selling products may not be feasible for other businesses.

Argument No. 86   Video-game companies

In this argument the author reasons that the failure of Company B portends a similar fate for Company A. The grounds for this prediction are similarities that exist between the two companies. The line of reasoning is that since both companies produce video-game hardware and software and both enjoy a large share of the market for these products, the failure of one is a reliable predictor of the failure of the other. This argument is unconvincing.

The major problem with the argument is that the stated similarities between Company A and B are insufficient to support the conclusion that Company A will suffer a fate similar to Company B's. In fact, the similarities stated are irrelevant to that conclusion. Company B did not fail because of its market share or because of the general type of product it produced; it failed because children became bored with its particular line of products. Consequently, the mere fact that Company A holds a large share of the video-game hardware and software market does not support the claim that Company A will also fail.

An additional problem with the argument is that there might be relevant differences between Company A and Company B that further undermine the conclusion. For example, Company A's line of products may differ from Company B's in that children do not become bored with them. Another possible difference is that Company B's share of the market may have been entirely domestic whereas Company A has a large share of the international market.

In conclusion, this is a weak argument. To strengthen the conclusion the author would have to show that there are sufficient relevant similarities between Company A and Company B as well as no relevant differences between them.

Argument No. 87   Color vs. black-and-white photography

The author concludes that photographers who work in color hold a competitive advantage over those who work in black-and-white. To support this conclusion, the author claims that the greater realism of color accounts for its predominant use in magazines and portraits. The author also points out that newspapers now use color photographs, and that there are more types of color film than black-and-white film available today. This argument is problematic in several important respects.

First, the argument unfairly assumes that working in color is necessary in order to gain an advantage. The author identifies only two areas—magazine and portrait photography—where color predominates. It is possible that the overall demand for black-and-white photography remains high. Moreover, the author provides no evidence that the realism of color photography is the reason for its predominance. The predominant use of color may be due to other factors—such as consumer preferences or relative costs of film—which might change at any time.

Second, the argument unfairly assumes that a photographer must make an either/or choice between the two types of photography. This assumption presents a false dilemma, since the two media are not necessarily mutually-exclusive alternatives. Common sense tells us that a photographer can succeed by working in both media.

Third, the fact that more kinds of color film are available than black-and-white film accomplishes little to support the argument. The difference in number might be insignificant, and the distinctions among the types of color film might be negligible. In fact, by implying that more choices in film type affords a photographer a competitive advantage, the author actually undermines his larger argument that working solely in color is the best way to succeed in the field of photography.

Finally, the argument ignores other factors—such as initiative, creativity, technical skills, and business judgment—that may be more important than choice of medium in determining success in photography. A poorly skilled photographer may actually be disadvantaged by working in color insofar as color work requires greater skill, and insofar as color photographers face keener competition for assignments.

In conclusion, this argument oversimplifies the conditions for gaining an advantage in the field of photography. To better evaluate the argument, we need more precise information as to how large a portion of all photography work today is accounted for by color work. To strengthen the argument, the author must convince us that a photographer must choose one medium or the other rather than working in both.

Argument No. 88   **Age of eligibility to drive**

The conclusion of this argument is that 15-year-olds should be eligible to obtain a driver's license. The author employs two lines of reasoning to reach this conclusion. In the first, the author reasons that since older drivers can retain their driving privileges by simply renewing their licenses, 15-year-olds should be eligible to obtain a license. In the second, the author reasons that 15-year-olds are physically more capable than older drivers of performing the various skills associated with driving a vehicle and thus should be eligible to get a license. This argument is unconvincing for a couple of reasons.

In the first place, the author assumes that there are no relevant differences between 15-year-olds and older drivers that would justify treating them differently. This assumption is clearly mistaken. The major difference between the two groups, and the major reason 15-year-olds are denied driving privileges, is their relative lack of emotional maturity and social responsibility. This difference is sufficient to justify the policy of allowing older drivers to renew their driving privileges while at the same time denying these privileges to 15-year-olds.

In the second place, even if it is granted that fifteen year olds possess better night vision, reflexes, hand-eye coordination, and are less disoriented in unfamiliar surroundings than older drivers, these abilities do not qualify them to obtain a driver's license. The author assumes that physical capabilities are the only attributes necessary to operate a motor vehicle. But this assumption is clearly mistaken. In addition to these abilities, drivers must be able to exercise good judgment in all types of driving situations and conditions and must be cognizant of the consequences of their decisions and actions when driving. It is because 15-year-olds typically lack these latter abilities that they are denied driving privileges.

In sum, the author's argument fails to take into consideration important differences between older drivers and 15-year-olds that justify denying driving privileges to the younger group while at the same time allowing older drivers to retain their privileges by simply renewing their license.

Argument No. 89   **Writing screenplays**

This advertisement for "How to Write a Screenplay..." concludes that a writer is more likely to be successful by writing original screenplays than by writing books. The ad's reasoning is based on two claims: (1) the average film tends to be more profitable than even best-selling books, and (2) film producers are more likely to make movies based on original screenplays than on books because in recent years the films that have sold the most tickets have usually been based on original screenplays. I find the ad unconvincing, on three grounds.

First, the mere fact that ticket sales in recent years for screenplay-based movies have exceeded those for book-based movies is insufficient evidence to conclude that writing screenplays now provides greater financial opportunity for writers. Ticket-sale statistics from only a few recent years are not necessarily a good indicator of future trends. It is possible that fees paid by movie studios for screenplays might decrease in the future relative to those for book rights. Moreover, the argument is based on number of ticket sales, not on movie-studio profits or writer's fees. It is possible that studio profits and writer fees have actually been greater recently for book-based movies than for those based on original screenplays.

Another problem with the ad is that it assumes a writer must make an either-or choice from the outset between writing books and writing screenplays. The argument fails to rule out the possibility that a writer engage in both types of writing as well as other types. In fact, a writer may be more successful by doing so. Writing in various genres might improve one's effectiveness in each of them. Also, writing a book may be an effective first step to producing a screenplay. In any event, the ad provides no justification for the mutually-exclusive choice it imposes on the writer.

A third problem with the ad is its ambiguous use of the word "successful." The argument simply equates success with movie ticket sales. However, many writers may define writing success in other terms, such as intellectual or artistic fulfillment. The ad's advice that writing screenplays is the best way to achieve writing success ignores other definitions of success.

In conclusion, this quick pitch for a book is based on simplistic assumptions about ticket sales and writer fees, and on an overly narrow definition of success in writing. To better evaluate this argument, at the very least we would need to know the number of years the cited statistic was based on, and the extent to which ticket sales reflect movie studio profits and writer fees.

Argument No. 90   **Onboard warning systems**

In this argument the author reasons that the installation of computerized onboard-warning systems in commercial airliners will virtually eliminate the problem of mid-air plane collisions. The author's line of reasoning is that by enabling one plane to receive signals from another that reveal its course, the warning system will alert the crew to the likelihood of a collision and allow them to take evasive action. As a consequence, the problem of mid-air collisions will be solved. The author's argument is questionable for two reasons.

In the first place, the author assumes that all mid-air collisions involve collisions between commercial airliners. This assumption is clearly mistaken. In fact, most mid-air collisions take place between private aircraft or between military aircraft and only rarely between commercial airliners. Equipping all commercial airliners with the warning system would only help to solve the problem of mid-air collisions between commercial airliners. It would not solve the problem of mid-air collisions between aircraft in general. To solve the latter problem all aircraft would have to be outfitted with the warning device.

In the second place, the installation of warning systems in aircraft would not by itself prevent mid-air collisions. In order to be an effective deterrent to mid-air collisions the system's information must be noticed and understood by persons capable of taking the appropriate evasive actions. Moreover, there must be agreement among all parties regarding what these actions should be. Consequently, in addition to installing the warning systems it will be necessary to train aircraft crews how to use the system and it will also be necessary for all aircraft to abide by commonly agreed upon evasive procedures.

In conclusion, the author's argument is unconvincing. While installing warning systems in commercial aircraft may reduce the number of mid-air collisions, it would not solve this problem. Moreover, installing warning systems in aircraft would only be effective in reducing mid-air collisions if there were standardized evasive procedures in place and aircraft crews were trained in these procedures as well as in the use of the system.

APPENDIX

How To Obtain the 180 Official AWA Questions

In August of 1997, ETS first published all 180 AWA questions (90 Issue questions and 90 Argument questions) on the Internet. ETS has used this same bank of questions since October, 1997 (the inception of the CAT). Neither the GMAC nor ETS publishes the questions in *printed* form, and we are not permitted to reprint the questions here.

To get the most out of this book, you should generate a computer printout of the questions. You may already know someone who has a printout. If not, crank up your PC, go on-line, and follow these 8 steps:

Step 1 Go to the GMAC Web site, then find the AWA topics page.

Point your Web browser to the official GMAT Web site (*www.gmat.org*) and follow a series of links to the AWA topics page; or you can go directly to the AWA topics page by typing the following in your browser's location window:

> http://www.gmat.org/gmat5230.htm

Click on "Analytical Writing Assessment Topics" at the top of this page; you'll automatically move down the page to another link that takes you to the downloadable file containing all 180 AWA questions. You'll also see a link for downloading Adobe's *Acrobat Reader* software (see step 3 for details).

Step 2 Download the file that contains the AWA questions.

The file is only about 153 kilobytes in size, so it shouldn't take long to download. (*Note:* you may also have to use the "Save Next Link As..." or "Save to Disk" function of your Web browser.) Unless you are using a client-server system, the file will download onto your PC's hard drive—in the directory you've specified in your Web browser as your download directory.

Step 3 Download Adobe *Acrobat Reader* onto your computer (the software is free).

The file you just downloaded is in Adobe *Acrobat* format (*Acrobat* files are denoted by a .pdf extension at the end of the file name). You'll need special software called *Acrobat Reader* to view and print the material. The GMAC provides a link on its AWA topics page (see Step 1) to Adobe's site for downloading *Acrobat Reader*. Or you can go directly to Adobe's site to download the appropriate version for your system (e.g., Windows 95 or Windows 3.1):

---

http://www. adobe.com/prodindex/Acrobat/readstep.html

Step 4   Install Adobe *Acrobat Reader*.

Once you've downloaded *Acrobat Reader*, you'll need to "install it" or "set it up" on your computer. Your computer system may be enabled with a utility that does it automatically. If not, quit your Web browser, double-click the newly downloaded file (the filename should look something like either "ar32e301.exe" or "ar16e301.exe"), and follow the instructions on your screen.

Step 5   View the AWA questions on your computer screen.

When you install *Acrobat Reader* on your computer's hard drive, a program icon will be added to your desktop. You can open the *Acrobat Reader* program just as you would open any other application. Once you've opened *Acrobat Reader*, open the AWA file that you downloaded, just as you would open a file in any other application. In *Acrobat Reader* you can view an entire page, part of a page, or multiple pages. The 90 Issue questions run 9 pages in length altogether. The 90 Argument questions run 13 pages in length altogether.

Step 6   Print the AWA questions.

In *Acrobat Reader*, you can generate a printout of all 180 AWA questions. Your printout will include the same number of pages—22 altogether—and look the same as the version appearing on your computer screen. *Note:* You can also copy and paste the material into a word-processing program (such as *Word* or *WordPerfect*), then format and print from that program.

Step 7   On your printout, number all 90 Issue questions and all 90 Argument questions.

On your printed copy of the Issue and Argument questions, take a pencil and number all questions in each list, sequentially from 1 to 90. Why? Because we've numbered our essays in Parts 2 and 3 of this book in the same manner. As you read a numbered essay in this book, refer to one of your two numbered lists for the corresponding AWA question.

Step 8   Congratulate yourself for successfully completing Steps 1–7!